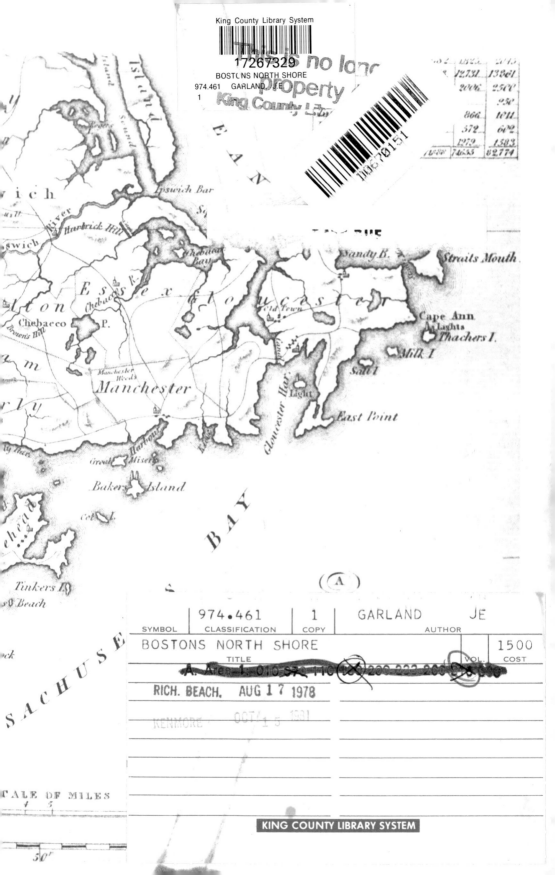

# Books by Joseph E. Garland

*AN EXPERIMENT IN MEDICINE: The First Twenty Years of the Pratt Clinic and the New England Center Hospital of Boston*

*EVERY MAN OUR NEIGHBOR: A Brief History of the Massachusetts General Hospital 1811–1961*

*TO MEET THESE WANTS: The Story of the Rhode Island Hospital, 1863–1963*

*LONE VOYAGER*
 (The biography of Howard Blackburn)

*THE GREAT PATTILLO*
 (The biography of James William Pattillo)

*EASTERN POINT: A Nautical, Rustical, and Social Chronicle of Gloucester's Outer Shield and Inner Sanctum, 1606–1950*

*THE GLOUCESTER GUIDE: A Retrospective Ramble*

*THE CENTENNIAL HISTORY OF THE BOSTON MEDICAL LIBRARY, 1875–1975*

*GUNS OFF GLOUCESTER*
 (Cape Ann in the American Revolution)

*BOSTON'S NORTH SHORE*

*Editor*

*HISTORY OF THE TOWN OF GLOUCESTER, by John J. Babson: 350th Anniversary Edition*

*GLOUCESTER RECOLLECTED: A Familiar History, by Alfred Mansfield Brooks*

# BOSTON'S
# NORTH SHORE

*The presiding cottage of Judge Edgar J. Sherman overlooks the bones of a
wreck on Good Harbor Beach. Procter Brothers, Howard collection*

# BOSTON'S NORTH SHORE

*Being an Account of Life Among
the Noteworthy, Fashionable, Wealthy,
Eccentric and Ordinary
1823-1890*

Little, Brown and Company

# Joseph E. Garland

Boston  Toronto

FIRST EDITION

T 05/78

LIBRARY OF CONGRESS CATALOGING IN PUBLICATION DATA

Garland, Joseph E
  Boston's North Shore.

  Bibliography: p.
  Includes index.
  1. Boston region, Mass. — Social life and customs.
I. Title.
F73.44.G37     974.4'61     77–28345
ISBN 0–316–30425–5

*Designed by Susan Windheim*
*Published simultaneously in Canada*
*by Little, Brown & Company (Canada) Limited*

PRINTED IN THE UNITED STATES OF AMERICA

*To*
*Becky*

# Contents

# Northeast of Boston

THE NORTH SHORE IS NOT WHAT IT USED TO BE, LAMENTED AN OBSERVER of the fast-passing scene in 1922: certain Boston owners of summer estates are known for a fact to be renting to westerners, and if this were not alarming enough, several properties have actually fallen into the hands of Chicagoans, Detroiters and even a party from Kansas City.

A columnist in that arbiter of all matters Bostonian, the *Transcript,* responded reassuringly. "No doubt this is true, but it is no new tendency. The Listener can well remember when, about 30 years ago, one place on the Beverly shore was occupied by a Chicagoan and the adjoining one by a Washingtonian. And one reason, perhaps, why these people of wealth from the West and South are attracted to the North Shore is that it is so Bostonian. That it still is, and it is to be hoped that it always will be. Perhaps some of these newcomers or summer visitors from a distance are as careful guardians of the Boston spirit and traditions as many of our natives. The Listener has heard of cases of this kind."

Fifty-five years later the object of these solicitudes is still keeping its guard up. A Manchester lady with credentials advised in chilling tones that to write about the North Shore and not restrict it to Manchester and Beverly — *The* North Shore in *her* book — was to advance a fraud on the reading public. *Her* North Shore consists of the dozen Social, wealthy and well-walled miles of it that wind from

Beverly's Woodbury Point through Pride's Crossing, Beverly Farms, West Manchester and Manchester, terminating at the east property line of the Manchester Bath and Tennis Club just short of Magnolia Point.

That is about twelve percent of the coastline between Boston and Ipswich. Fortunately for the upwardly mobile, however, the mantle of exclusiveness is by nature almost infinitely stretchable. The whole cloth, in actual fact, originally covered Nahant; not for years did Beverly and Manchester get even a corner of it. Summer settlers at Eastern Point and Bass Rocks drew another corner down to Gloucester. A third was tugged the length of Argilla Road in far-off Ipswich. The fourth has been draped over most of the horsey country-side that buffers the Myopia Hunt Club crowd from the madding herd. In between all this pulling and hauling, the residents of various worthy sections of Swampscott, Marblehead, Salem, Gloucester, Rockport and Essex have claimed their shares of the sacred cloak of ambience, while the remainder of the coast northeast of Boston, including Winthrop, Revere and its beach, Lynn, Danvers and everything and everyone else so far excluded, presumes perfectly legitimately that *it* is part and parcel of the North Shore.

Thus are all the Outs in, and we can get on with the geographically and demographically irrefutable definition of the North Shore of Massachusetts Bay as the hundred or so curious, twisting miles of rock and strand from Point Shirley to Castle Neck where Boston society — capitalist and uncapitalized, castebound and classless — and not a few visitors from a distance have for 175 years found summer resort suited to every civility, every vulgarity, every frivolity and every purse.

In the interests of accuracy it should probably be mentioned in passing that Massachusetts Bay has another shore on the other side of Boston, which holds some pretensions as a watering place, called the South Shore. Languorous and low, this other shore lazes around the shallow bays of Quincy and Hingham, along the graceful spine of Nantasket Beach and down through the friendly towns of Cohasset, Scituate, Marshfield and Duxbury to Plymouth, where Cape Cod

takes over. Except where the Cohasset ledges bare their teeth behind the warning wink of Minot's Light, the South Shore is a sandy
prelude to the Cape. Its few small harbors, though filled with pleasure boats, are half-emptied by every tide. Miles of flats, marsh and
bog provide a haven for waterfowl and avaricious insects. It is simply
incomprehensible to the North Shore summerer how his counterpart below Boston can, with evident satisfaction, spend the season
sweltering and smacking skeeters while *he,* enlightened soul, enjoys
the ten- or fifteen-degree discount on Fahrenheit with which geog-
raphy and climate have rewarded his good sense.

Actually, the North Shore is at first nothing much to brag about.
Across Boston Harbor there is little in either the Logan International Airport, the no-man's-land of tanks and pipelines known
ironically as the "Oil Farm" or the contemporary aspect of Chelsea
to delight the soul. In years gone by, though — before Chelsea was
irredeemably devastated by the Great Fire of 1908 — a serene summer resort was spread upon the riverbank, and the town occupied a
tract of farmland and salt marsh that undulated north as far as the
eye could see and oceanward to the four shining miles of what was
then called Chelsea Beach.

Settled as resorts of Boston when they broke away from Chelsea,
Winthrop and Revere are in fact the beginning of the North Shore,
notwithstanding that they alone are in Suffolk, not Essex, County
and with Lynn suffered systematic excommunication season after
season from that now-defunct synodicon of snobbery, *Who's Who
Along the North Shore: Being a Register of the Noteworthy, Fashionable & Wealthy Residents on the North Shore of Massachusetts
Bay.* The snooty rural seats of Hamilton, Wenham and Topsfield,
on the other hand, extend over some of the most handsome spread
in eastern Massachusetts — not an inch of it closer than a mile to salt
water — and were season after season baptized and anointed *in
absentia* . . . not without precedent, because the gerrymander, after
all, is an Essex County invention.

Once across the Essex County line, the great Chelsea marsh gives
way to solid ground. Hanging out to sea from Lynn by a thread of

sand, the rocky demi-isles of Nahant portend the geology to come. At Swampscott the rusty ledge breaks through and from Marble-head on rules the coast in ridges, miles of them, erupting and sub-merging and erupting again in parallel with the long Atlantic swells that seethe upon the shore. Scoured and scarred by the glacial sheet, the bedrock subsides into gullies and swamps and ponds and streams, deep harbors, coves and crescent beaches, and heaves up into bald domes and hard heads, scrawny necks and islands barren of all but boulder and brier, and lurks beneath the wave in silent menace. Along this surf-crashed coast, rock and sea have shaped human destiny.

Beyond Cape Ann the ledge sinks below the billowy borders of Ipswich Bay, and sand takes over again in the dazzling dunes and windy beaches of Wingaersheek, Coffin's and Crane's. Behind them in the marshes and tidal creeks of Essex and Ipswich, where land and water meet uncertainly, the North Shore ends.

From the June day in 1823 when Colonel Perkins threw open the doors of his summer hotel at Nahant to the ocean breeze and invited the upper crust of Boston to come and cool off on his verandas, this patch of coast has been America's most durable seaside resort be-cause it *is* so *Bostonian,* so redoubtably the preserve of Bostonians of all shades of propriety and of successive transfusions of newcomers who have bought, rented or toured their way in, only to turn into the fiercest guardians of them all, as often happens to converts.

Besides Presidents, members of cabinet and Congress, and justices of the Supreme Court, there have been a few victorious and less than victorious generals, an embarrassment of ambassadors, some denfuls of literary lions, heirs and heiresses real and apparent, various princes and princesses of the blood, and one capital fellow who was a Knight of the Bathroom. In the checkered course of its history the North Shore has been the refuge or the hunting ground, as the case may be, of crooks and confidence men both high and low, of writers by the bushel and artists by the basket, of idols of the matinee and others who idled all the hours away, of knaves, jokers and jacks of both sexes and of all trades and of none — and the destination for a few weeks or hours of surcease from the baking sidewalks of several million citizens, with neither credentials nor pretensions, who took refuge in their cottages or merely bought ten-cent round-trip tickets to the beach for the day.

Summer styles perforce have changed forever. War, death, taxes, automobiles and other such markers on the road of time have taken care of that, and of a good lot else. Today most of the more conspicuous monuments to consumption along the golden strip of *The North Shore* have been torn down, truncated or turned over to the tax-exempt (rest assured, though, that if the glitter is gone, some of the gold remains), and Revere Beach's naughty, gilded strip is giving way, fun house by boarded-up arcade, to high-rise apartments.

The liveried carriages, haughty coachmen in the boxes, that dashed along the manicured avenues of Pride's Crossing and through the woods of the Big Heater are slipping over the edge of memory. So are the glorious Glidden Tours, the steam yachts with sterling silver toilet pulls and the private Pullmans, followed by strings of boxcars for horses and grooms, that squealed to a stop on the owner's private siding for the season.

Gone is that shadowy line of chauffeurs outside the Casino at Magnolia, awaiting the final wail of the saxophone, cigarettes aglow like fireflies in the night. Gone up in smoke, most of them, are those vast warehouses of hotels with their full-blown piazzas piled one upon another, their fringed barges that met every train in a day when there were trains and the family arrived for the summer with servants and twenty-eight pieces of baggage, gone their billiard parlors, gaslit ballrooms, Thursday night charades, bumpy croquet fields, and bathing machines on the beach below the lawn.

Long gone over the horizon is the last excursion steamer, jammed rail to rail, brass band blaring away, churning off from the Great Ocean Pier with a white plume of steam and a blast on the whistle that dissolved every spine on board.

This first volume traces the colonization of the North Shore as city people found more time to get away from it all and enjoy themselves, its *Bostonization* town by town with the extension of public transportation northeast along the coast, much as the American frontier followed the rails and the clipper lanes westward during the same years. The sequel will chronicle the Shore in its maturity as a resort through the nineties, the Edwardian Era, the First World War, the twenties and the Great Depression wherein were finally laid to rest the last ghosts of a lost day.

J. E. Garland

# PART ONE

 olonization
ommenced

1823–1861

# 1

# So Near and Yet So Far

THE FIRST EXCLUSIVELY SUMMER RESIDENTS OF ITS NORTH SHORE WHOSE footprints have survived the flood tide of their successors were the Indians who gave their name to Massachusetts Bay. By most accounts the Massachusetts struck the white men as tall and brawny yet lithe, and handsome though distinctly red of skin under their paint and tattoos. They spoke the lilting tongue of the Algonquin nation. They may or may not have been happier with their wilderness life than, say, the European peasantry. Anyway, the natives had no reason that they were aware of not to extend the open hand of friendship to the palefaced strangers. The act was their ruin, not, ironically, because the white man's heart was evil but because his palm was contaminated.

Every spring, in response to the climbing sun, the sweet scent of the shadbush bloom, the softened swish of the surf and the twitter of peep and plover, the Massachusetts pulled up the stakes of their villages where they had wintered in the wooded vales. Following the still-swollen streams coursing to the sea, they padded and paddled back to their summer campgrounds at the edge of the lush salt marsh, above the ruddy ledge, on the borders of the beach or among the dunes. And there they whiled away the moons of a smiling sun, burning and clearing more forest as they needed it, planting corn and reaping the harvest of the ocean, and taking their pleasure in sport, canoeing, bathing, feasting, dancing and amorous play.

When the sun lowered in the southern sky, and the days shrank, and a harsh wind stripped the forest and whipped the inshore waters and stirred the birds to flight, the Massachusetts withdrew to the protection of their hunting grounds and left beach, bluff and bay to the mewing gull.

Sailing along the North Shore in July of 1605, the French explorer Samuel de Champlain and his men saw many smokes, and many natives running to the edge of the surf to observe their ship. "All along the shore," he wrote, "there is a great deal of land cleared up and planted with Indian corn. The country is very pleasant and agreeable, and there is no lack of fine trees. The canoes of those who live there are made of a single piece, and are very liable to turn over if one is not skillful in managing them."

Among the most popular aboriginal playgrounds was the sand spit of Long Beach, all two miles of it, by which Nahant is reached from the Lynn shore. Colonial chronicler William Wood was impressed with this sandbar arching into the bay, especially at high tide when the surf was running, and recorded that "when a storm hath been, or is likely to be, it will roare like Thunder, being heard sixe miles; and after stormes casts up great stores of great Clammes, which the Indians, taking out of their shels, carry home in baskets. . . . Shoales of Bass have driven up shoales of Macrill, from one end of the sandy Beach to the other; which the inhabitants have gathered up in wheelbarrows."

When the moon of the Massachusetts withdrew her waters from Long Beach she left behind a sheet of strand whose eastern slope drifted off almost imperceptibly into the open Atlantic for five hundred feet, scrubbed and packed so smooth by the retreating waves that a running foot would leave scarcely a trace.

Walk way out here and imagine that a line has been scratched in the sand. The naked contestants advance and shake hands across it (but have painted their faces lest a careless victor be recognized by a poor loser). They spring, they jump, they grapple, they vie for the mark with bow and arrow. They leap into a free-for-all with a ball that they kick, bounce and toss. They come together to squat on the sand and play *puim* with small sticks, and another game with five flat pieces of bone, white on one side, black on the other, that they place in a wooden bowl; the bowl is struck upon the beach, and the bones bounce up and fall, black or white, call win or lose, while the circle of crouching players tightens, intent on the play, shouting *hub! hub! hub!* — come! come! come! Suspended above the hubbub from poles driven into the sand, beaver skins, wampum and other prizes swing in the summer breeze. The betting runs high.

To the white settlers who came upon them, the less tumultuous pleasures of the maidens of the Massachusetts in the twilight of these Indian summers "must have been in the highest degree interesting and beautiful." So thought the mid-Victorian Lynn historian Alonzo Lewis. "The light birchen canoes of the red men were seen gracefully swimming over the surface of the bright blue ocean; the half clad females were beheld, bathing their olive limbs in the lucid flood, or sporting on the smooth beach, and gathering the spotted eggs from their little hollows in the sand, or the beautiful shells which abounded among the pebbles, to string into beads or weave into wampum, for the adornment of their necks and arms."

Their idylls were as fleeting as the footprints of the frolickers in the sand. Captain John Smith inspected the shore of the Massachusetts in the summer of 1614 and reported to Prince Charles that "surely by reason of those sandy cliffes and cliffes of rocks, both which we saw planted with Gardens and Corne fields, and so well inhabited with a goodly, strong and well proportioned people, besides the greatnesse of the Timber growing on them, the greatnesse of the fish and moderate temper of the ayre . . . who can but approove this a most excellent place, both for health and fertility? And of all the foure parts of the world that I have yet seene not inhabited, could I have but meanes to transport a Colonie, I would rather live here than anywhere: and if it did not maintaine it selfe, were wee but once indifferently well fitted, let us starve." Within three years ninety-five percent of the strong and well-proportioned people admired by John Smith had been exterminated by a pestilence that probably was a common European contagion communicated by the immune explorers.

Three years after the Plymouth landing of the Pilgrims in 1620 a fishing company from Dorchester in England settled on the western shore of Gloucester Harbor; from there the fishermen were driven by three more years of bad luck and worse weather to Naumkeag, which they soon named Salem, a few miles along the coast to the westward. Pastor Francis Higginson arrived at Salem in 1629 and wrote home to England of the *commodities* of this North Shore, of the fish, fowl, grain, fruits, nuts and berries, and of lobsters weighing twenty-five pounds "that the least Boy in the Plantation may both catch and eat what he will of them. For my owne part I was soon cloyed with them, they were so great, and fat, and lussious." As for the *discommodities,* in summer "we are troubled much with little Flyes called Musketoes," also mortally poisonous "Rattle Snakes," while the winter brings snows and "sharp biting Frosts" . . . though the clergyman protested sturdily in a paean on the weather (which qualifies him as New England's pioneer meteorologist) that "there is hardly a more healthful place to be found in the World that agreeth better with our English bodyes. . . . A sup of *New Englands* Aire is better than a whole draft of old *Englands* Ale." His first and only winter in Salem was a sup too much for the pastor: already racked with tuberculosis, he died in August 1630, fifteen months after he discovered his "store of blessings."

The white man's guile dispossessed the sorry remnant of the red men who survived his plague. Poquanum, alias Duke William or Black Will, is said to have sold Long Beach and Nahant in 1630 to Samuel Dexter for a suit of clothes and a plug of tobacco, and thought he had the better of the bargain, doubly so after he conveyed the same lands to William Witter for two pestle stones shortly after. In 1638 John Winthrop, Jr., paid Masconnomet twenty pounds for Agawam, now Ipswich and Essex (the sagamore's realm took in the whole coast between the Merrimack River and Salem before the English came), and in 1700 the citizens of Cape Ann and Beverly voted the chief's grandson fourteen pounds for his claims to the land they had been squatting on for sixty years.

When Nahant seceded from Lynn in 1853 the minority of year-round Nahanters eligible to vote adopted a town seal as a reminder to themselves and to their neighbors along the still native-owned mainland of the North Shore how insidiously one man's birthright may be converted into another's quitclaim deed. The insignia showed Black Will complacently accepting his suit of clothes and plug of tobacco from Sam Dexter. By that time most of the blue-chip acreage in Nahant was owned out of town. It had taken only thirty years for the palefaces from Boston, armed with a few paltry dollars, to dispossess Dexter's successors and assigns and transform a windy pasture into America's first coastal resort.

Once and once only did Boston ever literally grab a piece of the North Shore. In the 1630s the town reached across the harbor and annexed Pullen Point (years later named after Governor John Winthrop, one of its original royal grantees), and across the Mystic River, the deserted tracts of Winnisimmet and Rumney Marsh. The tide ran so strong between Pullen Point and Deer Island that mariners passing through the gut had to jump ashore with lines and pull their boats when it was against them. (Hence the name, so it's said.) The island supposedly memorializes the deer chased over from the point by wolves; pursued turned pursuer after a couple of centuries when Boston set up a penal institution there. William Wood called Winnisimmet "a very sweet place for situation . . . being fit to entertaine more planters than are now seated." Its flatness was relieved by five smoothly rounded drumlins. The great beach lay to the east across the emptiness of Rumney Marsh, which Wood described as half-marsh, "halfe upland grasse, without tree or bush: this Marsh is crossed with divers creekes, wherein lye great store of Geese, and Duckes."

After a hundred years Boston had still found no great use for its annexation, and in 1739 the lonely territory regained its independence as Chelsea. Fourteen more years passed, when Colonel Thomas Goldthwait and a syndicate of Boston men bought the end of Pullen Point and leased Deer Island for the purpose of a fishery. As a promotional scheme they invited Governor William Shirley, his entourage and the General Court to sail over for an outing, during the course of which the proprietors announced that they had His Excellency's permission to name the place Point Shirley.

Within five years the fishery had failed, and there were contentions that the promoters, who included the Hancocks, Quincys, Otises and their crowd, spent more time and money building summer villas at the delightful spot than tending the business. More likely the fish weren't biting. At any rate, during the smallpox epidemic that raged through Boston in 1764 an inoculating hospital was erected on the point. The presence of this grim facility cast a pall over the resort life, and then came the trouble with the mother country. By the end of the Revolution, Point Shirley had reverted to the seagulls, and Boston's first summer colony was only a memory.

Exactly two hundred years elapsed from the founding of the colony of Massachusetts Bay to the opening of the Nahant Hotel, for the North Shore two centuries of almost total immunity from the pleasure brokers that owed as much to Boston's isolation from the countryside as to the rest of the coast's from Boston.

Until the filling of the Back Bay in the 1850s the state capital was as nearly cut off by water as Nahant and Winthrop. The sole mainland access was across the narrow neck to Roxbury. To the south and east were South Boston Bay and Boston Harbor, and to the west the Back Bay, a filthy backwater of the Charles River. After mixing its muddy waters with the tides, the Charles united with the Mystic, which poured into the harbor betwixt Charlestown and the Winnisimmet shore of Chelsea; the two then surged torpidly around Noddle's Island (now East Boston) south and east to merge with the Atlantic, and east and north into Chelsea Creek and the brackish marsh of Rumney beyond.

Chelsea was the closest stepping-stone from Boston to the North Shore, whose chief port and commercial center was the Essex County seat of Salem. The most direct route to Salem until 1803 lay a mile and three-eighths across the broad Mystic aboard the Winnisimmet ferry, which sailed, weather permitting, from its landing next northwest to Constitution Wharf in the North End of Boston. Once over on the Chelsea side, the traveler took to the Old Boston Road, a route which today follows close to the Northeast Expressway through Chelsea and Revere to become Washington Avenue along the Everett line, ducks in and out of Malden, rides Lincoln

Avenue into Saugus through Cliftondale, East Saugus and over Saugus Great Bridge (first to span the Saugus River in 1639) to Lynn, where it becomes Boston Street, which takes it to Flax Pond. Here, under the guise of Broadway, it passes Sluice Pond (ex–Wyoma Lake, ex–Tomlyn's Pond) to Peabody (once South Danvers), then as Lynn Street wends north by Brown's Pond, turns east as Washington Street, resumes the banner of Boston Street at the Salem line, and so marches wearily to its destination.

One of our French allies set out upon this Old Boston Road from Salem one November day in 1782. The countryside at first was "arid and rocky," while from Saugus south to the Winnisimmet ferry "you travel over disagreeable roads, sometimes at the foot of rocks, at others across salt marshes. It is just eighteen miles from Salem to the ferry, where we embarked in a large scow, containing twenty horses; and the wind, which was rather contrary, becoming more so, we made seven tacks, and were near an hour in passing."

A longer route by several miles involved ferrying the Charles to Charlestown, then ferrying the Mystic to Malden and meeting up with the Old Boston Road for Salem at a junction west of the North Chelsea line. A third and exceedingly roundabout and tiresome connection was resorted to only by those whose business required and by females who must be spared the company of twenty horses and the risk of *mal de mer* while being tacked across the Mystic against a headwind. One of the ladies, setting out from as far along as Malden, "had to rise early, and travel by wagon, side-saddle or pillion [two-on-a-horse] through Medford, Charlestown [the part which is now Somerville], Cambridge, Little Cambridge [Brighton], Roxbury, and over the Neck, to the great metropolis; and, on arriving, was so fatigued with her day's journey, that she had to rest a day or two before she was able to make her calls."

So jolting were these trails-turned-cart-tracks, and so grudging the improvements, that no one would risk a stagecoach on them until the eve of the Revolution, when in 1774 Salem was made a stop on the first scheduled route in Essex County, between Boston and Newburyport. Peace, independence and the resumption of commerce turned the new republic's attention necessarily to the primitive state of the no longer royal highways.

Ferries fell under scrutiny first. In 1786 the Charlestown ferry from Boston was replaced by the Charles River Bridge. Next year Penny Ferry over the Mystic from Charlestown to Malden gave way to Malden Bridge. A more proximate benefit to Cape Ann at the far end of the shore was the celebrated drawbridge that put the Beverly Harbor ferry out of the running in 1788 and finally and firmly established a communication between Salem and Beverly — though not without such rancor as to inspire one wag to remark that there never was a bridge built *without railings on both sides*. Hardly had the last plank been spiked when Jonathan Lowe whipped the first regular stage from Cape Ann over this wonder of engineering that would attract the inspection of President Washington himself. Lowe's was a two-horse open carriage, and since the trip consumed a day, twice weekly was enough, for besides avoiding potholes, rocks, mud, washouts and ditches, he had on his mind the wolves, bears, wildcats, *Rattle Snakes, Musketoes,* highwaymen and other such discommodities lurking in the wilds between Cape Ann Side (as Beverly was first called) and the West Parish of Gloucester.

Salem was pressing Boston as one of the busiest American ports in the world trade, and in both a clamor arose for a more direct and efficient communication between them than by sea, which was wretchedly slow and uncertain, or by the Old Boston Road, which was simply wretched. Lacking a local Paul Bunyan to tie one end of this serpentine road to Derby Wharf, hitch Babe the Blue Ox to the other and pull it straight, a syndicate of Salem citizens in 1802 organized the Salem Turnpike and Chelsea Bridge Corporation. Captain Moses Brown, a local veteran of the Revolution, was put in charge and finished the job in the astonishingly short time of sixteen months.

This prototype turnpike closely followed the crow seaward of the Old Boston Road all the way from Essex Street in Salem to the Chelsea shore a quarter of a mile west of the Winnisimmet ferry landing and over the Chelsea Bridge, which the corporation

*Black William trades Nahant to Thomas Dexter for a suit of clothes. From* History of Lynn, *by Alonzo Lewis (1829)*

*Lynn Mineral Spring Hotel. From* History of Lynn, *by Alonzo Lewis (1829)*

*Floating bridge, Salem Turnpike, looking south, about 1890. Essex Institute*

*Tollhouse, Salem Turnpike, 1860s. Beverly Historical Society*

built across the Mystic, to Charlestown Square. The successor of that span is the soaring Mystic River Bridge, and the Salem Pike carries a greater load than ever today, as Highland Avenue in Salem, Western Avenue in Lynn, still the Salem Turnpike in Saugus, and Broadway in Revere and Chelsea. It opened for traffic on September 22, 1803, the $189,000 cost to be defrayed by tollhouses at Chelsea Bridge, Halfway House on Breed's Island in the Saugus marsh and in Salem's Great Pasture; the tolls were lifted after sixty-six years of profitable operation.

The doubters didn't think Captain Brown could ever make it across the four miles of Lynn and Salem salt marshes, where one claimed he had thrust a pole twenty-five feet into the muck without striking anything solid. But the builder laid a mattress of brush over the marsh and cartloads of gravel from the Chelsea hills atop of that, and, though spongy, it worked.

Captain Brown's other problem was Collins Pond in north Lynn near the Salem line. It lay athwart his transit line, deep and soft of bottom. Nothing deterred, he built a raft 511 feet long and twenty-eight feet wide, buoyed by massive logs. The famous Floating Bridge opened for horse-drawn vehicles in 1804 and was still floating for the first automobiles a hundred years later. Farmers herded their cattle across until the day several steers from a large drove paused to duck their heads under one railing for a drink. Others followed until their weight buried under water the rail and the heads of those drinking, in which predicament they drowned; the rest slipped and slid over the submerged barrier, swam to shore and scattered. Some years later the elephants in a traveling menagerie declined, in their greater wisdom, to board the bridge at all, choosing to break for the woods and plow across through the water.

The Turnpike passed half a mile to the east of Spring Pond, from whose Lynn shore (it lay mainly in Salem) gushed a mineral spring first tapped by Dr. Johannes Kaspar Richter von Kronenscheldt, sire of the Crowninshields of Salem. Kronenscheldt arrived mysteriously in America — in flight, some said, after dispatching his adversary in a duel at the University of Leipzig — made his way to Lynn, married a young patient and around 1700 bought the therapeutic spring and enough land for a farm from her family. Here the Herr Doktor entertained largely and presumably prescribed widely.

A hundred years elapsed, and in 1802 the resort of Saratoga Springs opened near Albany, New York, on a renewed wave of enthusiasm for the waters. Word of its success, and the proximity of the new Salem Turnpike to Spring Pond, led to the erection of the Lynn Mineral Spring Hotel on the old Crowninshield estate in 1810. For a few years the spa rivaled Nahant as a mecca for the carriage trade, attracting a lively and not so lively clientele of afflicted fishers, fowlers, hikers, riders and the less active, hypochondriac and otherwise. After the vogue passed, Richard S. Fay, a rich Bostonian and amateur conservationist, bought the hotel and five hundred acres in 1847, named it "Lynnmere," planted a forest of imported trees and shrubs, drained the lowlands, set sheep to graze upon the pastures and made an agricultural showplace of the North Shore's one and only spa.

"How much the new route, only twelve miles and a fraction long, did to bring us and the metropolis together," wrote the Salem historian Robert S. Rantoul of the Turnpike, "will be recalled with pleasure by some yet living who enjoyed for the first time, in the early years of the century, an evening ride to Boston with a ball, a concert, or a play in prospect to give zest to the excursion."

Two more Essex County turnpike corporations were chartered in 1803 while the Salem Pike was under construction. One built the Andover Turnpike from Salem through Danvers and Middleton to the Andover Bridge over the Merrimack River, connecting with the new road from New Hampshire through Methuen and Reading to Boston. It thrives today as Route 114.

The other syndicate took the summary view that a road running straight as an arrow from Newburyport to Boston over the Salem Turnpike's Chelsea Bridge would overnight become the spinal cord for activating central Essex County from a sleepy back country into a bustling commercial region and summer resort of golden proportions. The engineer in charge of imposing this mirage on the landscape was directed to aim his transit twenty-four degrees west of south from Newburyport and follow it thirty-one miles to Boston. He succeeded with hardly a deviation until he came up against the impassable ledges of Saugus, finally emerging at Malden Bridge rather than Chelsea Bridge because of land-taking problems. The Newburyport Turnpike cost the lives and limbs of several laborers and a half a million dollars. It was the biggest public works boom ever undertaken in New England, and proved to be the biggest bust.

Unmoved by the proposition that the way may not be so very much farther around an obstruction than over it, the builders pushed their pike, and the horses and coaches of the Eastern Stage Company after it began operating in 1818, groaning up the steep slopes of the four Topsfield hills, only to dash almost out of control down the other sides. Exhausted teams, short-tempered coachmen, petrified passengers, broken axles and some horrible accidents were the result. Many of the stage company's best drivers and uncounted traffic boycotted the turnpike; tolls declined, and the coming of the railroad in mid-century completed the rout.

Long before the final evaporation of the mirage, the two resort hotels which the promoters built beside the Newburyport Turnpike in South Lynnfield and Topsfield were sold, and all sorts of other attractions came to naught. At the former location they had laid out a trotting track for a mile alongside the pike and installed ambitious sailing facilities on Suntaug Lake. All they lacked was the clientele to brave their road. The Topsfield hotel fared better. It was bought in 1844 by two Marblehead men, who dismantled it, moved it and reassembled it on the beach at Clifton. Here at the seaside, as the destination of excursionists ferried to its door from the steamer, the turnpike's Topsfield hotel fulfilled its destiny at last for two happy seasons before burning to the ground.

Sixty years after it opened the Newburyport Pike was regarded as a curiosity, "a *modern ruin* for miles and miles, suggesting some greatness, certainly, but so vaguely, that one can hardly guess what the greatness may have been. . . . And thus it lies, right through the center of the county, a long line of admonition and counsel, teaching all to beware of ill-considered enterprises, and not to risk the fruits of honest industry for the dazzle of a fancied scheme, or the glitter of a happy possibility."

Though in thirty more years the Model T Ford would bring the road back to life, the happiest possibilities for the maritime county of Essex were, after all, not to be found in the interior but along its north shore, which the turnpike to Newburyport bypassed, demonstrating once again that the shortest distance to a desirable objective is not always a straight line.

# Summer Pioneers at Nahant and Danvers

DURING THE SIXTEEN-ODD HOURS OF THE TWENTY-FOUR WHEN THE TIDE was down, long before the road along the crest was built, the two exposed miles of Long Beach that spin off through the sea from the Lynn shore to Nahant served the traveler as a harder, smoother highway than any that the hand of man could grade. A century and a quarter after the last of the Massachusetts hubbubed on the gleaming sands, British officers raced their best horses up and down the length of it. Then they too were evicted. The Revolution was over when a few of the more venturesome first citizens of the United States of America became aware of the cool, islandish dream world that lay out there in the ocean at the far end of the shimmering beach.

The pounding hooves of their horses made barely a mark, nor the wheels of the chaise a sound. Silently above the surf the Nahant-bound sped along the sea-smoothed sand as if upon the surface of a mirror. "On a cloudy day," Alonzo Lewis mused, "the traveler may see the perfect image of his horse reflected beneath, with the clouds below, and can easily imagine himself to be passing, like a spirit, through a world of shadows — a brightly mirrored emblem of his real existence."

First met, Little Nahant was without a house, all pasture and a single clump of cedars, the absolute domain of the herds driven over from the main. Great Nahant (both then were part of Lynn) lay across a second, much shorter, beach and was owned by three families in three houses. Both Nahants had been divided into planting lots in 1657 on the condition that the grantees clear them of the forest within six years, which they did, completely. Once the cover against the elements was gone, all efforts for generations to replant it failed.

Nahant's cart tracks crept around boulders and along stone walls, sending cow- and footpaths scouting through meadow and brush to the freshwater springs and beaches. Great Marsh expanded south from behind Little Nahant Beach to Bear Pond. Nipper Stage Point separated the pair of coves on the southwest lee where the Johnsons kept their fishing boats and quantities of cunners — "nippers" — began the journey to the frying pan.

A narrow footpath skirted sixteen beaches of sizes, shapes and seclusion to suit every taste and hugged the crest of a weirdly Gothic ocean parapet of cliffs, bluffs, ledges, caves and queer rock formations eroded and carved into glowering and romantic shapes by the glacier and the sea — a geologist's fantasy in strange contrast to the upland, which Lewis dismissed as "a barren waste, covered by short, brown grass, tenanted by grasshoppers and snakes."

In February all was barren indeed, gale-lashed, spray-whipped, snowdrifted and bitter. But when summer rolled around every pasture invited a romp, every breeze caressed the cheek, every vista of the bright blue bay entranced the eye, every breaking wave beguiled the ear.

This was the Nahant of young America recalled to writer James L. Homer by his mother, when ladies "(and she was certainly one who moved in the *respectable circles of society*) came here with their husbands and friends, plainly attired, in a humble sail-boat, bringing with them all the necessary implements for cooking, to have a clever, out-and-out, rational jollification." After landing the ladies, the men sailed off to try their luck. "On their return to the rocks, with their fish well cleaned, they would find the women prepared to receive them — with their tables neatly spread, for luncheon or for dinner — their fires brightly burning, and their pots and pans ready to make the fish sweat. The men would throw themselves carelessly on the grass, or lounge about the rocks, while the women made the chowders and fried the fish. Dinner being ready, a horn was sounded and the wanderers came in. What followed, it were quite as easy to imagine as describe, for, in those days, the ladies would drink and enjoy a generous glass of punch, or a modest dash of gin and water, as heartily as their lords."

And then, Homer continued, "three or four hours having been spent in innocent hilarity, in dancing and singing, and talking about tender infants, the party, after partaking of an early cup of tea, would get under way for home. If the wind was fair, they would have a pleasant sail and a speedy return; if it was calm, they would be compelled to do — what you and I have often done, colonel: —

> 'Dance all night,
> 'And go home with the girls in the morning.'"

From his ordination in 1784 until his death thirty-five years later Nahant was the regular summer retreat of Salem's tireless diarist, the Reverend William Bentley. Of an early visit he wrote: "It was the fashion of the antient families to resort to Nahant . . . by a kind of removal for a week or a given term in which the whole family had an interest. The last of which I was present was of the Faneuil family, 28 July 1787. The Seat at Cambridge was left to the farmers & the Father, Mother & all the children with the domestics spent a week at Nahant. It was at the house of Mr. Breed." Bentley stayed with his "very good friend Mrs. Bethune & her family." His hostess was a daughter of Benjamin Faneuil, Jr., inheritor of the family fortune from his brother Peter, who built Faneuil Hall and gave it to Boston. Benjamin's sons, Benjamin and Peter, were Loyalists in the Revolution and fled the town.

Perhaps because the Breeds, Hoods and Johnsons, the only native families, were Quakers and avoided politics, the first Boston family to board at Nahant for the summer, that of Frederick William Geyer, was more than tinged with Toryism. Merchant Geyer occupied the old Vassall mansion on Summer Street (later the site of Hovey's and Jordan Marsh department stores) and kept one of the finest gardens in town. Like the Faneuil brothers, Squire Geyer watered the wrong roses in the Revolution and had to take his family on a voyage to England, leaving his house behind. It was confiscated, but he also left friends behind, among them Paul Revere. The patriot arranged for the expatriate to ship him a large consignment of goods from London within days after the signing of the Treaty of Paris in September 1783. With such connections Geyer, who happened also to be the grandfather of the English novelist Frederick Marryat, was soon back in his Summer Street mansion.

The opening of the two new bridges connecting Boston, Charlestown and the Malden shore in 1787 made Nahant easier to reach, with the result that more custom than pleased the Breeds passed through the door of their rude tavern. Dr. Bentley often ate with them and recalled that "at first the entertainment was free, but the many youth from Boston occasioned . . . some complaints & Mr. Breed refused to keep a public house & friend Hood opened one opposite to him."

The natives were certainly islandish. One exasperated mainlander complained that they were "very shy of visitors — they disliked the intrusion — would run affrighted when they saw them coming — and it was with great difficulty that anything in the nature of cooking utensil or food could be obtained from them. They would shut their doors in the faces of strangers and escape to their back rooms or chambers of safety." But the Nahanters caught on quickly and were soon extracting "most unconscionable prices for the smallest favors."

In 1800 Captain Joseph Johnson of Lynn (not a Nahant Johnson) opened the first summer hotel on the North Shore, and probably the New England coast, at Bass Point, overlooking Lynn Bay and the distant line of combers breaking along the four-mile sweep of Chelsea Beach. It was a small and tentative operation, and he was closed in 1801. But the next year he advertised:

## NAHANT

Joseph Johnson informs the public in general and the valetudinarians and sportsmen in particular, that he has reopened a House of Entertainment on the most delightful, pleasant, airy and healthy spot on Nahant, where he will be found ready furnished with every "good thing" to cheer the heart, to brace the frame, or to pamper the appetite. His house is commodious and neat — in the vicinity of the best fishing and boating on the peninsula; and he keeps a neat sail-boat always afloat for the accommodation of his friends. To the other inducements he adds his respectful invitation; and while he will attend his guests with delight, he assures them that every favour shall be remembered with gratitude.

> *Friend to pastime, foe to care.*
> *Come, enjoy our sports and fare!*
> *Come, and stay a week or so —*
> *But if uneasy, haste to go.*

Nahant, July 26, 1802.

On the fifth of July, 1803, Dr. Bentley rode out. "The hot weather has driven much company to this favourite spot. Nearly 100 daily, for the warm days. . . . We found a few invalids stationed here from the southward." Next month the hotel burned down, only weeks before the opening of the Salem Turnpike. Johnson rebuilt and was back in business in June 1804 in the undoubted expectation that he was at the golden end of a rainbow from Boston. His example was followed to their regret by some Salem men with large plans for Nahant as a coming resort; the time was not yet ripe, and their spectrum collapsed.

On his July outing in 1806 Dr. Bentley counted fifty carriages, chiefly from Boston; the British consul was with one party. The Salem minister's opinion that "the increasing number which visits this healthy spot for the sea air in summer will oblige more buildings" was on the mark; within a year the Hoods and Nahant Johnsons added two more boardinghouses, making eight dwellings in all. The affrighted had seen the light. The hand of hospitality was now fully extended, palm up. And the first of the publicists was at work. *Nahant, or A Day in Summer* flowed from an anonymous pen which used up nineteen stanzas just to get there. In the twentieth,

*We gain the beauteous beach of smooth hard sand,*
*That from the shore extends in gentle curve,*
*And, like a giant causeway, joins the land*
*To fair Nahant; whose aged cedars serve*
*As beacon-marks, to guide the certain way*
*Of weary fishermen along the bay.*
*. . . At length we reach Nahant's romantic height,*
*And rest our weary steed at friendly door;*
*. . . Gladly we seek the profferr'd shelter bland,*
*And sweet refreshment meets a welcome hand.*

The Embargo of 1807 squeezed Salem out of the world trade and brought on the War of 1812, which ended in February of 1815. That summer was the occasion of relief and celebration for a coast that had been under the guns of British warships for almost three years. Gay parties of as many as twenty chaises set out at daybreak from Boston and the surrounding towns, wheeling across Long Beach with everything packed but the fish chowder. Once upon Nahant's romantic height, they scattered for Swallow's Cave, Spouting Horn, John's Peril, Roaring Cavern, the Grotto and the other quaint deformities of the shore, "the ladies with their sewing and books," as Alonzo Lewis pictured the scene, "while the men amused themselves in shooting or fishing, and the children in picking up pebbles and shells on the beaches," as children always have.

Then the steaming fish chowder, cooked up over a driftwood fire by the native hired for the purpose — perhaps Joe Nye, who, nothing fazed when the fish declined to bite, made it without them. More ease and sport, a last call, the caravan of carriages gliding back over Long Beach in the eye of the setting sun, supper at the Lynn Hotel, the trot down the turnpike by the light of the moon, and so, everyone red as boiled lobster, to bed.

Dr. Bentley's summer partiality for Nahant was shared by numerous of his townsmen. Embayed behind Marblehead, Salem could gasp quite as breathlessly as Boston when the ocean ran out of wind. "The extreme heat seemed to endanger the citizens," recorded the diarist of the blistering July of 1811, "but we had no riots & a quiet evening found all at home . . . the heat increasing . . . 90° in my bed chamber at 11 at night . . . many examples of suffering by the great heat . . . many abroad on account of the heat in their little parties." And early in September two years later, "emphatically one of the warmest days ever experienced . . . three times I changed my cloaths from the violence of sweat, with which I was drenched." Hardly less bearable than Boston, Salem — almost alone on the North Shore — was not only avoided by the relief-seekers but was similarly abandoned summers by at least a few of its best-heeled citizens who could afford to escape to estates in the country.

Living as they did at the edge of the sea, though deriving more profit than cooling comfort from it, wealthy Salem shipmasters and merchants at first turned their backs and retreated to the tidewater creeks and rolling countryside of Danvers in their search for a breeze atop rural elevations from which they could survey their gentlemanly farms; not until the 1830s and 1840s, when Nahant and Beverly came into vogue, did their sons and grandsons accept the fact that the rest of the North Shore was not the stifler that Salem could be.

The first of the first was the colony's first governor, that unyielding Puritan John Endecott, who in 1632 was granted 300 acres of Danversport looking across the Waters River, the more southerly of the fingers of the tidal Danvers River that sweeps back and forth into Beverly Harbor under the famous bridge Beverly and Salem built with railings on both sides. Governor Endecott cut Orchard Farm out of the wilderness with such energy that within fifteen years he was able to spare five hundred fruit trees in exchange for another 250 acres.

The Peabodys and the Crowninshields followed the lead of the Endicotts (who had by now changed the *e* to *i*), all Salem names of note, all intertwined in marriage. Joseph Peabody, brave privateersman of the Revolution, who gave up the quarterdeck to amass one of the great shipping fortunes of his time, bought a large farm in the west of Danvers in 1814 after renting it as a retreat for his family just in case the British should throw a few broadsides into Salem during the War of 1812. Glen Magna Farms passed by death and marriage from Peabodys to Endicotts to the Danvers Historical Society, which today maintains it on thirteen of the original acres between routes 95 and 62, an elegant amalgam of the landscaping and architectural tastes of four generations of Salem aristocracy.

Fulfilling wealth's usual tendency to agglomerate, Peabodys drew other Peabodys to Danvers and eventually gave South Danvers their name. Endicotts attracted Endicotts, and Crowninshields, and Derbys such as Elias Hasket, *King Derby,* who added Canton to the gazetteers of Salem. And Captain Stephen Phillips, who made his money from the sea and sank so much of it into the soil of his Beaver Brook Farm that he sheepishly burned all his bills behind him before he died lest his heirs find out. And the most aspiring of them all, Colonel William Browne.

Born in Salem in 1709 and educated at Harvard, Browne was, in the admiring words of a visitor from New York rather worse versed than he, "a Gent'n of Excellent Parts well Adversed in Leaturate a good Scholar a Great Vertuosa and Lover of the Liberal Arts and Sciences." When he was about forty he bought the highest hill in the west of Beverly, since annexed by Danvers, 207 feet above the tidal Porter River, which is the northern of those fingers of the Danvers River that embrace the once busy little port of Danversport. On this bald eminence, with the grandest view in three towns spread out before him, Browne set his men building Browne Hall.

His summer mansion was still unfinished when the Colonel rode out from Salem with the impressionable New Yorker one October day in 1750 to show it off.

"We arrived there at 4 a Clock," wrote his guest in his journal. "The Situation is very Airy Being upon a Heigh Hill which Over Looks the Country all Round and affords a Pleasant Rural Prospect of a Fine Country with fine woods and Lawns with Brooks water running through them, you have also a prospect of the Sea on one Part an On another A Mountain 80 Miles distant The House is Built in the Form of a Long Square, with Wings at Each End and is about 80 feet Long, in the middle is a Grand Hall Surrounded above by a Fine Gallery with Neat turned Bannester and the Cealing of the Hall Representing a Large doom Designed for an Assembly or Ball Room, the Gallery for the Musitians &c. the Building has Four Doors Fronting the N.E.S. & W. Standing in the middle the Great Hall you have a Full View of the Country from the Four Dores, at the Ends of the Buildings is 2 upper and 2 Lower Rooms with neat Stair Cases Leadeing to them, in One the Lower Rooms is his Library and Studdy well Stockd with a Noble Colection of Books, the others are all unfurnish'd as yet Nor is the Building yet Compleat." Colonel Browne was grieved over the loss of his first wife, the New York visitor observed, "as he was doateingly fond of her Being a Charming Ladie when married. But he is now determind to Compleat it. We drank a Glass wine haveing Feasted our Eyes with the Prospect of the Country."

William Browne resumed work on Browne Hall (Danvers became independent of Salem in 1752, meanwhile), put up adjacent quarters for his slaves and for nearly five years entertained grandly in the great hall under the circular gallery, with its mosaic-painted dancing floor and spectacular views in all directions, once roasting a whole ox for his guests . . . that is, until November 18, 1755, eighteen days after a holocaustal earthquake killed sixty thousand people in Lisbon. In the wee hours of that day wave upon wave of terrifying tremors shook New England to its eyeteeth and gave Browne Hall such a rattling that windows broke and chimneys tumbled. Its ambitious master, fearing that his private Olympus offended the gods and that the walls themselves might fall in on him, moved "Browne's Folly" in 1761 down off the hill — ever after Folly Hill — to a location above the Porter River, but lived only two more years to enjoy it.

Folly Hill remains a landmark just south of Route 128 in Danvers. Where once the most celestial country seat in Essex County graced its summit, ten million gallons of water slosh about in the reservoir that the city of Salem dug around the cellar hole of Browne Hall after the great fire of 1914. Ah, the ancient Horace said it all:

> *No ascent is too steep for mortals.*
> *Heaven itself we seek in our folly.*

# 3

## Cold Roast Boston

NOTHING ESCAPED THE CURIOSITY OF DR. BENTLEY, AND WHEN HE HEARD that a "steamboat" had actually made it from Boston as far as his pastorate of Salem in June of 1817, he must have a ride on her. *Massachusetts* was not a queen, though she breasted the wave with a figurehead. Her enormous, ugly, belching engine cranked a walking beam that in some mysterious fashion caused banks of oars to flail away at the water — an ingenious circumvention of the patents of Robert Fulton, whose sidewheeler *North River* had introduced commercial steam navigation on the Hudson River ten years previously.

A tour of Boston Harbor and a voyage around Salem Bay convinced the hearty bachelor minister that the odd contraption was safe enough for him to invite his favorite pupil, Miss Hannah Crowninshield of the Salem Crowninshields, for a day's cruise along the North Shore to Gloucester. All went swimmingly until a bit of chop kicked up on the return, and "most of us Landmen" were seasick passing Manchester's Kettle Cove. However, they "had a band of music which contributed not a little to relieve the unpleasant circumstances of the weather. The Boat did all her duty & upon the last part of the voyage had all the celerity [they] had ever observed in the best state of the weather."

Cape Ann was still buzzing over the steam monster when Dr. Bentley "heard from Gloucester that a Narway Kraken had visited their harbour within ten pound Island. We have had letter upon letter. Many attempts have been made to kill him. The general representation is that his head is like a horse & that he raises it several feet out of water. That his body when out of water looks like the buoys of a net, or a row of kegs, or a row of large casks. . . . At the last dates he had not been taken."

His usual curiosity failed Dr. Bentley, and he did not trouble himself to confirm or deny with his own eyes these reports of a sea serpent (which he mistakenly referred to as the Norway Kraken, a legendary giant squid) in local waters. Colonel Thomas Handasyd Perkins, Boston's leading China merchant, did, however, and rode down on August 16 with a friend identified in one account as Daniel Webster. From high on the western shore of Gloucester Harbor the eminently sober financier vowed that he saw through his spyglass an undulating, chocolate-colored sea serpent, some forty feet in length, whose flat head, raised a yard or so above the water, was equipped with a single horn in the shape of a marlinspike.

The unquestionably sober Linnaean Society of New England listened gravely to the sworn testimony of a parade of supposedly sober citizens that they had sighted and in a couple of instances encountered the monster along the North Shore. The savants published a scholarly report, solemnly naming the visitor *Scoliophis Atlanticus,* Greek for "Atlantic worm-snake." The craze, thus officially canonized, was on.

*Scoliophis* (or the single-file school of tuna fish some of the more skeptical old-time fishermen took him for) returned the next summer and was greeted with gunfire and harpoons in Gloucester Harbor; he fled to Salem, and then to Annisquam. *His Snakeship,* as the newspapers called him, was joined off the North Shore in September by a new steam monster, *Eagle,* smaller than *Massachusetts* (which had been sold, only to burn en route to the Gulf Coast) but evidently faster and rated for two hundred passengers, which left no room on deck for a lifeboat. *Eagle* thrashed out of Salem September 17, 1817, on the four-hour trip to Boston with only two passengers. Dr. Bentley supposed that her first run would be her last, for "the certainty of reaching Boston in two hours at two thirds of the distance by water, gives every advantage to the Stage. We have 21 miles to the Town & then all the inconveniences of entering & leaving the boat when 13 miles may carry us to the bridge from the entrance of the Turnpike & we can be taken up & put down at the places we may chuse."

The diarist was wrong. He underestimated the power of steam and the changes that had come over Nahant, where "they have now more houses, more company, less distinctions, and more luxuries. The simplicity & diet of former times is no more." That was in May of 1819, but he had not been on the peninsula in several years, and when he rode out in July he found much new building and expansion of old for the accommodation of summer visitors, a bowling green, and even a small stone schoolhouse built by wealthy Boston men to remind their vacationing children that all play and no work also makes Jack a dull boy.

That summer *Eagle* inaugurated the first scheduled steamship service in Massachusetts Bay with three round trips a week from Boston to Nahant, alternating with Hingham. For lack of a pier, passengers were landed and taken on at Nipper Stage Point in dories. Thus did James L. Homer first visit Nahant with thirty other excursionists under Captain John Wood, whom he found "a gentleman of the old school — a man of polished manners, good conversational powers, and hospitable feeling [who] had commanded a Liverpool packet for many years out of Boston, but now had 'fallen into the sear and yellow leaf,' as regarded both his property and health. The *Eagle* was usually *three hours* in making her trip to Nahant, and the same time back; and she was considered a wonderfully swift boat. Six hours only upon the water out of nine!"

The well-promoted chance of a glimpse of *Scoliophis Atlanticus* while on the Nahant excursion soon doubled *Eagle*'s passenger complement. On the morning of August 13 "the something" (in Dr. Bentley's doubting words) obliged off Long Beach before two hundred spectators. James Prince, the highly respectable Marshal of the District of Massachusetts, was rolling along the beach with his family and coachman for a few days at Nahant when they caught sight of "an animal of the fish kind" with thirteen and possibly fifteen "bunches" on its back (there was disagreement over the number), making much wake as it raced back and forth before its fascinated gallery. The Marshal said he had a good look through his "famous masthead spyglass," which elicited James Homer's comment that Prince was "a most worthy and estimable old gentleman — a little near-sighted, and at times somewhat passionate and enthusiastic; in a word, he was just the man to see the sea-serpent!" So was Samuel Cabot, apparently, who had his family at Nahant and was crossing Long Beach the next morning in his chaise, returning to Boston on business, when the performance was repeated. The Prince and Cabot accounts were published in the papers and revived the sensation a hundredfold. Probably it is only coincidence that Prince was the first treasurer of the Massachusetts General Hospital and a close friend of the chairman of the board, the doyen of sea serpent–sighters, Colonel Perkins, who happened also to be Sam Cabot's father-in-law.

Long of nose, cool of eye, Perkins was fifty-five and the patriarch of an extensive family hierarchy that had been joining him off and on for several summers at Nahant, where the members boarded, usually with Abner Hood. A few weeks of sea air this season had worked such wonders with an ailing Cabot grandson as to persuade the Colonel to stake Sam to land and house on the spot if Perkins could have the occasional use of it. In the fall Perkins bought from Hood a bluff piece on the north shore of Nahant, west of that wonder of natural hydraulics, Spouting Horn, and overlooking the ocean crag of Eagle Rock, and another lot from the Breeds, and construction began.

Dr. Bentley died of a heart attack on the twenty-ninth of December, and with him the era of simplicity whose decline he had bemoaned. The next summer, 1820, the energetic Perkins clan moved into their stone house, the first summer cottage on Nahant, and in so doing founded the first enduring summer colony on the North Shore.

Such was the contagion of sea serpent–searching while steamboat-ing along the North Shore (a shed was built near Faneuil Hall to exhibit the monster after its expected capture) that *Eagle* extended her thrice-weekly run as far as Salem, and a second *Massachusetts* started a daily schedule between Boston, Nahant, Marblehead, Salem and Beverly. This froth of activity was not unnoticed by the Colonel, relaxing above the sea and Spouting Horn, and the one sighting that summer was reported, obligingly, from his terrace.

Nothing if not a born entrepreneur, T. H. Perkins no doubt pe-rused with interest a paean from an unidentified but "very intelligent correspondent" in the *Patriot* of August 14, 1819, the day after Mar-shal Prince raised his famous masthead spyglass with exclamations of wonder and delight. Omitting mention of *Eagle,* which seems not yet to have proved to him that it was any less a freak than His Snakeship, the writer extolled Nahant as superior to every watering place in New England; approached "over a most excellent turnpike road, surpassed by none in the United States; and across a beach of surpassing smoothness, on whose hard level the wheel leaves no mark." Visitors, he remarked, "have hitherto resided among the few Quakers of the place, and partook of such homely accommodations as they could conveniently provide, but their ability has not equaled their good disposition. It is only necessary that a hotel and bathing-houses should be erected to make Nahant one of the most fre-quented places in New England. The advantage of attracting here the company which annually seek amusement or health abroad is prodigious, if calculated only in a pecuniary point of view. A cir-culation of at least sixty or seventy thousand dollars in specie would be annually derived from the people who frequent any well estab-lished watering-place, and with the superior natural accommoda-tions of Nahant, the assistance of a small capital would place it on the most desirable establishment."

The fact is that the ability of the Breeds had been so outstretched by their disposition, which was never any too good, that they forsook Nahant for Lynn in 1817 and leased their land and farm to Jesse Rice, who ran the homestead as a tavern, which he shortly tore down and replaced with the larger Rice House. The Hoods opened a small hotel in the summer of 1819. Johnson's still operated at Bass Point. Frederick Rouillard, an amiable Frenchman, kept a guest house in the village. Actually an *hôtelier* of some note, he once presided over Julien's Restorator, an excellent French restaurant at Congress and Milk streets in Boston. James Homer recalled him as "a very competent man, and 'while he had money he had friends;' but unfortunately Rouillard had a fast trotting horse, called Buckskin, and a few unprincipled social companions made sad work with his funds, on the turf and elsewhere. The few last years of his life were passed in penury."

A further rationale for going into the resort hotel business on the grand European scale, rather the same that had induced Colonel Perkins to build his cottage, was advanced by Dr. Walter Channing, Professor of Obstetrics and Dean of the Harvard Medical School, in *The New England Journal of Medicine and Surgery* in January 1821. The author argued warmly that Nahant's cool summers offered the invalid "a perpetual inducement to exercise," while the beaches were the best on the coast for the *sea bathing* which so braces the constitution. "What more is wanted to render this place a most desirable residence for invalids during the excessive heat, the variable atmosphere, the impure air of our summers in town? It wants *accommodations.*"

Moreover, Dr. Channing had learned that a desirable tract was on the market but would be withdrawn by March. He urged its purchase by someone for the construction of a grand hotel, which, if properly managed, would offer the invalid guest "something positively salutary in the excitement of a gay and happy society. . . . Whatever the plan be . . . none probably will be very successful which does not offer ample accommodation for the healthy, the gay, and the fashionable, as well as for the sick and convalescent. It seems absolutely necessary, that a watering-place should receive the patronage of fashion, in order that its various means of usefulness should be brought into operation. . . . The remedial influences of such places owe much of their power to the intellectual excitement they produce and sustain."

Dr. Channing happened to be married to the Colonel's niece,

Barbara Higginson Perkins. Uncle Tom required no further urging; that July of 1821, with William Paine, a business associate, he bought nearly all of East Point from Nehemiah Breed for $1,800. While he set about recruiting a syndicate to build the hotel, his observant family was recruiting potential patronage: from their terrace they again spotted *the something* and were not backward about informing the press.

Work started in 1822. Perkins sent prospective backers a testimonial on the medical advantages of sojourning at Nahant. As he was a large benefactor and chairman of the just-opened Massachusetts General Hospital, its founders, Doctors James Jackson and John Collins Warren, were happy to prescribe that "there is not a spot probably on the whole coast of our country which offers so many natural advantages for this purpose as the peninsula of Nahant." Indebted as the Boston profession was to him, the proprietor could anticipate a healthy flow of unhealthy guests referred to the remedial atmosphere of his hotel.

Set upon the crest of East Point high above the crashing surf, America's number one resort hotel flung open its doors on June 26, 1823. The core was stone, like the Perkins cottage. An observation cupola commanded the ocean and the coast. Bold decks of broad porches embraced seventy chambers (most offered "recesses" for beds), a dining room seating 124 and facilities patterned after the continental. The Nahant Hotel cost the Colonel and his associates $60,000, an impressive figure for the day. The newspaper puff touted *this magnificent establishment* as "the most delightful spot on the American coast for health or pleasure. . . . Located in the bosom of the ocean, the air is salubrious and inviting; while the spacious bay continually presenting the fleets of commerce, with the hills, verdant plains, islands, villages and country seats, extending from the heights of Scituate to the peninsula of Cape Ann, form a panorama unrivaled in any country. . . . In truth, Nahant is the chosen domain of the youthful Hygeia, the pleasant summer residence of the invalid and of all those who seek enjoyment or require relaxation from the cares and business of life; whether they flee from the sultry clime of the South, or the 'stir of the great Babels' of commerce, there they can be at ease and KEEP COOL."

There were hot and cold fresh- and salt-water baths and showers, bar, billiard rooms, bowling alleys, sailing, fishing, riding and "a beautiful marine hippodrome," in reality a small and rather pebbly beach. A singular feature of the hippodrome was "a machine of peculiar construction for bathing in the open sea," which may be the first appearance in America of the popular European bathing machine, a bathhouse on wheels that was rolled into the ocean to whatever depth suited the occupant desiring privacy and protection from the waves.

Boston had achieved cityhood the previous year, and it would not do for the newly urbane who chose the water route to Nahant to endure ferriage between steamboat and beach in dories, as in former days, like so many quintals of codfish. A road was therefore cut from the hotel to the ledge above Swallow's Cave, terminating at a six-sided belvedere from which steps descended to a wharf and landing just below Joseph's (alias Joe's or Josie's) Beach.

Down at the Boston docks *Eagle* and *Massachusetts* strained at their lines, steam up. On Beacon Hill the best-groomed steeds fretted in their stalls. The Colonel's hotel was primed for the influx. The missing catalyst was His Snakeship. But lo! he surfaced, a fortnight after the opening, before the disbelieving eyes of Francis Johnson, a youthful Nahanter who pursued in his fishing boat what at first he thought was a parade of porpoises near shore until all his old doubts had been dispelled, or so he swore in a deposition which happened into the hands of the press.

And they came, a flood by land, a tidal wave by sea. They drained every drawing room in Boston worth the draining and engulfed Nahant in a Babel of fashion quite as stirring as those great Babels of commerce which the pied pipings of the Perkinses had enticed their set to desert. All that season and the next. Swept along in the stampede to see and be seen were Margaret and Eliza Quincy, daughters of Josiah Quincy, the relentless reformer now beginning his second year as the new city's second mayor. The sisters were bound to make the ball at the Nahant Hotel notwithstanding reports that Boston was empty and every house at the exciting new resort "absolutely crammed." They left the family home in Quincy on the morning of August 12, 1824. Margaret brought her diary.

Coming down the Salem Turnpike they paused at the Lynn Hotel, where dozens of carriages were pulled up, all headed for Nahant. The road to Long Beach, the beach itself and the approaches to East Point were clogged with vehicles and promenaders; the hotel grounds were "a forest of parasols, veils, shawls, hats, caps and leghorns"; the piazzas were jammed to the railings with guests; every room was taken.

Five hundred had applied for dinner. The Quincy name found seats for the sisters at three in the afternoon. "The tables were laid in two hollow squares, on the piazza was stationed the six musicians, who had come for the ball, playing with all their might, which, joined to the clattering of knives and forks, the jingling of plates, the screaming to the waiters, the shrieking to one another, and the shouts of laughter formed a concatenation of sounds that was almost deafening."

After the bedlam of dinner Margaret and Eliza strolled to the billiard room, found it packed to the walls, and then were lucky or well connected enough to get a room being vacated. They rested, dressed and descended to the ball that was by now bursting with a fresh contingent from the steamer. After cotillions, Virginia reels, quadrilles and the like, supper was announced and the couples marched in to be squeezed along tables set up in two drawing rooms. Then more dancing and earlyish to bed soon after eleven because, after all, "the gentlemen informed the ladies in general that they should not be able to serenade them, as Mrs. Dexter was sick and of course it would disturb her, so the house was very quiet after 12 o'clock."

That night the overflow of young eligibles from Boston was stretched out on chairs, tables, the floors, in carriages and in the stables. A Mr. Moody told Margaret that "he last night 'wished to *hire* some clean straw, every blade of it was engaged,' 'a tolerably clean bench, not one to be had for love nor money.' 'And what did you do at last,' exclaimed I, in vain endeavoring to keep a decent gravity. 'With much difficulty I hired *part* of one of those horrible hard sofas in the drawing room, *whereon I stretched my limbs,* but as to sleeping, I never closed my eyes all night, and therefore intend returning in the boat as fast as possible.' Mr. Dawes . . . moaned forth, that he 'took up his quarters over the chicken house, and was serenaded by at least a hundred hens, to say nothing of geese, turkeys and ducks.' "

By 1825 a definite Nahant punctilio had developed. One magazine writer reported that the new resort "bears the marks of rapid improvement. The honest old inhabitants are fitting up their houses, and seem to catch the spirit of courtesy and improvement from their neighbors. . . . There is no aristocracy there — every one is on equal terms, in riding, walking, or in the other amusements, — there is no shunning *this one* and cutting *that.* Gentlemen are found in the fishing boats or bowling alleys together, who never saw each other before. Every one according to the *lex loci* is put upon his own good behavior, and the slightest deviation from the manners of a gentleman, is marked with instant contempt, neglect, or expulsion."

The *beau monde* at the hotel was invidiously contrasted, all the same, with the rustic beauty of its Gothic setting in *Nahant, or "The Floure of Souvenance,"* an anonymous romance of 1827 spun around the tragic end of Faustino, the swain who ventures out in a small boat to a nearby island, probably Egg Rock, to pluck a forget-me-not for his Alice and drowns on the return to Nahant. Like the floure, she soon withers and expires. As for the hotel, "the rooms were gaily decked and lighted; violins, tambourines, and drums echoed through them, and the ladies dressed in full ball costume, were dancing lightly and merrily. . . . Flowers, manufactured by Nicollati, and perfumed by Richardson, lent their artificial brilliancy to the loveliest of Nature's works; feathers, laces and gauzes. . . . Matrons, in gay attire, not weary of a winter's campaign of light amusements, were there. . . . Many gay and gallant chevaliers were there, tight laced, in white gloves, and perfumed 'kerchiefs, contending for the honour of the maidens' smiles."

*Eagle on the Nahant run, 1817. First regular steamship service in Massachusetts Bay. Nahant Public Library*

*"Monstrous Sea Serpent as seen at Cape Ann," reads the caption to this contemporary print. Nahant Public Library*

*Colonel Thomas Handasyd Perkins. Nahant Public Library*

*The Reverend William Bentley. Essex Institute*

NAHANT HOTEL.

*Earliest view of the Nahant Hotel. From* History of Lynn,
*by Alonzo Lewis (1829)*

It was too much. The nameless writer had "fled from brick walls, paved streets, and 'conversaziones,' to breathe the air of heaven, uncontaminated by the smell of lamp oil, and sickly perfumes; to see the young and happy, free from the restraints of fashion and prejudice; but behold, here are the same violins, the same drums, and the same waiters that I thought I had left behind me; the very paraphernalia of a Beacon Street drawing room."

For the first time in eight years the supposed sea serpent was not reported in Massachusetts Bay in 1825, not even by the Perkinses, nor was he "sighted" again for another eight. The initial two summers of his absence were the Nahant Hotel's third and fourth and were not especially successful. *Eagle* had been sold for scrap and *Massachusetts* relieved of the run. Their places were taken by *Patent,* then *Housatonic.* Steamer service was not what it had been. Perhaps the spectacle, finding smaller and rather more jaded audiences on land and sea, had recoiled and departed in a huff. James Homer, a frequenter of Nahant, conceded that "it has been insinuated — with what truth I am unable to say — that the people of Nahant themselves, the hotel keepers, or some wag of an editor for them, often raised the cry of sea-serpent! when, in fact, his majesty was more than a thousand miles off. I plead guilty to a part of the indictment. And all this was done to induce unsuspecting people to flock to Nahant, to see the monster wag his tail and eat mackerel, while they themselves ate chowder and drank old wine."

Another writer cogitated on the coincidence of the apparition with the opening of the Nahant Hotel and the genteel crowds drawn there. "Whether the serpent was emulous of being reckoned in with such company, or was merely summoned as an outside attraction, it is not the purpose here to enquire. No matter what the envious keepers of other establishments and their friends surmised."

Even the gentle poet John Gardiner Calkins Brainard was unable to suppress his suspicions in an ode to the sea serpent:

> *But go not to Nahant, lest men should swear*
> *You are a great deal bigger than you are.*

No question that the hotel builder and his family were the champion snake-sighters on the coast and that *Scoliophis Atlanticus* was an inspired and inspiring subject, or object, of the potency of suggestion on the popular imagination at precisely the moment that Boston's first ocean resort and steamship line were in need of a few launching columns of publicity.

But His Snakeship was merely a passing diversion. Having been made accessible by the Salem Turnpike and the steamers, and fashionable by Colonel Perkins, Nahant assumed a new life of its own. Let East Point and the hotel contain the glamour; the deeper beauties of the peninsula proper were coming into the possession of the Boston friends of Perkins who followed his lead, one after another, in buying up the shore and building secluded cottages above the sea.

Cornelius Coolidge, a speculator, architect and builder of Beacon Hill mansions in Boston, bought enough Breed and Hood land to lay out streets and sixty-two lots, making him the North Shore's first summer real estate developer. After installing the steamship wharf for the Nahant Hotel, he built a small competitor, the Nahant House, and several cottages before the financial panic of 1829 caught him short.

Nahant's early summer houses verged on the austere. They were rarely more than a story and a half, flanked by piazzas whose supporting posts were half-hidden in rose bushes, and linked sociably by footpaths through field and copse. The usual New England clumps of lilacs in the dooryard bloom'd, but not a tree around. From the cottage colony the gloss of civilized Boston was banned. None of the rich and powerful owners was far from the Yankee dirt of his sires, and the annual removal to Nahant was undertaken as an instructive and refreshing reminder to each family of the fact.

The little stone schoolhouse the Bostonians built before any of them owned a foot of Nahant doubled for divine services until 1831, when some of the new summer residents, led by Colonel Perkins, got up a fund to raise a nominally nonsectarian chapel of distinctly Episcopalian cast ("a modest-looking, Grecian temple–like wooden building," wrote a foreign visitor), ever after known as "The Boston Church." With their neighbors, who endowed it with a bell, they make a fair sampling of the men who were moving New England commerce, shaking Massachusetts politics and shaping Boston's cultural influence from their counting rooms and studies in the city, and from their piazzas by the sea.

There was jovial Abbott Lawrence of infinite energy and shrewdness, partner with his ailing brother Amos (a Nahant-lover, too) in the firm of A. & A. Lawrence, the greatest textile manufacturers in America. Abbott gave the family name to the city he created around his mills. So to Lowell did the Lowells, represented among the churchly subscribers by John Amory Lowell, first trustee of the Lowell Institute and grandfather of the cigar-smoking poetess Amy and her brother, A. Lawrence Lowell, Harvard's bricks-and-mortar president.

There was William Appleton, merchant-shipowner who came down to Boston from New Hampshire "with a small bundle in his hand and a few cents in his pocket," as he liked to recall. William was a cousin of Nathan and Samuel Appleton, mill owners in league with the Lawrences and Lowells; he regarded the Nahant air as a tonic for the chronic dyspepsia to which his daguerreotype bears witness.

Peter Chardon Brooks, penniless apprentice in Boston at fourteen, retired on a fortune in insurance at thirty-six, was another; late in life he tried some very modest yachting, gave it up as an expensive waste of time and died the richest man in New England. And David Sears, merchant-philanthropist with a cottage on Swallow's Cave Road, a striking, curved business block on Cornhill in Boston called Sears Crescent and a granite mansion on Beacon Street, now the Somerset Club. And Thomas G. Cary, a Perkins son-in-law and partner. And an Amory and a Codman and a Russell, Boston names to be reckoned with.

There was Dr. Edward H. Robbins, who graduated from Harvard Medical School only to change course for the wool business. Coolidge built him a cottage near Sears. After two lean seasons the proprietors put the Nahant Hotel on the block in 1827, and Robbins, with Perkins as his silent partner, picked it up for less than $12,000, inspiring a parody on "Robin Adair" in the *Lynn Mirror* which began

> *Who bought Nahant Hotel?*
> *Robbins, I hear.*
> *Pray, will it turn out well?*
> *Oh, never fear.*
> *Will all the mirth and glee*
> *That we were wont to see*
> *Be all revived by thee,*
> *Robbins, my dear?*

and ended

> *Then will grasshoppers sing,*
> *Then will thy chowder bring*
> *Crowds. Oh! — this is the thing,*
> *Robbins, all hail!*

There were the aristocratic Eliot brothers, William H. and Samuel A. The former had a cottage on Vernon Street. His business association with Colonel Perkins in the Nahant Hotel inspired him to promote a landmark in hotel development, the Tremont House in Boston, which opened in 1829. Charles Dickens stayed there in 1842, and it had "more galleries, colonnades, piazzas, and passages than I can remember, or the reader would believe." William Eliot died soon after pledging to the chapel. Samuel built above Bass Beach. He was in the prime of a life of useful public service in politics, music and education, to which his most useful contribution was a son, Charles William Eliot, whose boyhood ABC's absorbed within the stone schoolhouse (when he might have been down on the beach) paid off in Harvard University's most imperial presidency.

Another subscriber in the Perkins circle was Jonathan Phillips, son of William Phillips, the lieutenant governor around whose legacy the Massachusetts General Hospital was founded. Jonathan was president of the New England Asylum for the Blind when the Colonel decided to follow the example of his late brother, James Perkins, in giving his Pearl Street mansion to the Boston Athenaeum, and presented his own neighboring one to the Asylum provided it raise $50,000 in endowment. It did so under the leadership of Judge William Prescott and took its benefactor's name as the Perkins Institution for the Blind when it outgrew his home.

Judge Prescott was a subscriber too. He built on Swallow's Cave Road when he retired from the bench in 1828 and shared his cottage with his son, William Hickling Prescott, already an historian of note. The judge's father, Colonel William Prescott, had commanded the patriots at Bunker Hill; his son, through a whimsy of Cupid, married Susan Amory, granddaughter of the Captain John Linzee whose British Sloop of War *Falcon* poured a merciless fire on Prescott's men that hot June day of 1775. The tall, handsome, gracious scholar had been nearly blind since his Harvard days, when he lost the sight of one eye and suffered impairment of the other during a student fracas; he wrote prolifically in a darkened room, relying on secretaries and the illumination of a prodigious memory.

The younger Prescott preferred the family homestead at Pepperell ("an acre of grass and old trees is worth a wilderness of ocean"), but summered at Nahant as much out of loyalty to his aged parents, with whom he had always lived, as from love of the place, of which he wrote: "The house stands on a bold cliff overlooking the ocean, — so near that in a storm the spray is thrown over the piazza, — and as it stands on the extreme point of the peninsula, it is many miles out to sea. . . . It is not a bad place — this sea-girt citadel — for reverie and writing, with the music of the winds and water incessantly beating on the rocks and broad beaches below."

Among all the merchant princes on Nahant that summer of the Boston Church, one was monarch, the "Ice King." Frederic Tudor, Esquire, furiously ambitious, fired with imagination, ruthless, despotic, creative, and, if necessary, charming, was the only one of the four sons of Judge William Tudor not to attend Harvard, and he never got over it. In 1805, when he was twenty-two, he and brother William were seized with the extraordinary notion that they could ship New England ice to southern climes and sell it at huge profits to the native innocents, who had never seen water in such form before. The brothers cut a shipload of blocks from the pond on the family country place in Saugus, bought a brig and loaded for Martinique; Frederic sailed as supercargo, as much to escape the jeers of his friends as to restrain the liquidation of their assets.

William went his own way, dabbled in business with Colonel Perkins and wound up a man of letters. Fred went it alone, went broke, went to jail for debt, went back to the ponds for more ice, and bore with him the motto he penned on the cover of his "Ice House Diary" when he began to climb: "He who gives back at the first repulse, without striking a second blow, despairs of success, has not been, is not, and never will be a hero in love, war or business." Overcoming a mountain of obstacles, inventing a technology of refrigeration, even designing vessels, Tudor by 1821 had the ice market cornered in Havana and Charleston, and in 1833 shipped his first cargo to cool the drinks of the English colonials in Calcutta . . . just in time, as Samuel Eliot Morison has pointed out, to save

Boston's East India trade from collapse. The Ice King was a legend before he was fifty.

The Tudors sold "Rockwood" to Saugus for its poor farm in 1822, and Fred's mother, Mrs. Delia Tudor, built a stone cottage at Nahant above Stony Beach, a quarter of a mile west of the Perkins place. Her son bought it from her in 1824 and was off on the avocation that, like everything else he tackled, would grow into an obsession. It would also change forever the face of Nahant.

One more pillar and we are done with the Boston Church. Benjamin Cutler Clark, a rugged, jut-jawed young capitalist, owned a fleet of topsail schooners and clipper brigs in the West Indies and Mediterranean coffee, fruit and wine trades, yet small boats were his passion. This joy in the thrill of a lively tiller, a taut sheet, a galloping hull, a spanking breeze and a wet tail was shared by many of his peers on State Street and his neighbors at Nahant, who had learned the ropes of their businesses from the quarterdecks, and not infrequently forecastles, of their own or their families' vessels on voyages to Canton and Gibraltar. Nahant appealed to Clark as a summer anchorage for small yachts, and when he was thirty-two, in 1832, he built a cottage on the brow of the forty-foot bluff of Bass Rock at the west end of Joe's Beach and dropped a mooring where he could keep an eye on a succession of smart little schooners swinging with the tide and the breeze in the cove below.

Ben Clark was a founder of organized yachting in Massachusetts Bay, and so loved the helm that by keeping fresh horses at Boston, at a stop on the Salem Turnpike and at Nahant he could reach his landing in an hour in his light sulky. How he thrilled to a patch of canvas, or a cloud of it! In his later years, after the invention of wet plate photography, he would direct the masters of his clippers when outward bound from Boston to stand in by Clark's Point with every sail flying and have their pictures taken.

During the decade following the business slump of 1829 the Nahant Hotel had slumped, too. As a small girl, Caroline Cary Curtis watched her parents starting out for an evening at Grandfather Perkins's famous spa. "I felt as if they were going off for all sorts of delightful experiences, but when I grew older and saw for myself the public drawing room with a row of seats against the wall on each side, giving it the name of the 'omnibus,' I thought it a little grim for a scene of gaiety."

So did Thomas Grattan, the incoming British Consul for Massachusetts. Four days after his arrival in America at the end of July 1839, Grattan fled the "fiery furnace" of Boston for Nahant, which he found delightfully cool, and its hotel, which was "large and uncomfortable — nothing better than a huge pigeon-house, with a number of sleeping cribs wretchedly furnished." Twenty years later, when he was safely back home, the diplomat published his bleak observations under the ironic title *Civilized America.*

If his bed was bad, the board — to which Her Majesty's Consul was summoned by "an infernal gong" — was unbearable; "the pleasures of the table, as combining indulgence of appetite and taste with intellectual intercourse between the sexes, are wholly unappreciated by the persons assembled in this hotel." Relief could not be found even in the awful American *mint julep* — "detestable — bad as a cordial, and worse as a physic."

An Anglican Irish snob whose wit was his saving grace, Grattan conceded that he met occasional "agreeable people among the promiscuous crowd," but the children raised a continuous bedlam, and though the ladies played ninepins avidly with the men (he hesitated to call them gentlemen), they were "indifferent instrumental performers, have the rudest notions of singing, and can at best but execute a feeble pencil sketch."

And Nahant kept early hours "to a ridiculous excess." Nine out of ten of the men were up before the sun for Boston by stage or steamboat and arrived back so late that they were no good for anything but the bar in the evening and certainly not for flirtation, the onus for which evidently fell on the one in ten who remained . . . that is, "judging from the goings on in this hotel, I should say that no proportionate given part of the Old World can furnish anything approaching to the quantity of flirtation which is so consumed in this section of the New. I find myself so much infected with the spirit of the place [as was Mrs. Grattan, who declared that she saw the sea serpent, ninety feet of him, as long as the upper piazza], as to rank almost everything as a commodity of barter and sale. The article just specified is of such very flimsy texture that it costs nothing and is worth nothing. This accounts for its being so freely thrown away."

When the first easterly storm of the fall swept the coast at the end of September, Grattan was astounded to witness an absolute exodus and then to be evicted himself from the hotel (though gorgeous weather followed), which was closed for the season on orders from the owners, "the worthy Doctor, who also managed a woollen factory, and the gallant Colonel, who speculated in land in Michigan, and opium in China, and in many other undertakings besides hotel-keeping at Nahant," This abortion of the season reinforced the consul's contempt for the shortsighted penury of the management, with its "loftiest pretensions to 'aristocracy,' yet descending to very low methods of money-making," with the result that the Nahant Hotel, "instead of being frequented for months as a place of elegant enjoyment, was resorted to merely as a refuge from the scorching heat of the dog days, and abandoned at the very first symptoms of a change."

The rest of Nahant, with the exception of Mr. Tudor and his improvements, was equally the object of consular condescension. "The most niggardly spirit pervades the place; not the least advance being made towards sociability among the visitors. To enjoy cool weather at the smallest possible expense, saving every dollar they can, is their utmost ambition. To spend one in entertaining their neighbors is out of the question, unless as a *very* rare exception on some unfavorable exigency." The crowning affront to the sensibilities of His Grattannic Majesty was the discovery that there was not a single bathing machine at the resort (though one had been advertised at the opening of the hotel), "a few huts . . . being the only accommodations for ladies: the rougher sex taking to nooks among the rocks."

Consul Grattan, whose vituperations rather suggest that his nose was out of joint in more respects than he was prepared to admit, liked Nahant well enough withal to take rooms in a cottage after three seasons of enduring the hotel. The penny-pinching partners sold out to Phineas Drew in 1842. Drew tacked on an addition which brought the rooms to a hundred, and restored an air of hospitality. James Homer was there in September of 1845 and gathered that Drew had "been blessed with a run of prosperity which must have been highly flattering to his feelings and grateful to his purse. . . . I may add that the company which usually assembles here embraces as much of intellect, good manners, kind feelings, and amiable social bearing, as you will find at any other watering place in the country. The sturdiest democrat in the land need not be afraid to venture here with his wife and daughters, while the proudest aristocrat must be satisfied with the facilities and comforts which are accessible to all."

To Homer, Nahant was everything the South Shore was not. Earlier that summer the public and private houses at Nantasket Beach and farther down the coast were crammed with Bostonians trying futilely to escape the heat, for the only cooling breeze came off the sea, and rarely at that. The writer found that the mosquitoes south of Boston, "like mackerel, have been unusually numerous, and active, and sharp-set. To a man of delicate taste, there is nothing so interesting as to slay one of these mischievous insects, while in the act of fastening itself upon the pure white bosom of a beautiful girl. I have watched many a long minute to get a chance to brush one of them away!"

While on the North Shore, "a night's sleep at Nahant," wrote another guest, "in hot weather, is a luxury no where else to be enjoyed — if ice is a luxury at Canton, so is a bed at Drew's, of a hot August night!"

Frederic Tudor's cleverly insulated wooden ships had been carrying frozen Yankee pond water to the Far East for a year when the Ice King made Euphemia Fenno his queen in 1834. Having shown how to cool drinks in Canton and Calcutta, he launched warmly, at fifty, into the project of fathering six young Tudors. And having entered the age of domesticity, he proposed to demonstrate that the barren waste of Nahant, created by the axes of the settlers and tenanted by grasshoppers, snakes and the cottages of a small colony of ascetic Bostonians, could be induced to bloom.

Tudor set about to buy every piece of land below his stone cottage on the west side of Great Nahant that he could get his hands on, including the Great Swamp, which he drained and made largely arable. Colonel Perkins had planted and persuaded a row of elms to survive along the road to the village. The King did him one better: beside the numerous roads he built, and everywhere else his neighbors would let him, he planted balm of Gileads; his idea was that these brittle poplars would rapidly grow up to be windbreaks for the slower shade trees, the elms and maples with which he reforested Nahant. It worked, and for the first time in two centuries the windswept peninsula had trees, and shade. As for the balm o' Gileads, Caroline Curtis in her *Memories of Fifty Years* complained of their "filling the air and covering the ground with fluff. I do not suppose that they committed suicide at his death, but they certainly disappeared."

The Ice King adapted his plan of windbreaks to shelter his orchards of apple, cherry, pear, peach and plum trees with towering fences of vertical slats on rails secured to posts as thick as telegraph poles and as high as thirty feet. His South Garden of fruit trees across Nahant Road from his cottage was popularly known as the Brick Garden from the tall slat fence he erected around it, veneered with a basket-weave pattern of bricks. Tudor tried to grow tobacco and some other alien plants without much success, although he refused to employ a professional gardener. He thought insects a great nuisance and hung three hundred bottles of sugar water in his trees, congratulating himself that in a few hours one June 108,000 flies, bugs and moths were enticed to their sweet sorrow.

Mr. Tudor was "a striking personality with his aquiline face and silver hair," in the childish eyes of another Perkins granddaughter,

Emma Cary. The bearded old gentleman with the frigid gaze, in his brass-buttoned blue frock coat, had his eccentricities, cultivated or not, and they were not especially appreciated in the neighboring Perkins-Cary compound. "To arrange a boundary line with Mr. Tudor," Caroline Curtis wrote tartly, "was to expend all you had of time and patience and good sense and good manners — and at the end he got the better by sheer persistence" — which reminded her of his "great gray bull, which was the terror of old and young Nahant, and therefore very dear to its owner, because he had the added pleasure of thinking all the rest of us fools for our fears." Another lady who seems to have run afoul of King Tudor described a sort of moat that he had his men dig so that the sweep of his lawns would remain unmarred by any visible barrier . . . his "Ha! Ha! fence," he called it.

Nahant's historian Fred Wilson had his favorite Tudor story, too, telling how the old man went about hiring a carpenter by first instructing the applicant to shingle the roof of a small shed. "He made the unusual stipulation that the shingles were to be laid upside down, butts up, beginning at the ridgepole. Several job hunters refused to do so foolish a thing, until finally one said 'twas nonsense but he would do it. Next day Tudor found the job done in a workmanlike manner, though wholly useless, and ordered the man to rip the shingles off and put them right, saying he only wanted to be sure he got a man who would obey his instructions."

Consul Grattan observed that Tudor's summer neighbors, who had done hardly a thing to improve their environment, regarded his innovations as "rather objectionable 'workings against nature.'"

By midcentury the railroad had breached the fastness of the North Shore. To Nahant's relief, it swept past in its rush toward the future, leaving the peninsula a complacent colony of Commonwealth Avenue and Beacon Hill except for two or three hotels quarantined behind a *cordon sanitaire* of private property lines. Thomas Gold Appleton of the summering Appletons, the sharpest wit of his day, regarded with amusement his neighbors from the city (and himself), congratulating themselves on the simple superiority of life in their simple cottages on Nahant's superior shore, and impaled them collectively as "Cold Roast Boston" on his spit. The sobriquet has stuck, but precisely what, one may ask, does it mean? *Cold roast* is slang, long out of fashion, for "something insignificant, nothing to the purpose." So time has left the point but dulled the barb . . . which would probably have relieved Tom Appleton, had he reflected on it, for no one loved Nahant more than he.

# 4

# Th' Haunt Is Not Newport (Thank God)

NEWPORT WAS DESTINED TO OUTSHINE NAHANT, FOR WHICH NAHANTERS thanked God and Thomas Handasyd Perkins. The natural attractions of Rhode Island's vastly larger peninsula had been appreciated since colonial days, but not until 1846 was there a glint of the glitter to come. That summer the Ocean House, Newport's first (and last) grand hotel, opened with a splash that turned the heads of the fashionable from Boston to Charleston, never mind that the "huge, yellow pagoda factory," in the sneering words of George William Curtis, was fully a mile from the water.

As he stitched away, the local tailor of Newport watched each new season of the Ocean House outdo the last. Pondering its distance from Narragansett Bay, Alfred Smith withdrew his life savings and with one Joseph Bailey bought 140 acres of intervening farmland for $22,700. Smith then proceeded to squeeze the camel through the eye of his needle by talking the town into extending Bellevue Avenue past the hotel and clean across the middle of their investment to the beach that perpetuates the name of his partner, whom he shortly bought out. In three years seventy-five "cottages," in the euphemism of the day, were up or abuilding on the lots he sold, strictly on his terms, to the New Yorkers queuing up to his door with their millions, and Tailor Smith was on the way to his first.

So spectacularly had Newport caught the fancy of fashion that

Nahant was already considered old hat when George William Curtis's *Lotus Eating: A Summer Book* appeared in 1852. The journalist's Rhode Island and New York background and his youth (he was twenty-eight) predisposed him to the excitement of Newport, while his two years at Brook Farm under the influence of Emerson had tuned his soul to the inner vibrations of Boston and Nahant.

Compared with America's newest watering place, its oldest was dull — dull as dishwater, though Curtis was too discreet to put it so crudely. "The beaux and belles have long since retreated into the pretty cottages whence they can contemplate the hotel, which has the air of a quaint, broad-piazzaed, sea-side hostelry, with the naked ugliness of a cotton factory added to it, and fancy it the monument of merry, but dead old days." Many former habitués of Nahant he talked with "now recoil from it, and only visit it with the same fascinated reluctance with which they regard the faded love-tokens of years so removed that they seem to have detached themselves from life. This will explain to you much of the surprise with which Bostonians listen to your praises of Nahant. 'Is anything left?' say their smiles and looks; 'it is a cup we drained so long ago.'" The younger generation finds it a bore, and "it has no variety, I grant. You stroll along the cliffs, and you gallop upon the beach, and there is nothing more. . . . Nahant would not satisfy a New Yorker, nor, indeed, a Bostonian, whose dreams of sea-side summering are based upon Newport life. The two places are entirely different. It is not quite true that Newport has all of Nahant and something more. For the repose, the freedom from the fury of fashion, is precisely what endears Nahant to its lovers, and the very opposite is the characteristic of Newport."

Alfred Smith was happily selling lots to the highest bidder when Curtis measured off the mile that separated the Ocean House from Bailey's Beach and made the sea at Newport a luxury, a distant presence . . . "in the silence of midnight as you withdraw from the polking parlor, you hear it calling across the solitary fields, wailing over your life and wondering at it." At Nahant, by contrast, the sea was supreme. Nahant was "the ante-chamber to the ball-room of Newport, where you may breathe the fresh air awhile, and collect your thoughts, and see the ocean and the stars, and remember with regret the days when happiness was in something else than a dance, the days when you dared to dream. . . ."

Curtis was wearing his melancholy cap when he wrote that. As it turned out, there was one last dance left in the hotel, one last dream to be dared, one last draught in the cup of merriment.

Possibly because he was as bored as his dwindling clientele, Phineas Drew sold the Nahant Hotel in 1852 to the owners of the Sagamore House in Lynn, the Rands, who were taken with the dream that they could revive the dead old days so lamented by young George Curtis (who of course never knew them) and give Newport a run for the money. In this delusion the Rands were encouraged by the man they chose to manage their new property, Paran Stevens, who had just been hired to run the Tremont House year-round in Boston after five years in the city at the Revere House, where he had established a reputation as "the Napoleon of hotel proprietors." They were further encouraged by Nahant's new-found identity as a town in 1853; Lynn had withdrawn its opposition to incorporation, with the same short sight that allowed Swampscott to cut loose the previous year, on the grounds that it would be cheaper to let Nahant go her own way than to stand the expense any longer of maintaining the road along the crest of Long Beach, first built in 1848, washed out by a storm in 1851 and recently relaid.

The new owners and their Bonaparte of hospitality spent $300,000 to clothe their vision with the appearance of reality. They boxed the old stone hotel on the verge of East Point within a spread of wooden wings four hundred feet long, five stories high. Four acres of carpeted floors. Three hundred rooms, every one claiming an ocean view, all with access to "bathing apartments" offering hot, cold, fresh and salt water, all connected to the annunciator at the main desk by nine miles of wire, all steam heated during the chills of early autumn, illuminated by gas manufactured on the premises and put in touch with Boston by telegraph strung across Long Beach. Stables for two hundred horses were built, and bowling saloons, a shooting gallery, and a remarkable Greek Revival billiard hall of stone. There were saddle horses and carriages for hire, and yachts and fishing boats, and hops, concerts, balls and extravaganzas. In their grandest splash, the promoters launched the steamship *Nelly Baker,* 153 feet long, in 1854. She was built expressly for the run from the city and was said to be the fastest vessel in Boston Harbor; she certainly was the most famous on the Nahant line during her brief civilian career, which ended with Civil War service as a hospital ship, and she left behind haunting memories of a fogbound coast, the *Nelly* somewhere out there blasting her whistle every minute or two, and the answering horn from the unseen shore directing her to the wharf.

Henry Cabot Lodge, who as an isolationist senator sixty-five years later led the opposition to the League of Nations, summered at his Grandfather Cabot's cottage. His childhood memory of the hotel, soon after it reopened in 1854 in its new magnificence, was of a "huge wooden barrack . . . ugly, tasteless, with no quality but size. . . . There was at the outset, however, a brief period of gayety and success, the hotel was full, and fashion seemed to justify the anticipation of Mr. Stevens." Full indeed. At the height of those first seasons the overflow slept on mattresses lined up on the hallway floors.

The resurgence of the hotel life at Nahant was regarded with amusement by Professor Cornelius C. Felton, Harvard classical scholar married to a daughter of Colonel Perkins. "Hither comes the youthful dandy, with the suspicion of a mustache on his lip, and a cigar in his mouth. Middle aged men and old men, fat men and lean men, stout ladies and slender ladies, disport themselves on the rocks, and repair the waste of exercise by the daily chowder, prefixed to the far fetched luxuries of a city dinner. . . . The morning concerts and evening dances at the hotel fill up the time and employ the heels and voices of the performers, as well as the ears and eyes of the spectators in the most agreeable manner."

Nothing in an anonymous bit of fluff entitled "Belle-Life at Nahant," which appeared in *Harper's Weekly* toward the close of the 1858 season, as much as hinted that the emperor of hotel men might be heading for his Waterloo or that Nahant might not soon put Newport to rout.

"I bowl, bathe, dance, dine, flirt, drive, sigh, smile, pick up mosses, and wander over the rocks in a broad-brimmed hat and a very becoming morning dress," chatters our visiting belle, who spends half the forenoon with her nice but not very smart Tom Dyce preparatory to bathing. . . . "Good heavens, what monsters we are in the water. I think that the baggy bathing-gowns, and the caps and hats, are the most hideous insults to the ocean. Why not put on India rubber dresses and take umbrellas?"

Then for a late morning nap, then lunch, and then for a drive over Long Beach with Tom's rival in his dogcart, his natty groom up behind, "lovers and flirters, and young married pairs in wagons, on horses, in carriages; papas and mammas, aunts and uncles, rolling by in closer carriages, beholding us upon the same beach, in the same sunset — laughing, loving, chattering — gay ghosts of their departed selves — brisk and beautiful spectacle of an hour, while the sea is down, and before it comes up lazily and wipes all our traces away."

Then back to the hotel for tea, the ball, the moonlight stroll on the piazza with Tom. And then to bed.

But hark! Belle springs to the window and peeps below. "It is only my Tom Dyce, and ten men he has hired for fifty dollars to blow and fiddle on brass and wood" . . . dear old Tom, empty of head, and empty of purse "because he has been filling the pockets of host, musicians, boatmen, hostlers, billiard saloons, bowling-alleys, and the bar-keeper, from his own."

The sharp-tongued English actress Fanny Kemble stayed at the Nahant Hotel that same summer of 1858 and in a letter home gave her own version of the "belle-life": "How you would open your eyes and stop your ears if you were here! This enormous house is filled with American women, one prettier than the other, who look like fairies, dress like duchesses or *femmes entretenues,* behave like housemaids and scream like peacocks."

In spite of Consul Grattan's fervent hope that Paran Stevens might "be, like his wealthier, but less liberal predecessor, every inch a colonel," the Nahant Hotel closed forever on the first of October, 1859, after a season fraught with false hopes. As George William Curtis had penned the obituary of the first hotel era, so Henry Cabot Lodge (with grim satisfaction, for the land on which it stood came eventually to him) wrote the epitaph of the last: "Nahant, divided as it was from the country of woods and fields by three miles of beach and a growing manufacturing city, was too small and too remote from the mainland ever to be a great watering-place. She could not sustain so vast a scheme, and the panic of 1857, together with the gathering clouds of civil war, only served to hasten the inevitable catastrophe. Mr. Stevens was the first to hear the hand of fate knocking at the door. He disappeared quickly and adroitly from the scene, leaving his associates with the hotel and the mortgages."

Nahanters who sighed with relief over the closing of the ugly, tasteless barrack in their midst might better have held their breaths. The Ice King was at that instant of mutual congratulation thawing out a disagreeable surprise for them, the ultimate eccentricity of a long career. Frederic Tudor, now seventy-six, chose the demise of the hotel epoch on Nahant in 1859 as the moment of creation for one of the very earliest, possibly the first, full-fledged amusement parks in America. Amused, his neighbors were not. Most everyone had been delighted when the snowy-bearded tycoon with those frosty eyes had made Nahant bloom with trees and vegetation; but now he proposed, in the words of one who applauded his plan, to offer a refuge in the heart of the resort for the public, "who would otherwise be deterred by the fear of trespassing upon private grounds, where some unhospitable sign-board forbids eating your luncheon if you are hungry, or of overstepping certain imaginary boundaries if adventurous."

Unfortunately for the peace and quiet of his abutters, the awkward truth was that the open pasture behind North Spring's clear, cold trickle at the shore edge of Tudor's property, where he chose to launch his latest enthusiasm, was a public chowder and stamping ground by tradition. Furthermore, it was adjoined on the west by Cadet Field, which every July for a decade at least (and as it would be for another fifteen years) had been the tenting and marching ground of Boston's First Corps of Cadets, of which several prominent summer residents were members. Here the governor's honor guard paraded in brilliant uniform, put on band concerts and evening collations, and flirted with the flower of Nahant, the whole colorful excitement of Cadet Week climaxing with the appearance of His Excellency on Governor's Day for review.

Tudor bought the North Spring pasture between Ocean and Pond streets about the time a second freshet was discovered on the shore to the east of it. He built a circular wall around this new spring in 1859, called it the "Pool of Maolis" (a transposition of Jerusalem's Pool of Siloam) and "Maolis Gardens," the curious project which for the remaining five years of his life engaged his whimsy and his furious energy.

Around his pasture Nahant's master of the unexpected erected a ten-foot slat fence with entrance gate (adults five cents, children three). Inside, he planted trees and flower beds, built a restaurant on the edge of the cliff overlooking the ocean, a dance hall, a small hotel, several open pavilions, which could be hired for picnics that required cooking, and an ice cream parlor. His men installed seesaws and swings, one of which was fifty feet high with a collective seat. Flying horses were added, and a shooting range, a croquet field, bowling alleys, wheels of fortune, a Punch and Judy show, caged animals and two tame bears, Ben Butler and Jeff Davis, which took their keeper to the beach for dips. Indians from Old Town, Maine, sold baskets and trinkets, and concessions were let to the balloon man, the candy man and the tintype artist.

Was the Fun King in his second childhood? The teahouse of Maolis Gardens was a temple-like pavilion of marble, tiles and seashells. Nearby was an octagonal fancy of similar construction sheltering a pool in which stood the spouting statue of a boy covered with shells; a third pavilion consisted simply of a tilted circular roof, the Parasol. He blasted a den out of a cleft in the ledge and had a local mason carve a stone lion that glared out from behind the iron bars of its cage. A painted clay bull menaced little children from its pen under the trees. Everywhere was strange statuary, and on every surface playful paintings and murals such as the sea serpent, which writhed across a hundred feet of slat fence and appeared and disappeared as one walked by.

Frederic Tudor was eighty when he died in 1864. It was said that he spent no less than $30,000 a year the last thirty of his life on his eccentric projects at Nahant. His widow carried on valiantly after the Civil War and is credited with inventing the barge, the horse-drawn conveyance for guests familiar to every summer hotel, when she bought a boat-sleigh called *Cleopatra's Barge* and had it put on wheels to carry passengers from the Lynn depot to Maolis Gardens. By 1882, however, the crowds had shifted to Revere Beach, and that June, when Mrs. Tudor's amusement park opened under the strict temperance management of the Lynn Reform Club, it presented a "ragged appearance" to a visiting reporter, and the speakers almost outnumbered their hearers.

Before her death in 1884 the Ice Queen willed Maolis to the town of Nahant, but it was more than the taxpayers would support, and they refused the gift, settling eventually for Tudor Wharf. In 1892 most of what was left was removed. Today there remains a single intact monument to the driving, driven Despot of the Ice Trade, who wanted possibly more than all else to be loved by his fellows en masse. This is the Witch House, last remnant of his midway, standing on a private estate near the corner of Marginal Road and Ocean Street. Eight fieldstone columns support the octagonal gabled roof. Time has stripped away most of the weird carved ornaments and doodads, and it broods above the sea, a pseudo-Druidic put-on left there by Nahant's most extraordinary, and unfathomable, citizen.

At Newport the sea whispered in Italian to Henry Wadsworth Longfellow; at Nahant it roared in Norse. The poet listened to the accents of Newport one summer, but he settled for Nahant's, where the Atlantic crashed ashore as he made it crash against Gloucester's reef of Norman's Woe with "the sound of the trampling surf/On the rocks and the hard sea-sand," and where, by way of contrast, he could turn landward to the cows wending across Long Beach into the sunset from their pasture on Little Nahant and meditate on how "their red hides and the reflection of the wet sand light up the gray picture of the sky and surge."

During the Olympian era of his summer residence Longfellow by tacit acclamation occupied the highest nook among the literary *lares et penates* who accompanied Beacon Street's vernal flight from the heat of the American Athens to the coolness of Cold Roast. As a visiting journalist, George William Curtis thought the atmosphere seductive — "if a man had any work to do, Nahant opens its arms to him, and folds him into the sweetest silence and seclusion." Or so it seemed to him. Not quite so to William Hickling Prescott, who, unlike his brethren celebrities who throve on adulation, chafed increasingly in the ambient toils of the resort's embrace.

One day two strangers mistook the Prescott cottage, which perched on a cliff a short stroll from the steamboat wharf and the hotel, for an inn and mounted the piazza demanding sustenance. The historian's mother graciously obliged. They took their ease, took in the ocean view and an excellent lunch, and when they pushed back their chairs and prepared to pay up were advised crisply by their hostess: "This is Judge Prescott's house and you are entirely welcome to any refreshment it has given you." The judge's almost blind son was so imposed upon by idle lionizers, he wrote, that "I have lost a clear month here by company. . . . Yet how can I escape it, tied like a bear to a stake here? I will devise some way another year, or Nahant shall be 'Nae haunt of mine.'" Some other way he did devise, finally, and in 1853 forsook *Th' Haunt,* as the colony's domestic servants called it, and its blinding sea glare for a house on the beach at Lynn, where he spent the remaining six summers of his life.

The year previous to Prescott's desertion of Nahant, 1852, was marked by the permanent departures of a faded old "Haunter," Daniel Webster, and a brilliant new arrival, the sculptor Horatio Greenough, an early protégé of Colonel Perkins. Greenough was building the cellar walls of his cottage, where the Library stands today, when he died suddenly, at the age of forty-seven. Webster, on the other hand, had been visiting James W. Paige (a relative whose estate was across the road from Greenough's property) for years, though the Great Man's first loyalty, it must be conceded, was to Marshfield on the South Shore, where he had bought a Tory homestead and turned "a sterile waste of sandy hills to a charming landscape of fertility and beauty."

Webster was the political voice of the summering Lawrences and Lowells and their financial interests, a voice that echoed sonorously if briefly from the aristocratic throat of another summer Nahanter, Robert C. Winthrop, his former law clerk named to Webster's seat when he resigned from the Senate in 1850. Charles Sumner, the ramrod abolitionist who defeated Winthrop in his first run on his own in 1851, was a frequent Nahant visitor in later years. The whole town was invited to the reception Paige gave for Webster after he lost the Whig presidential nomination earlier in 1852. Just before the end, ravaged by drink, the most famous man in America made one last visit to the resort.

The departure of Prescott, literary conquistador of Mexico and Peru, left John Lothrop Motley as Nahant's historian-in-residence. Here he had summered since he had learned to read in the stone schoolhouse. Tom Appleton and Wendell Phillips were his boyhood chums in Boston, where Wendell tested his oratory and the three of them shouted poetry and strutted about in finery they found in attic trunks under the eaves of Mot's family home on Beacon Hill. "Cassandra in masculine shape of our long prosperous Ilium," said Dr. Holmes of the terribly handsome abolitionist, twitting affectionately his patrician cousin's "melodious prophecies." In 1840 the Phillips family (Wendell's father, John, was Boston's first mayor) bought the old Johnson House, archetype of the North Shore summer hotel, and made it their manor and the west shore of Bass Point

The Nahant Hotel achieved its grandest proportions under Paran Stevens, who was engaged to manage it in 1852. The polka was published two years later. Nahant Public Library

*Frederic Tudor. From* History of Essex County, *D. H. Hurd, editor*

*A column of the Ice King's trees marches along the south shore of Nahant toward Bailey's Hill in this enthusiastic 1860 drawing by Dr. Piper for* The Trees of America. *Nahant Public Library*

*Maolis Gardens, about 1870. The Witch House (above) stands today, though no longer guarded by the stone lion in his lair. Below, the Ice Cream Pavilion. Nahant Public Library*

*Louis Agassiz, March 1, 1860. Essex
Institute*

*Henry Wadsworth Longfellow.
Essex Institute*

*The Prescott cottage. Lynn Historical Society*

looking across the water to the Point of Pines their fiefdom. "Old Castle" was torn down in 1903, ending the fears and hopes of a couple of generations of Nahant youngsters that it was haunted by the ghosts of long-gone revelers.

Motley cut as fine a figure as Phillips and took himself less seriously. A sociable scholar, he was frequently tagged for diplomatic missions in Europe and never lacked for invitations to revisit Nahant, sometimes at the cottage of his brother, Edward, near Dashing Rock. While boarding with Mrs. Hood he wrote portions of *The Rise of the Dutch Republic,* a labor from which distractions were not always unwelcome, as he confessed to George Curtis. "After breakfast at Nahant I feel like Coeur de Lion, and burn to give battle to the Saracens. But the brave impulse ends in smoke, and musing and chatting, and building castles in the clouds, you loiter away the day upon the piazza, ending by climbing about the cliffs at sunset or galloping over the beach."

No beach-galloper, Longfellow surrendered sedately to Nahant's Norse beguilements about the time he took Frances Elizabeth Appleton for his second wife, in 1843. He was thirty-six, and she was a sister of Thomas Gold Appleton. After a few years the brothers-in-law built and shared a cottage above Curlew (inevitably renamed Longfellow) Beach. When Captain Arthur Clark, Ben Clark's son renowned in the clipper trade, demonstrated the ocean racing potential of Yankee yachts by sailing Appleton's forty-eight-foot sloop *Alice* from Nahant to the Isle of Wight in nineteen days in 1866, the owner's nephew, Charles A. Longfellow, was a crew member. One summer day when he was a greener hand, young Charlie sailed a small boat across the bay to Lynn to visit his Uncle Tom's brother, Nathan Appleton, but capsized, and was soaking when he arrived. Nathan loaned him a pair of slippers to wear home and next day received from Nahant a parcel on which was written in the poet's hand:

> *Slippers that perhaps another,*
> *Sailing o'er the bay of Lynn,*
> *Forlorn or shipwrecked nephew*
> *Seeing, may purloin again.*

No one relished a glass of claret with Tom Appleton any more than Wendell Holmes. The peppery little anatomist had not yet in the 1850s abandoned his country place in Pittsfield for Beverly Farms ("if you would be happy in Berkshire, you must carry mountains in your brain; and if you would enjoy Nahant, you must have an ocean in your soul"); but as the uncommon denominator of the Boston literati he knew everybody at Nahant and everybody knew him. Dr. Holmes wrote Motley of encountering a barouche one day in Boston "and out jumped Tom Appleton in the flesh, and plenty of it, as aforetime. We embraced — or rather he embraced me and I partially spanned his goodly circumference." Of Appleton's talk, it was "witty, entertaining, audacious, ingenious, sometimes extravagant, but fringed always with pleasing fancies as deep as the border of a Queen's cashmere. . . . I never heard such a fusilade in my life" — praise indeed from Boston's marathon monologist.

Longfellow entertained and walked the beach with Emerson and Whittier, and was entertained by the Ice King and his odd friend, Dr. R. V. Piper, and their talk of planting Iceland with trees, as Tudor had Nahant, thereby turning the frozen waste into one vast wheat field. Piper cut a comical figure in his green sash as surgeon of the Nahant Home Guards during the Civil War — the "Piper Guards" — and thought the Rebs had landed when some jokers dragged a cannon up behind his cottage and fired it off.

In the course of preparing a panegyric on the home life of Longfellow, Blanche Roosevelt Tucker-Macchetta visited the Longfellow-Appleton ménage when her hosts were advanced in age. She found a spacious Italianate cottage girt by a simple garden of roses and sweetbrier. The family assembled for breakfast in the airy dining room at the back which looked out over the porticoed terrace and the sea. On the wall were "some curious painted pebbles, framed in a background of velvet . . . faithful pictures of the surrounding scenery" by Appleton, who sometimes with his daughters (Edith was Mrs. Richard Henry Dana, Jr.) sat across the table from the bard, all in wicker chairs. Longfellow was a light eater, declaring that "most people have a famous appetite at the seashore, but I never had. I think the very sight and sound of it constitute sufficient nourishment." After he had finished, "a general sally takes place through the French window, and the broad balcony is soon peopled with animated faces . . . he sits at a round table drawn up near the edge of the terrace, with a light mantle thrown across his shoulders to protect him from the sea-breeze, which is always strong and brisk at Nahant." Later he took Blanche for a ride around the resort in his open Victoria behind his coachman and ebony black horses.

Mrs. Tucker-Macchetta quoted ample Tom Appleton on a proper Nahant fish chowder. "Chowder is only good when made in private houses. At hotels it is watery and insipid, while the fish and chowder crackers are usually boiled to rags. The way to make it is this. The fish (cod or haddock) should be broken into large flakes, and boiled twenty minutes with plenty of salt pork and milk and chowder biscuits."

Next to Appleton's, the most admired chowders at Nahant were served by Emelyn Story, wife of William Wetmore Story, the poet-sculptor; they had the cottage built by his mother, widow of Judge Joseph Story, east of the Perkins compound. On a visit to England, where she stayed at a castle filled with important guests, Mrs. Story was persuaded by the ladies to instruct her hostess's housekeeper in the preparation of a Nahant chowder. *"Chowder,"* they repeated, "how charmingly Indian that sounds!" Emelyn was rather put down by this factotum and stammered out the recipe, upon which, she told her friend Caroline King, the housekeeper sniffed, "I will do my best, Mrs. Story, but I cannot think it will be nice." When the "chowder" arrived only the old general who had taken Emelyn in to dinner "stood to his guns, and while the tears stood in his eyes from the effort, like the hero he was, gallantly took a second spoonful, murmuring to his neighbor, 'Capital, by Jove.' But Emelyn having meanwhile tasted the nauseous mixture came speedily to his relief, exclaiming, 'Oh, General B., don't try to eat this horrible stuff, it is not in the least like a chowder.' . . . Having no sea fish, they had made it from fresh fish from the pond in the park; having nothing that answered to our crackers, soft bread had been substituted; having no salt pork, slices of ham had been used; whole onions were added, and the dreadful mess boiled in milk."

Mrs. Story's disgust was reciprocated by Consul Grattan's revulsion from the Nahant chowder — "a thick mess . . . an odious compound."

Longfellow was an intimate friend of his Cambridge neighbor, Professor Felton. The robust Greek scholar had married Mary Louisa Cary in 1846, the year of the arrival at Harvard of Jean Louis Rodolphe Agassiz. The Swiss naturalist was thirty-nine, his reputation as a zoologist established, his glacial theory more than glacially advanced, and he came to America with all his manic magnetism to explore a new world "where Nature was rich, but tools and workmen few and traditions none." Agassiz and Felton hit it off from the day they met. Mrs. Agassiz had remained in Europe, too ill to accompany her husband, and died in 1848. Louis in the meanwhile was introduced to Felton's sister-in-law, Elizabeth Cary, and to the Nahant beloved by their circle. In 1850 the widower and Elizabeth were married.

Four years later the sisters' venerable grandfather, Thomas Handasyd Perkins, the founder of the Nahant summer colony, died at the age of eighty-nine, spurning all entreaties that he take to his bed: "Certainly not. I have always proposed to die dressed and sitting in my chair." And so, they say, he did. His stone cottage near Spouting Horn went to his daughter Mary and her husband, Thomas G. Cary; they moved a foursquare house, the "Butter Box," onto the family land above the bluffs and turned it over to their daughters and their learned husbands.

Almost surrounded and deeply eroded by the ocean, Nahant was an ideal natural laboratory for Louis Agassiz's studies of geology (in 1851 he discovered in the slate and limestone fossils by which the strata were proved years afterward to be Lower Cambrian) and marine zoology. A small lab was tacked on to the Butter Box for him, so near the ocean that he had a constant supply of salt water for his aquarium and a cornucopian one of specimens from the local fishermen, who brought him their exotic catches. "It is said the finny tenants of the sea already know the philosopher, who has done so much to sound their fame all over the world," Professor Felton joshed. "They surrender themselves cheerfully without hook or bait, bob or sinker, for the good of science, into his hands. . . . All the odd fish, star fishes, sea urchins, shovel sharks and the like find the way to the workshop of Agassiz, but none of them get back again. Perhaps they chose to remain; perhaps they prefer their lot; for they are forthwith thrown into bottles or casks and continue in liquor the rest of their days."

The great Agassiz would hole up for hours in this seashore laboratory; yet, as Emma Cary remarked, "he could come out of this state of absorption and join in the merriment of the young people like a boy free from care and responsibility." The gentle scientist radiated warmth, and but for the season of his residence, it equally could have been said of the Butter Box that "one has less need of an overcoat in passing Agassiz's house than by any other in Cambridge." Dr. Holmes regarded Elizabeth Agassiz "so wonderfully fitted to be his wife that it seems as if he could not have bettered his choice if all womankind had passed before him." As a measure of her devotion to the compulsive collector, she was dressing one morning while they were traveling and discovered a small snake in her shoe. "What, only one?" cried her husband. "Where is the other six?"

Cornelius Felton, too, loved the company of family and friends at Nahant, but like Agassiz he must have time for study and contemplation. The classicist was most content lolling upon the brink of the cliff, where he could watch the sails crossing the horizon and "the play of purple, blue, green, and the flash of the foaming waves as they break along the rocks; the march of the clouds across the sky, and now and then a fog-bank slowly and majestically sweeping landward and hiding all behind it like a solid wall." In the consummation of his career Felton was appointed president of Harvard in 1860, but he was in poor health and died in 1862. Louis Agassiz died in 1873. His widow then helped found Radcliffe College and presided over it from 1894 to 1902.

In 1934, when Robert Grant was eighty-two, he published *Fourscore — An Autobiography*. Better known as a novelist than as Suffolk County Judge of Probate, Grant described his boyhood summers at Nahant as if they were his yesterdays. The clouds of civil war, like that fog bank that transfixed the imagination of Professor Felton, were sweeping the land, and still no hint of the coming conflict seemed to mar the equanimity of Boston's summer colony, where the lad stayed with his grandmother, Mrs. Henry G. Rice, in her cottage almost on top of the sea at the tip end of the point of land between Irene's Grotto and Swallow's Cave.

"Cows on the place!" was the rallying cry that a neighbor's bossies had slipped through the Rice gate and were placidly trimming the grass. The men in the family commuted to Boston in the steamship *Nelly Baker,* leaving at 8 and returning on the 3:45 in time for an early dinner of partridge or squab, perhaps, delivered to the door by Mr. Blood, fruit and vegetables by Mr. Richardson, on their daily rounds from Lynn. Mrs. Rice's kitchen was set off from the main house, and meals were carried up the gravel path in covered dishes. "I can see as clearly as if it were yesterday my grandmother's very dignified and worthy butler John Nash on his way with the blue-and-white soup tureen which warned us that dinner was ready."

In the Boston manner, the routine was regular and predictable. Every weekday afternoon Grandmother Rice drove forth in her hired barouche, sometimes accompanied by young Robert up on the box with the coachman, always across the beach to Lynn, along fashionable Ocean Street to Swampscott, and back. Two or three times a season Grant's father and uncles would charter a schooner and take the boys along for a day's trip to the fishing grounds, with prizes for the first and biggest catch, and chowder for all steady enough in the stomach to partake. (Female athletics stopped at the last wicket on the croquet field.)

For all Nahant, the great event of the summer was Cadet Week, whose "semblance of roughing it in tents on the verge of the ocean served as a stimulus to midnight flirtation under the trees or on the improvised parade ground."

The scandal of the decade was staged by Grant's aunt after she ran off and left her husband, Henry Gardner Rice. In August of 1860 the aggrieved spouse was awarded custody of their son, Charles Allen Thorndike Rice. One day soon after, the cousins were in summer school in the Nahant church when three kidnappers swept in and abducted Charlie. Two were captured and identified on the testimony of a witness, Henry Cabot Lodge, who was eleven and a playmate of the cousins. The third, believed to have been Mrs. Rice herself in disguise, escaped with the boy to Europe, where he was educated. In time, C. A. T. Rice recrossed the Atlantic, became the sensationally successful editor of the *North American Review,* organized archeological digs, ran for Congress and almost made it, and was about to embark as Minister to Russia in 1889 when he suddenly died.

The boy who fingered Charlie Rice's abductors was not to be the least distinguished of the summer chums, and like Judge Grant, Senator Lodge reverted to those carefree days at the North Shore's first resort, which would be his lifelong home, in *Early Memories*.

"The love of the sea," Lodge wrote, "which a child acquires who has been reared at its very edge deepens through life, and nothing can ever replace it. I played upon the beaches and climbed among the rocks; I loved the sea smiling and beautiful in the midsummer heats, and I loved it even more in the great gales of the autumn, when the huge waves broke over the cliffs and ledges, filling me with interest and excitement as I watched them by the hour together." Cabot learned to swim and row and sail a boat, "accomplishments really worth having and one of the rare portions of my education which have been of use and pleasure to me my whole life through. There was, too, a certain enchantment about the place — the mystery and magic of the sea, I suppose — and such dreams and imaginings as I had were all connected with Nahant and not with Boston."

On September 12, 1861, five months to the day after the bombardment of Fort Sumter and the onset of the Civil War, the Nahant Hotel caught fire ("as empty mortgaged buildings sometimes do," in the skeptical words of Henry Cabot Lodge, who inherited the real estate on which it had stood since Colonel Perkins put it there) "and after making a most magnificent blaze for the benefit of onlookers along miles of coast, was burned to the ground."

That was the utter end of the hotel period at Nahant. Along the rest of the North Shore the breezy days of piazzas measured by the mile were in the offing, over a dark horizon, somewhere beyond the approaching firestorm of war. The storm descended, and in the midst of it one of the summer people returned, and reflected as if in a dream: "Nahant is very solitary and deserted this year. I stood looking down at the steamboat landing opposite — not a fishing boat, not a human being in sight; then the ghostly little steamer comes in, and the phantoms go over the hill towards the ruins of the burned hotel, and all is still and lonely again."

# 5

## nter
## the Iron Monster

NEVER ONE TO BE LEFT STANDING AT THE STATION, COLONEL PERKINS in 1826 had bankrolled the first railroad in America, the Granite Railway Company, to horse-haul the stones for the Bunker Hill Monument from his Quincy quarry over rails of wood to the Neponset River, whence they were sailed to Charlestown. Four more years and he was promoting a steam road between Boston and the textile mills of Lowell, in which he held a large stake. By then the rail age was hissing down the track.

So it is no great surprise to find the builder of the country's first seaside resort hotel at Nahant, as a stop on New England's first steamship line, asking the Massachusetts General Court in 1832 to charter the first train service in Essex County, between Boston and Salem. The five hundred horses of the Eastern Stage Company were pulling 77,000 passengers a year over that route alone. Its stock was at double par and nowhere higher than under the golden dome of the State House, where the sympathetic legislators stopped the "Iron Monster's" incursion into the stage's territory on its tracks.

Never mind. One way or another the prescient Perkins was bound to hitch this radical new source of energy to his hobby of exploiting the attractions of the North Shore, so near to Boston and yet so far away. It happened that in precisely the two hundredth year of its operation in 1831, the easygoing Winnisimmet ferry had gone broke. The bankruptcy trustees replaced the sisterly sailboats that since colonial days had tacked back and forth to Boston at the weather's whim with the small steamer *Robin Hood,* which shortly gave way to the new steam ferries *Boston* and *Chelsea.* In the bargain they also acquired the Williams Farm, covering a large area of lower Chelsea. The immediate attraction was the homestead that crowned a knoll above the ferry landing and long had doubled as a drinking and watering spot for Bostonians, who for generations crossed the harbor in the heat of summer to shoot in the marshes and creeks of Chelsea and to quaff punch in quantities requiring a washtub for the mixing. The new managers rebuilt the old place as a small resort hotel.

After two years the trustees conveyed their franchise and lands to the Winnisimmet Land and Ferry Company, of which Colonel Perkins was a principal. A single season of steamers had seen the end of Ferry Farm as a languid landing, painted by Robert Salmon and Charles Hubbard and described in the words of Walter Merriam Pratt, where the green hills "ran down into the salt water and were divided by stone walls, overgrown with barberry bushes; with here and there a great elm or Lombardy poplar, or a huge clump of weeping willows, as a landmark, [where] on and between the gentle hills, composing the town, were hawthorn hedges which blossomed white in spring and in fall had red berries."

Now Bostonians sped across on the new steam ferries to swarm over the balconies of the hotel and gape at the several balloon ascensions of Lewis A. Lauriat, who one summer floated heavenward and landed in Lynn, faring differently, if not better, than a Mr. Durant, who arose from Boston in 1834, transited Nahant and dropped into the ocean, where he was rescued after fifteen minutes by a passing schooner.

And there were dramas at this lively and now-forgotten resort on the bank of the Mystic — acrobatics, tightrope walks, even a circular railroad for children, some thirty feet across and drawn by flying horses spurred by a sweating minion who cranked the affair by hand (evidence of the Perkins hand again, perhaps). Some fine mansions were built on the Chelsea slopes, with broad views across the river to

Boston and the harbor, excellently terraced and gardened. Ferry Village bid fair, with its hotel and cottages and steamer landing, to rival Nahant.

But the steamer that brought the charms of Chelsea within reach of the spreading city across the water also placed that pleasant countryside within its grasp; the Perkins group closed the fingers. The twenty souls in the Ferry Village of 1831 increased eightyfold in ten years, and to five thousand by midcentury. Outpriced for residences, the waterfront sprouted factories spawned by the industrial revolution. Rows of brick tenements, planted on the flatlands for the workers who poured in from Boston and abroad, overripened into slums. Even the lovely hill graced by the balconied hotel was leveled. By 1857, when Chelsea attained cityhood, its population exceeded twelve thousand. Eighty years later Walter Merriam Pratt, survivor of an early Winnisimmet family, wrote a bitter obituary. "Grasping and unscrupulous avarice found a pretty village and turned it into city slums. Where once on a summer day cattle could be seen standing knee-deep in the shining tide overflowing the broad creek . . . now flourishes the greatest rag market of the United States."

The brief triumph of oats over steam evaporated with the opening of three different railroads out of Boston in 1835, and when a group headed by the Danvers-born financier George Peabody proposed that year to lay a fourth line of tracks through Salem to Newburyport, the General Court approved the line; the Eastern Stage gave way to the Eastern Railroad Company the following spring. From the East Boston Company, which had renamed and was developing Noddle's Island, the railroad bought a right of way to the landing for its steam ferries that would shuttle the two thousand feet across the harbor to Lewis Wharf. The tracks coursed from East Boston in a nearly straight line over the expanse of salt marsh behind great Chelsea Beach, over the Saugus River, through the heart of Lynn and the west of Swampscott, and on to Salem. Gangs of Irish laborers dug and piled the bed and laid rails "chaired" high above the ground to prevent their blockage by snow.

The Eastern's inaugural train clattered and jerked with high fanfare, disgorging clouds of smoke and showers of sparks from its wood fire, into the Salem depot on August 27, 1838. Although they were the first to boast ladies' and toilet rooms, the twenty-four passenger cars were so loosely chained together that anyone standing when they started and stopped was thrown to the floor. Time from Salem to Lewis Wharf, including the ferry ride across the harbor, was thirty-five minutes. The fare was fifty cents, half that charged by the stage company. Six trains a day. Before most departures from Salem, Corporal Joshua Pitman, a one-legged local character who claimed to be a Revolutionary veteran, clanged the bell in the station's belfry; he always said he could tell if someone else had rung it and not he, by the tone.

The corporal's bell tolled for the competition. Already the Boston and Lowell road had penetrated to Haverhill, and now the Iron Monster threaded his way through Essex County, "enfolding in his fatal coils," as Salem historian Robert S. Rantoul put the matter, "the poor struggling Stage Companies whose nightly dreams were disturbed by the scream of the whistle, and whose waking eyes, turn where they might, were blasted with those words of doom, *Look out for the engine.*" From twenty-three trips a day to Boston from Lynn alone, Eastern Stage dashed into runaway bankruptcy and ruin on June 26, 1838, two months before the railroad had even got up steam.

Pushing on through Salem, Irish immigrant laborers dug a huge trench along Washington Street and laid up a granite arch inside, 718 feet long, which they covered with earth for a tunnel. Past the city, the tracks bridged Beverly Harbor, traversed the meadows and glens of Beverly, Wenham and Hamilton, reached Ipswich at the end of 1839, then Newburyport in the summer of 1840, and Portsmouth, New Hampshire, on New Year's Eve, linking in 1842 with the Portland, Saco and Portsmouth Railroad, which became the Boston and Maine in 1843. Meanwhile, prospering at the zenith of their fishery and nursing along their shoe factories, Marbleheaders subscribed enough Eastern shares to finance their own branch from Salem, which opened on December 10, 1839.

The effluent Back Bay, which drove affluent Boston to the North Shore, photographed from the dome of the State House in 1857. The Mill Dam, later an extension of Beacon Street, separates the miasma from the Charles River. The new tree-lined Arlington Street and recently filled Public Garden extend to the left. Boston Public Library, Print Department

*The idyllic Chelsea waterfront, painted by Robert Salmon in 1832, shows the old Winnisimmet ferry landing and, above it, at right, the new resort hotel. Peabody Museum of Salem*

Early Eastern Railroad summer timetable. F. B. C. Bradlee collection, Essex Institute

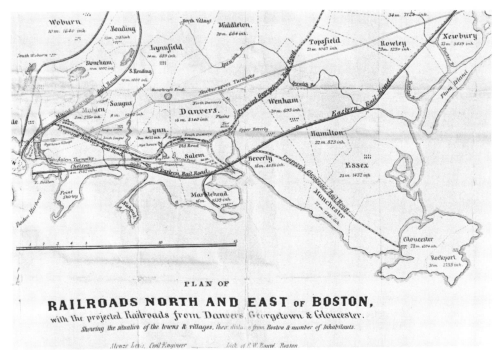

Alonzo Lewis's map of about 1845 shows the Salem and Newburyport turnpikes and the Eastern Railroad when it still connected with Boston by ferry. Essex Institute

*Enoch Redington Mudge's "Elmwood," Swampscott. From* History of Lynn, *by Alonzo Lewis and James R. Newhall (1865)*

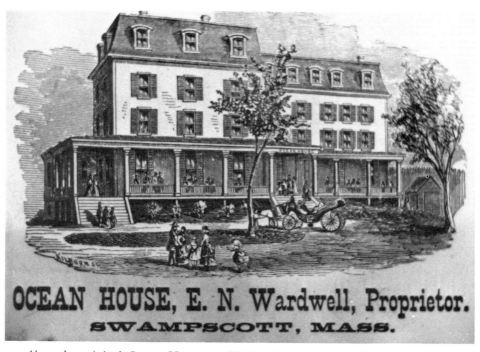

# OCEAN HOUSE, E. N. Wardwell, Proprietor.
## SWAMPSCOTT, MASS.

*After the original Ocean House on Phillips Point burned, the "Anawan" was moved to the site and renamed the Beach House; Wardwell bought it in the late 1860s, took it to Whale Beach and renamed it, again, the Ocean House. Lynn Historical Society*

Like it or not, the North Shore, Essex County, New England, America, followed the shining rails where they might lead. Many balked at "that giant," as one mossback groused, "that has stretched forth its arm, and laid, literally, a hand of iron upon the bosom of Essex County." And they were still grumbling in 1872 when a spur darted off from Wenham to Essex, where a native grieved: "Yes, the road has got here; we've fought it off for thirty years, but it has come after all, and I suppose it will stay." It did — for seventy years.

Others, like Salem's Rantoul, rejoiced: "If Boston is the Hub, the Railroads seen from the State House dome are the living spokes, which bind it to an outer circle of social and business relations. If these have carried off our men of enterprise in search of a larger market, they have brought back the wealth they accumulate, to beautify our estates and elevate our culture, and make of Massachusetts Bay, from Plymouth to Cape Ann, one great suburb in which the arts of cultivated life are brought to aid the native charms of country living."

The railroad penetrated the North Shore just as the charms of country living were looking more attractive to Bostonians of means with every passing summer. Again, Thomas Handasyd Perkins was behind it. Back in 1814 he had led a move in the General Court to build a mill dam westward across the middle of the Back Bay as a source of water power for factories that would presumably spring up in response. His intention was not to drive his wealthy friends to the beds and bars of his Nahant Hotel, for that had not yet taken shape in his mind; yet the fruition of the project provided the push for the railroad's pull that populated the resorts of the North Shore.

The Colonel did not carry all with him on this one. A truly clairvoyant reader wrote the Boston *Daily Advertiser:* "What think you of converting the beautiful sheet of water which skirts the Common into an empty mud-basin, reeking with filth, abhorrent to the smell, and disgusting to the eye? By every god of sea, lake, or fountain, it is incredible." All the same, the Milldam was completed in 1821.

Hardly a hope of its backers, and all the fears of its foes, materialized. Built across the flats as an extension of Beacon Street, the Milldam failed to provide significant water power, and although it gave the city another land access as an alternative to Boston Neck, it shut off most of the cleansing tidal circulation of the Charles River, which had previously watered the 680 acres of the Back Bay. This sorry deterioration coincided with the displacement of the Boston establishment from its traditional strongholds by the influx of European immigrants and the rise of the working class. The reaction of the uprooted was to escape westward down the only route they trusted, Beacon Street, which now, of course, led straight through the muck.

By 1849 the Board of Health was condemning the Back Bay as a "nuisance, offensive and injurious to the large and increasing population residing upon it." To Justin Winsor it was in "an abominably filthy state . . . an open cesspool, receiving the sewage of a large community." Public pressure (and the dreams of speculators) forced the issue; the state intervened, and the famous filling that turned the melancholy miasma into Commonwealth Avenue and Copley Square and the Fens of the Muddy River, tributary of the Charles, began in 1858 and continued for several years, the building upon it for many more.

Bishop William L. Lawrence remembered the Back Bay when the filling had barely started. "The Public Garden," he wrote, "was then a dirty waste, and at Arlington Street was the city dump, where ashes and other refuse were thrown by tipcarts into the Back Bay." The southwest air of summer, hot as blazes, drifted torpidly over the flats before assailing the nostrils of Beacon Street, where the boy George Santayana moved with his family in 1872 into number 302, one of the last west on the Charles River side; nor could he forget "the stench from mudflats and sewage that the sluggish current of the Charles and the sluggish tides that penetrated to the Basin did not avail to drain properly. However, this was chiefly noticeable in summer, when Beacon Street people were expected to be out of town."

Beacon Streeters had been summering out of town for half a century when the stink that drove them first tested Santayana's capacity for philosophical resignation, and in such growing numbers that Cold Roast Boston's capacity to contain them all (not to mention its own children and grandchildren) had long since been exhausted. The first to grasp the railroad's potential for opening up the frontier of the North Shore mainland to summer colonizing on a scale that would turn Nahant from proboscis to appendage was not a Beacon Streeter but the proprietor of a well-known restaurant in Theatre Alley (now Devonshire Street), William Fenno.

Eastern Railroad's petition was before the legislature in the summer of 1835 when Fenno and a friend went fishing one day in a boat off the Swampscott shore. As they passed Phillips Point, the northern headland of Nahant Bay, the restaurateur remarked that it would make a fine summer resort. On September 14 he bought nineteen acres of the point known as New Cove from the heirs of Walter Phillips for $1,600; on a rise commanding the Atlantic he built the Ocean House, the first summer hotel on the mainland of the North Shore.

The infrequent summer visitor had been lodging in Lynn's picturesque fishing and farming village of Swampscott since 1777, when William Allen sojourned above Phillips Beach; there were only five houses in the center then. Farmer Jonathan Phillips put up his first guest at Phillips Point in 1815, while west a mile, at Blaney's Beach, Mrs. Jonathan Blaney took in a Medford family in 1830, the first in that section; they grumbled at paying Aunt Betsy three dollars a week and having to wait on themselves. James L. Homer boarded at Phillips Beach in his youth. "The old lady who made the chowders, and fried the fish," he wrote, "will ever live in my memory, for I remember that she wore spectacles, that she was an excellent cook, that her tumblers and wine-glasses were always wiped with a clean napkin, and that it delighted her to see a visitor enjoy a good cigar."

William Fenno and the Eastern Railroad put Swampscott on the map. He ran his Ocean House for two years, and when the locomotive's first toot scattered the cows at Cherry Brook he leased it out and built a second hotel nearby, Fenno Cottage.

Fenno was a character. After wining and dining old friends he would invite them down on the beach if it happened to be low tide. At a certain spot he would clear away the sand and gravel, revealing a hidden spring; into this depression he would empty a flagon of Hennessey's best brandy, "and bid them drink it before it became diluted, and they generally effectually did it."

One of Fenno's first guests at the Ocean House, Philo S. Shelton of Boston, was so taken with the Swampscott shore that he hastened to purchase land on Whale Beach, bordering Phillips Point on the west, where he built a summer cottage that was probably the first on the North Shore inside of Nahant. Thurlow Weed, the Whig party boss, visited Shelton in 1851 and hooked a codfish weighing sixty-seven pounds off the Point. His host happened to be visiting the famous Astor House in New York not long afterward when he was buttonholed by their mutual friend, its equally famed proprietor, "General" Charles A. Stetson: "You are just the man we want to see. At a dinner in that room are a dozen public men, all friends of yours, and a heavy bet is made that Weed did not catch a codfish weighing fifty pounds." Shelton vouched for sixty-seven, and Boss Weed won his wager. "General" Stetson fell for Swampscott too, and retired to his Woodside Farm there soon before the Civil War.

Shelton's nearest rivals as the pioneer summer residents of the North Shore "off Nahant" were Benjamin Tyler Reed, financial angel of the Episcopal Theological School in Cambridge, and Enoch Redington Mudge. Reed put up his cottage on Ocean Street (now Puritan Road) above Blaney's Beach on land he bought in 1842 from Joseph Ingalls, who was haying when the philanthropist approached him:

"Good afternoon, sir. Is this your land?"

"Yes, sir."

"Will you sell it?"

"Yes."

"I will give you four hundred dollars per acre for it."

The owner threw down his rake in astonishment. "Do you mean it?"

"Yes, sir." And Mr. Ingalls straightaway hustled off to a lawyer to have the deed drawn for fear the crazy man from the city would change his mind.

The scenario would change but the dialogue would oft be repeated up and down the rural North Shore over the next decades. A mere forty years later Reed's land was worth $8,000 an acre.

Enoch Redington Mudge was the commanding possessor of flowing side-whiskers and features as stalwart as his name. He made a start on his fortune running the St. Charles Hotel in New Orleans. In 1843, at thirty-one, he bought the 130-acre Burrill estate above King's Beach for $8,000 and brought with him the four members of the slave family he had owned since 1840, and freed them. He built a Gothic stone summer cottage on the upland and wintered in New York, and then Boston, after taking up the textile business in 1845. "Elmwood," with its tree-lined drives, fountains and "Paradise Road," which Mudge cut through his forest for public use, was an early North Shore showplace long before its owner died in 1881.

On the heels of Reed and Mudge, the Bates and Curtis families settled Fishing Point and the adjacent Cedar Cliffs for the summer. Addison Child got hold of a tract at Beach Bluff at the east end of Phillips Beach and catalyzed a cottage development around the old Jacob Phillips farmhouse, which he enlarged into an estate he leased to Chickering, the piano manufacturer. On Phillips Point Dr. G. H. Lodge acquired "John's Field" from the heirs of Farmer Phillips in 1847 and made a summer estate of it, while the same year his neighbor, James L. Little, Boston dry goods importer, bought up the northeast head of the Point and built "Blythewood," the nucleus of a family compound of summer mansions he raised as he enlarged his holdings — "Greenhill," "Grasshead," "Shingleside," "The Cottage," "Beach End" and "Brier Gate" — until, at last, his end of it had to be known as Little's Point. Most of the first families left their best carriages at their winter homes lest the salt air tarnish them.

Suddenly, with the arrival of the railroad and its leavening effect on land values, Swampscott awoke to the fact that she was beautiful and desirable. Not Mother Lynn's ugly duckling at all. Her head was further turned, indeed nearly out of joint, by the mass descent

on the sixth of September, 1844, of twenty-five thousand Massachusetts Democrats, who assembled at the Eastern Railroad depot in
Lynn and marched to Clambake Hill. It was the year of James K.
Polk's successful Democratic campaign for the presidency against
the pride of the Whigs, Henry Clay.

The friendly assault strung out for a mile of marchers and bands
and banners, led by a platoon of Swampscott fishermen in red shirts
and sou'westers. Up on the hill overlooking the ocean seven pits
awaited the faithful, each ten feet across and hot enough to roast a
dozen Whigs; in the absence of the enemy, 170 barrels of clams and
a thousand lobsters were tossed in for a starter. In the eye of the
maelstrom stood a stage in the guise of a rural temple, garlanded
with wreaths and flowers and dedicated to the Genius of Democ-
racy. Order was called at one. Robert Rantoul shouted out an ora-
tion, followed by numerous high-spirited toasts, of which the highest was raised to "the Democrats of Swampscott — men of sterling
worth, and true friends to the people, ever ready, when duty re-
quires, to march shoulder to shoulder to the polls and vote for
honest men and liberal measures; but the dread of all those who
vote for corporations, log cabins, hard cider, and last but not least,
[Clay] the Mill Boy of the Slashes!"

Pretty heady stuff for the "droll, queer place" remarked on by one
visitor at about this time.

Swampscott's transformation was hastened by the ambitions of
her parent Lynn, which felt puffed-up and important enough by
1850 to adopt cityhood, with unexpected and most deflationary con-
sequences. Swampscott by then was a coming resort of the affluent
and the influential, and resented relegation to mere ward status. She
declared herself a town in 1852 (one old soul was *agin* a separate
post office on the grounds that he neither wrote nor received any
letters). Independence called for another parade, more oratory and
an encore of fireworks, and encouraged Nahant to go and do likewise the next year.

These defections stripped Lynn of three-quarters of her finest
coastline and of any significant future as a watering place. But she

was always stodgy. One July afternoon in 1851 a bevy of young ladies from Boston romped off the train in bloomers, just then all the rage, prompting Alonzo Lewis to comment that they created "considerable observation if not admiration by their short tunics, full trowsers, bright sashes and jaunty hats. Quite a number of the young ladies of Lynn arrayed themselves in the new style, but such a strong prejudice against the innovation began to manifest itself, that they soon laid aside the unappreciated garments."

Nor would Lynn lift a finger to encourage the nearest to godliness of all the attractions of the shore. "There are many people in Lynn," chided her impatient historian, "who never washed themselves all over in their lives, and who would as soon think of taking a journey through the air in a balloon, as of going under water. . . . Some of these water haters a few years since made a law that boys should not bathe in sight of any house; yet they have furnished no bathing houses; and there are no secluded places, excepting where the lives of children would be endangered. . . . Perhaps nothing is more conducive to health than sea bathing."

Swampscott was as tolerant as Lynn was tight-lipped. One Bostonian in 1846 rejoiced that ladies from the city enjoy a sea bath at Swampscott Beach "in just such costumes as they please, in elaborate costumes or in old cast-off dresses, without fear of talk."

# 6

# Beverly and Manchester Are All but Subdued

EVERYBODY COMPLAINED ABOUT THE TERRIBLE SERVICE ON THE STEAM ferry that shuttled North Shore passengers across Boston Harbor between the Eastern Railroad's terminal at East Boston and the city's Lewis Wharf. And as the ears of the road's new president had not yet become fully anesthetized to the utterances of his clientele, he threw his weight in 1851 behind an alternative approach to Boston entirely overland through Chelsea, South Malden (Everett), Somerville, Charlestown and across the Mystic River bridge, entering the city at Causeway Street.

The new route opened in 1854 over the objections, this time, of a stockholder minority that it was both circuitous and dangerous: it seems that the new right of way crossed the tracks of both the Boston and Maine and the Fitchburg railroads; moreover, Eastern's Boston terminal was so small that locomotives had to be uncoupled and switched off the main line a half a mile away while the passenger cars rolled into the station on their own momentum.

These were the bold days of railroading. Witness the separation of the Gloucester Branch cars and spares from the noon Portland train. At the end of the Beverly bridge the Gloucester coaches were uncoupled from the moving Maine-bound train. The engine and the Portland cars steamed into the triple-track Beverly depot. At just the right moment the switch was thrown. The Gloucester cars were shunted off onto the middle track and coupled with their waiting locomotive. The spare cars were then separated from the Gloucester train (everything still rolling along); another switch was thrown with split-second timing, and the spares swung onto the third track, from which they were switched a third time to a spur to await pick-up for the trip back to Boston. Eventually such sleight-of-hand was outlawed.

From Beverly on, Eastern's tracks ran due north for Newbury-port, bypassing the Beverly, Manchester and Cape Ann shores and all the verdant saltwater farm and woodland that drifted and tumbled down to the sea. At first the Iron Monster was no more than a distant whistle wafted in on a westerly breeze. Life went on as ever for the farmers and fishermen and their families, uncompli-cated by contacts with Boston and Salem that were rendered the more distasteful to country people by the high toll at the Beverly bridge; they were perfectly content with the scraps of news dropped in his passage by Jake Winchester, the Gloucester stage driver.

Such was the Farms section in the east part of Beverly when Mary Larcom Dow was a girl in 1840. The long green fields and deep woods skirted the shore, a peaceful hamlet inhabited by kind and honest folk and here and there an Uncle Jimmy Woodberry, who wrote a letter to the rats that had taken over his barn, informing them that there was more and better corn in David Preston's across the road. Uncle Jimmy kept watch, "and on a beautiful moonlight night had the satisfaction of beholding a long line of rodents with an old gray fellow as leader, crossing the road on their way to Uncle David's."

That was a good story, and not a few firmly believed that not only barns but woods and beehives were haunted, and spirits were all about. When John G. King, a Salem businessman, first brought his family to board at Beverly Farms in the summer of 1840 at the Isaac Prince homestead above the west end of West Beach, his daughter Caroline was impressed that the beehives around the place were draped with black bows, "the belief being universal that if on the death of a member of a family, the bees were not told of it, and their hives put in mourning, they would fly away."

One afternoon, Caroline related, her father arrived back at the Farms with the news from Salem, where he commuted by the stage, that the children's music teacher was bringing the Manchester Brass Band out to serenade them that evening. Expecting twenty musicians, Mrs. King divided her only cake into as many slices and concocted a well-watered sangaree with her only bottle of claret. Meanwhile, the eight Prince children carried word of the great event to all corners, so that by seven-thirty the surrounding fields were filled with country people, who, to pass the time away, sent a deputation to the house with the request that Miss Gusty give them a tune on the "argin" (the piano the Kings had brought from Salem — a mystery to the neighbors, who had never seen one before). Sister Augusta obliged until the arrival of the band in a huge hay wagon.

"Oh, Miss King, ma'am says there are twenty-*six* men!" reported a little Prince girl, rushing into the parlor. "Much to our amusement," wrote Caroline King, "my mother instantly cut six of the largest wedges of cake in two, and drowned her claret with another pitcher of water." The band arrayed itself before the house, and in half an hour, when its repertoire was exhausted, partook with satisfaction of Mrs. King's cakes and wine. "Then to make some return for the compliment they had paid us by offering this 'serenade' (Heaven save the mark!) William Story stood forth on the doorstep and sang as loudly as he could 'A Life on the Ocean Wave' and 'The sea, the sea, the blue, the fresh, the ever free,' which were received with great applause from Band and neighbors. Then the Band brayed out 'Auld Lang Syne' . . . the haycart was brought round, and amid a chorus of thanks and goodnights, the Manchester Brass Band departed, giving a cheer to their entertainers as they passed down the avenue."

Genial and courtly John King was credited by Warren Prince, a contractor who built many of their summer cottages, as the first to bring the beauties of the Beverly shore to the attention of "the cultivated people from our cities," such as other Prince farm boarders in the early 1840s, including this same William Wetmore Story, the answering serenader, to be better known as a sculptor, and his close friends the poet James Russell Lowell, author Thomas Wentworth Higginson and the newlywed Dr. Oliver Wendell Holmes.

Serenades, sangarees and "argin" playing were cut short on April 29, 1844, when attorney Charles Cushing Paine of Boston bought the Prince farm of 101 acres with its half a mile of ocean frontage for $5,500, and for another $500 the house, tools, chickens, stock, old Charley the horse, and a yoke of oxen that Farmer Prince threw in to ease his conscience with the remark that "these Boston fellows don't know anything about values." Paine was the grandson of Robert Treat Paine, a signer of the Declaration of Independence; his own son, R. T. the Second, who made a career of giving the family's money away, claimed years later that this germinative acquisition came about after "the previous summer [when] Father took some of us boys on a drive from Marblehead around the Beverly Farms shore and so on to Gloucester. The beauty of the shore has since then become famous. You might almost say we discovered it, for in April, 1844, Father made the pioneer purchase, selecting the most beautiful mile of sea-coast in Massachusetts, the side lines converging to a point where now is Pride's Crossing station. . . . Thus our family were the first settlers by purchase on this justly famous and now too fashionable shore; and as I went down in April to live with farmer Isaac Prince before our family moved down, I suppose I am the original pioneer."

Paine's was the pioneer purchase of summer property on the North Shore east of Swampscott, if one excepts John Cushing's premature acquisition of Eastern Point at Gloucester, but only barely: three weeks after the Prince farm changed hands John King bought John Thissell's house and five acres above Mingo Beach (named supposedly for a black slave, Robin Mingo, who once had a shack there) on Hale Street half a mile back toward Beverly, for $900. On the fifth of October another Boston lawyer, Charles Greely Loring, did likewise; for $4,000 he relieved Benjamin Smith of twenty-five acres on Plum Cove and Smith Point adjoining Paine's new property and engaged Warren Prince to build Beverly's first summer mansion.

Loring wanted to establish friendly relations with his neighbors and when his house was in frames had Prince stage an old-fashioned raising, to which he invited all the farmers and fishermen on the Beverly shore. The house attracted curiosity-seekers from as far as Marblehead, who poked around the grounds peeking in the windows. One noontime soon after the family moved down from Boston for their first summer, Mrs. Loring and a relative had withdrawn to the pantry hoping to escape the snoopers when a small boy hitched himself up to the narrow windowsill and shouted to his pals, "Here they are! Come and see them eat!"

Charles Cushing Paine sliced the Prince farm into building lots and offered them at auction in 1846; none of the bids was satisfactory, so he abandoned speculation, farmed the estate in gentlemanly fashion and kept it intact until its subdivision in 1875 after his death. Up the road Charles Greely Loring built a huge barn and hung swings from the loft for the local children. He kept horses, put up henhouses, provided sties with a room and yard for each pig, which got a brushing every morning and a hot bath on Saturdays. And he imported Norway firs and Chinese fowl, and Alderney stock and swine from the Royal Farm at Windsor, and shared their progeny with his neighbors. Of his land he gave away none save to his son Caleb William Loring, lawyer and trustee of Boston, and before he died in 1868 he owned a hundred acres gathered in with the object, as he calmly told a friend who chided him for his acquisitiveness, that "I never want any land except the piece next to my own." Every worthy cause in Beverly had his support, and the poor his benevolence, and he was respectfully known as Squire Loring. Warren Prince had the Squire in mind when he reflected that "although these families were all accustomed to wealth and its comforts, the poor were always remembered; no stain of ostentation or snobbery ever emanated from their escutcheons; these were the true nobility."

The lawyers and businessmen of Boston and Salem knew better than most that ever since the Eastern Railroad was first agitated and then carried on to Newburyport in 1840, an offshoot to Gloucester was in the cards. In September of 1844, three weeks before Loring bought the Smith land, a meeting of citizens convinced the railroad, and surveyors began laying out the Gloucester Branch to take off from the main line (by a process of multiple switchings and shuntings, as we have seen) just north of the Beverly depot.

Next May builder Warren Prince was the go-between in the sale of twenty acres west of Mingo Beach, adjoining John King, to Franklin Dexter of Boston, a noted trial lawyer and the United States Attorney for Massachusetts. Samuel Obear, the owner, thought Dexter's offer was too high, and his conscience drove him to seek the advice of William Endicott, Beverly's leading citizen:

"Here's a Boston man wants to buy my land for two thousand dollars. 'Tain't worth it. What am I to do?"

"I think he knows what he wants. Let him have it."

"But it ain't worth it."

"Never mind. Let him throw away his money if he wants to."

Prince built a stone mansion for Dexter, who kept Sam Obear on as his caretaker. Mrs. Dexter was the sister of William Hickling Prescott, the historian and a Nahant summerer, and had lived in England. "I want to have a lawn like an English lawn," she instructed the former owner. "It must be watered, rolled and cut regularly." "Well," said Sam, "if you will send out your maid to hold up the grass, I will undertake to cut it with a pair of scissors."

After Franklin Dexter, the next to succumb to the Beverly shore was the tall and tempestuous textile tycoon, Patrick Tracy Jackson, Newburyport-born, cofounder of the city of Lowell and organizer of the Boston and Lowell Railroad. In September 1845 he paid Peter Obear $1,800 for ten acres on Hale Street east of Mingo Beach and hired Warren Prince to build his cottage, which served him but two summers, for he died there of dysentery in September 1847. The ink was hardly dry on Jackson's deed when John Amory Lowell, the Boston philanthropist, abandoned Nahant for a premium piece of Woodberry Point, next on from Hospital Point to the west of Beverly Cove; he was joined on the east by son-in-law William Sohier in 1854. Lowell anchored the west flank of the Beverly colony beyond the Cove. Three days later P. T. Jackson's brother-in-law,

Colonel Henry Lee, idealistic (and unsuccessful) merchant, shy (and unelected) politician, staked out the eastern limit with three acres on the other side of West Beach. It remained for Franklin Haven, president of the Merchants National Bank of Boston, to nail down the rest of West Beach with twenty acres, for which he paid Josiah Obear $500 in April 1846, a beachhead he and Franklin, Junior, had quadrupled before the century was up.

The Gloucester Branch pushed on from Beverly to Manchester in August 1847 and to Gloucester on December 1. The initial stop for the convenience of the summer residents was three hundred yards from the cottage of David A. Neal, the president of the Eastern Railroad, and was first designated West Beach, then Beverly Farms. Three-quarters of a mile to the west the tracks transected Hale Street near the north corner of the Paine estate, at the colonial seat of the Pride family, and the crossing was given their name. It is difficult to ascertain when the depot there was built, no later than 1871 anyway, and for years Pride's Crossing was no more than a flag stop tended by a superannuated Pride, stone deaf and so indifferent to the approach of the train that the passengers had to do their own flagging.

Pride's Crossing was in the nature of a private stop and was not included in the railroad's published timetable until the 1900s. In the early days of the Gloucester Branch, though, the road showed no reluctance to tout the shore to one and all, as in 1851: "The excellent conveniences for sea-bathing, the invigorating sea-breezes, together with the charming views, walks, and rides, cannot fail of refreshing and strengthening the feeble, while they gladden the devotees of pleasure, and afford pleasant instruction to the inquisitive and reflective. . . . As a proof of the wholesome moral tone of Beverly, it has been said that no conviction for crime has occurred within its limits for five successive years."

James Russell Lowell was inquisitive and reflective, and he afforded some pleasant instruction about Beverly Farms to Miss Jane Norton, a young friend, in a letter dated August 14, 1854. The dislodged Prince farm boarder, who had lost his wife the previous

October, was staying at "Underhill": "Now — in order that you may
not fancy (as most persons who go to Rhode Island do) that Newport is the only place in the world where there is any virtue in salt
water — I will say a word or two of Beverly. Country and sea-shore
are combined here in the most charming way. Find the Yankee
word for Sorrento, and you have Beverly — it is only the Bay of
Naples translated into the New England dialect. . . . We are in a
little house close upon the road, with the sea just below, as seen
through a fringe of cedar, wild cherry, and barberry. Beyond this
fringe is a sand-beach where we bathe. . . . We are at the foot of a
bay, across the mouth of which lies a line of islands — some bare
rock, some shrubby, and some wooded. These are the true islands of
the Sirens. One [Cat Island] has been disenchanted by a great hotel,

*Beverly summer cottages of Charles G. Loring and his son, Caleb W., above
Plum Cove, 1861. From "The Earliest Summer Residents of the North Shore
and Their Houses," by Katherine P. Loring*

*William D. Pickman's summer house at Beverly Cove. Beverly Historical
Society*

*The first summer cottage in Manchester, Richard Henry Dana's, built in 1845 above
Graves (Dana's) Beach. Manchester Historical Society*

*Captain Robert Bennet Forbes moved into "Masconomo" at West Manchester in July 1857. Note the novel ventilator on the roof. Manchester Historical Society*

*The Russell Sturgis house, vintage 1863, behind Singing Beach. Manchester Historical Society*

to which a steamboat runs innumerably every day with a band — the energetic *boong! boong! — boong! boong! boong!* — of the bass drum being all we hear. Our sunset is all in the southeast, and every evening the clouds and islands bloom and the slow sails are yellowed and the dories become golden birds swinging on the rosy water."

"I would not have told you," Lowell wrote Miss Norton, "how much better this is than your Rhode Island glories — only that you Newport folks always seem a little (I must go to my Yankee) *stuck up,* as if Newport were all the world, and you the saints that had inherited it. But I hope to see you and Newport soon, and I will be lenient. You shall find in me the Beverly grandeur of soul which can acknowledge alien merit."

Money picked off the loose lots along the shore — the city wealth of Captain Israel Whitney, Boston merchant and one-time East India shipmaster, of Ellis Gray Loring, abolitionist lawyer, of Augustus Lowell and Benjamin Franklin Burgess of the West Indies trade, father of the yacht designer. John H. Silsbee and William Dudley Pickman, Salem shipmasters, bought up vantages "from which they could watch their ships as they came into midship channel from any old port of the world, at any time," in the words of their grandson John S. Lawrence. "With a horse and chaise ever ready, they could drive to Derby Wharf in Salem, and then attend to the merchandising of their cargo while their families remained at the beach." In 1860, sixteen years after Charles Cushing Paine's coup of the Prince farm for $55 an acre, Richard T. Parker of Boston bought an acre and a few poles of Curtis Point for $3,000, and the last of Beverly's coast from Mackerel Cove to the Manchester line, five miles of it, was the domain of the rich men from Boston and Salem. Seventy years after that, the 101 acres and house for which Paine paid $6,000 were assessed, with their "cottages," for $2,144,325.

The poet's appreciation of their shore — and Paine's and Loring's and Haven's and the rest of the Boston men's — had been miscalculated by the country Princes, the Thissells and the Obears to the sorrow of their descendants, one of whom, Frederick A. Ober, would lament in his town history of 1888: "It does not appear that our ancestors were heedless of the attractions nature had so lavishly spread around them; but, in the stress of their life of toil, these may have seemed of secondary importance. . . . This 'fatal gift of beauty,' which was to them a thing imponderable, attracted strangers to their birthright, and it passed from their possession."

Like that of Beverly, Manchester's coast was captured by city Yankees following the trail cindered along the North Shore by the Gloucester Branch. But not so rapidly. Manchester was more remote, more rustic and more inbred, and the spectacle of the country Yankees across the town line so shrewdly bargaining off their birthrights gave the natives pause to reappraise their own. Perhaps a further deterrent to the enthusiasm of Boston men (and women) for the Manchester shore lurked deep in the majestic, mysterious woods behind, so densely populated with rattlesnakes as late as 1844 that they fetched a bounty of a dollar each; unlike His Snakeship of Nahant and Gloucester glory, Mr. Rattler was not a summer attraction.

Manchester was "discovered" by Richard Henry Dana, the poet and essayist of Boston and father of the author of *Two Years Before the Mast*. Actually Dana had leapfrogged the town from Boston and "discovered" Rockport in 1840, the year of John King's "discovery" of Beverly. The fresh granite quarries of Pigeon Cove and Sandy Bay had been bestowing a moderate prosperity and an immoderate sense of independence upon the northeast coast of Cape Ann which the same year came to a head with the secession of the two villages from Gloucester as the town of Rockport, a name chosen by the voters over "East Gloucester," "Granite," "Brest" and "Cape Ann." The retiring and aloof Dana found the retreat he was seeking in an old tavern on the south side of the hamlet that clustered around and above the rockbound pocket of Pigeon Cove. He was joined in the summer of 1842 by his friends William Cullen Bryant, the poet and editor, and the sculptor Edward Augustus Brackett, who did a bust of Bryant. "A summer to be remembered by the village people," extolled Henry C. Leonard, their chronicler, "for men with seeing vision and acutest faculties and clearest utterance made a survey of their little seaside hamlet and its environs, interpreted the marvels all about them and shed the light of their presence upon the common things of sea and land always within sight."

While at Pigeon Cove a summer or two later, Dana was induced by the reputation of the Reverend Oliver A. Taylor to illumine a pew in the Congregational church at Manchester, "and it was Mr. Taylor," according to Richard Henry Dana III, "that suggested his coming to this beautiful town and staying here. My grandfather then drove up and down, and hearing the sound of the surf, he said, 'There must be a beach,' and following up an old wood road he came to the spot which he afterwards selected."

That spot was a tract of wild land and shore between the old Gloucester-Salem road and Graves Beach. On April 9, 1845, Dana's lawyer-author son, Richard Henry Dana, Jr., bought all thirty acres in his behalf from the Allen family for $225. The elder Dana, then fifty-eight, built a simple, square, gray cottage on the bluff above the beach and moved in as Manchester's first summer resident. By 1877, two years before his death, the venerable pioneer's desire for privacy had swelled his thirty to a hundred uncultivated acres, as to the impenetrability of which *The Beetle and Wedge* testified that "thanks are due to Mr. Dana for suffering his estate to remain in its original state of Nature; and it is a genuine pleasure to get stuck in the brambles that grow unchecked in the wild woods." Senator Charles Sumner, a veteran of the political cat brier, pronounced his host's outlook more stunning even than Biarritz, the watering place of Napoleon III on the Bay of Biscay.

One might almost imagine that Dana's hideaway had been plunked down on the edge of the ocean by the wishful thinking of Alonzo Lewis, who displayed the prescience of the contemporary-minded historian when the year previous to the poet's purchase he took to task the environmental philistines of his native Lynn: "I have long endeavored to introduce a style of architecture which shall be in harmony with the wild and natural beauty of the scenery — a style in which the cottages shall appear to grow out of the rocks and to be born of the woods. . . . When the hills and cliffs shall be adorned with buildings in accordance with the scenery around — and when men, instead of cutting down every tree and shrub, shall re-clothe nature with the drapery of her appropriate foliage, Lynn will appear much more lovely and interesting than at present."

Manchester's number two summer settler, Charles Frederic Adams, trailed Dana by three years. The Gloucester Branch had just penetrated the town in 1848 when Adams bought Crow Island from William Hooper and built a summer cottage on the nob of this small sentinel of five acres, not far east of the Dana estate. Like Charles Greely Loring of Beverly Farms, the island's new proprietor made a point of courting his long-established neighbors, and it was said that "in cases of sickness he would often with his own hands supply such articles as he thought might be needed in the sick room. Frequently on the approach of winter he would distribute flannel among the more limited for their personal comfort." Adams died in 1862 and left Crow Island to his daughter, Emily, who married Caleb Curtis, owner of the Goldsmith Farm across Kettle Cove on what was later called Coolidge Point. The island remained in the family until 1935, when E. Hyde Cox made a year-round estate of it.

That most singular of the singular among Bostonians, Robert Bennet Forbes, was the third to find summer harbor on Manchester's wild shore. In April 1856 he bought seventeen acres near the Beverly line from Israel F. Tappan for $800 and set his cottage on the hill west of Black Cove Beach; he called it "Masconomo" after the last sagamore of the Agawams and moved in on July 24, 1857. "Black Ben," as Captain Forbes was hailed in his handsome and dark-complexioned youth, had been a shipmaster in the China (and opium) trade under the aegis of his Uncle Thomas Handasyd Perkins. He made, lost and made again a fortune, devised all kinds of improvements in vessel design, sailed a relief ship to Ireland during the famine of 1847, plumped for better lifesaving methods and shipwreck patrols, organized a farsighted though premature coast guard at the outbreak of the Civil War, threw himself into sport and yachting as commodore of the first informal boat club at Boston in 1834 and at last wrote up his adventures, achievements, and even a few failures with ebullient immodesty in his *Personal Reminiscences*. Strange for a born seafarer, Captain Forbes in 1865 sold his Manchester estate (to B. G. Boardman, a merchant who paid him in gold as a hedge against wartime inflation), then removed his summer residence to Milton, one of the coming country suburbs south of Boston. One year later, Boardman's purchase, by his own account, had doubled in value.

A few months after Black Ben bought at Manchester in 1856, John Crowninshield Dodge, a Chicago native, picked up two lots behind Singing Beach. Adjoining him, Dr. Jedidiah Cobb built his cottage in 1857. Dodge built on the upland and sold his beach frontage in 1861 to Russell Sturgis, Jr., son of Captain Forbes's salty old ex-partner in the shipping and mercantile firm of Russell and Company of Boston. Major Sturgis built in 1863, war or no war. At the height of it, in 1864, Benjamin W. Thayer, a Boston real estate man who had been boarding in Manchester for thirteen seasons, talked Andrew Ruffin into selling him his land and boardinghouse on Singing Beach.

The end of the Civil War found the courtly carpetbaggers in complete control of the Beverly seaside and holding down most of Manchester's except for such few holdouts as the Smith family, who had refused $16,000 for their thirty-two acres of farm point on the east of the harbor, which they claimed was worth twice that. "Next to gold, for certainty of value both present and prospective," declared Thomas P. Gentlee, the railroad's land agent and a large investor himself in the North Shore, "I had rather hold such land now than any other property I know of."

Gentlee was not the only speculator who spotted gold onward and eastward in the granite of Cape Ann, or bypassed and ignored among the gleaming sands of Winthrop and North Chelsea, or under the cowflops on Marblehead Neck. The rush to the North Shore had only begun.

# 7

# Gloucester
# Keeps On Fishing

THE MOST IMPRESSIVE APPROACH TO CAPE ANN BY LAND HAS ALWAYS been along the shore road that Jake Winchester's stage pursued from Salem, winding through Beverly and Manchester with enticing glimpses of the ocean across beach and cove, then plunging inland into the West Gloucester wilderness of swamp and forest, as dank and dark as if the depth of it were a thousand miles from the fresh breath and sparkle of the sea.

The clattering coach encounters Sawyer's Hill. The sound of surf excites the ear above the hoofbeats in the dirt. The salt smell savored with the iodine pungency of seaweed quickens the pulse. The horses labor up the grade.

Abruptly at the crest the woods give way to pasture. The stage leaps into the sunlight, and there under the canopy of the blue, spread out below like all creation, is Freshwater Cove, pocketed within Dolliver's wooded Neck. Beyond the Neck is the shimmering sheet of Gloucester Harbor, rockbound behind the thrust of Eastern Point. Still farther beyond and out, lies the dazzling Atlantic.

In a few seconds the stage sways down the slope in billows of dust, and the electrifying vista evaporates into the roadside rock and brush. Then, as suddenly again, the curtain parts, this time fully, to reveal the arc of Cressy's Beach bit up against the sprouting ledge of Stage Head and that grassed-over fort of the Revolution upon its brow. Now the whole of Gloucester Bay spreads forth, crisscrossed with a hundred sail tacking through the lee of Eastern Point. There, to the east, is little Ten Pound Island, abaft of it the thumb of Rocky Neck, and across from it the inner harbor's opposing, beckoning forefinger of Watchhouse Point, squatted on by another grassy fort, inviting the traveler to bide awhile around the wharves and among the white clouds of houses that hover above the Neapolitan arc of Gloucester's portal beach.

Some summer in the early 1830s the verve of that first fresh vision froze a visitor in his horse's tracks, as it had Samuel de Champlain two and a quarter centuries before, and Freshwater Cove, where the explorer had refilled his casks from the tumbling stream, was adopted as their annual summer campground by the stout hearts of the Boston Pioneer Seashore Club. They were young businessmen of a musical turn, a score of them, and they brought flutes, trumpets, accordions, tambourines, Jew's harps, clappers and snare drums, besides their camping outfits and tents.

Charlie Sawyer had two wharves on Freshwater Cove where a pair of pinky schooners landed their fares; he cured and sold fish, ran a fisherman's outfitting store, stocked West India goods and owned a cluster of fish houses just above the tide. The Pioneers pitched their tents on his land, and Charlie let them inhabit one of the fishhouses during their month-long stay. In part payment for this hospitality the Boston boys played evening concerts which drew Gloucester people from miles around, but particularly the belles of the Cove Village, whose nightly presence for some reason resulted in the following pledge to Mr. Sawyer: "The girls will always be welcome here as our guests, and we assure you, sir, that they will be in the best of company for reputation, honesty and protection under the name of the Boston Pioneer Seashore Club!"

After a few years the campsite of the Pioneers was inherited by the 999th Battery, a fraternity of Charlestown merchants and politicians, numbering two Sawyer brothers who sprang collaterally from the Freshwater Cove Sawyers, which probably explains their welcome there. The 999th camped in style, bringing tents, tables, chairs, beds, cooking utensils and a brass fieldpiece. The members carried on the

Pioneer tradition of concerts and entertainment for the locals, not without the cooperation of one of their number, who was a wealthy distiller. Their signal cannon awoke Gloucester at every dawn, proclaimed high noon and shot down the sun resoundingly. One Sunday this venerable armament was primed and placed in hiding by the roadside to welcome the Honorable William H. Kent on a mayoral visit from Charlestown. As His Honor strode around the bend toward camp, they commenced to give him twenty salutes, and he was halfway to Manchester before the reassurance caught up with him that no harm was intended, 'twas merely "dry times and no powder" at Freshwater Cove, whatever they meant by that.

Nonetheless, the Batterymen of Freshwater Cove, like the Pioneers before them, were summer soldiers, who struck their tents and left no wounds except on the hearts and eardrums of the local populace. Furthermore, the subsequent land grab under cover of the smoke and cinders of the advancing railroad lost steam with every mile as the tracks pushed toward what many regarded as the bitter end of the North Shore. And it must be admitted that for all Gloucester cared — preoccupied with the comings and goings of the fleet, the weather, the price of fish and its cost in lives and fortunes, and bastioned from the rest of humanity behind the wilderness of the West Parish and the moat of the Annisquam River — Boston, save as a market, could be a thousand miles away.

Under such unfavorable circumstances, investment in summer property on a relatively distant coast whose climate, albeit cool, was not so cool as the welcome of its inhabitants was undertaken by few, and they were intrepid. They were also farseeing: the imminence of the Gloucester Branch and the diminishing supply of available remaining shoreline were the inducement.

George Hovey, for one, was a Boston wholesaler who may have been a Seashore Pioneer and is thought to have summered at Freshwater Cove for the first time in 1843. But it was his brother Charles, a dry goods merchant in the city, who made the first move and on March 10, 1845, paid the town $700 for a piece of pasture on the slope south of Granite Street, midway above the curve of Gloucester's frontal beach. Nine months later George followed suit by giving Charles and Samuel E. Sawyer $400 for the Lookout Lot, so called, on Sawyer's Hill commanding Freshwater Cove and the harbor. The summer houses the brothers built, sumptuous for Gloucester, were the first on Cape Ann. Charles's sons wheeled through the dirty streets of Fishtown in a willow carriage behind a brisk team of ponies. George in time reached out and bought up Dolliver's Neck and adjoining Mussel Point, which made Freshwater Cove practically his private anchorage, and took up yachting.

Even as Charles Hovey was in the act of taking title to his $700 summer estate on what is now Hovey Street, an astute Gloucester Surinam trader with business connections in Boston and an ear for the approach of the railroad train was laying out the handsome sum of fifty dollars for the first of many tracts of pasture he would gather to himself in the Bass Rocks section of Eastern Point. There will be more in a later chapter about George H. Rogers, who would patiently assemble his great holdings in a series of sorties. South of him, a Boston livery stable owner named Thomas Niles, who also heard the whistle in the distance, did it in one fell swoop when he purchased the four hundred acres of the Eastern Point Farm, comprising the entire end of the peninsula, except for the acre on which the government's lighthouse stood, for $5,000 and some small real estate in the city. This was in July 1844.

The buyer was my great-great-grandfather by the coincidence of his daughter's marriage many years later to John Kimball Rogers, my great-grandfather — and the great-grandson of the Gloucester merchant Daniel Rogers, who by further coincidence had owned the very same farm after the Revolution. Grandfather Niles was a naval veteran of the War of 1812, most of which he seems to have fought from England's Dartmoor Prison following his presumed capture. He next turned up in Boston, as a liveryman; the high point of his career in this line was the day he took the reins himself and drove the aged Lafayette through the streets of the city when the French hero of the Revolution visited America in 1824.

Thomas Niles intended his coup of Eastern Point as a long-term

*Freshwater Cove from Dolliver's Neck, 1870s. Procter Brothers' glass plate negative, Stephen B. Howard collection*

*Thomas Niles.*
*Author's collection*

*Bathers swim the polka at Gloucester's Pavilion Beach, 1856. Essex Institute*

*The Niles farmhouse at Eastern Point, sketched in 1871 by the owner's grand-daughter, Sarah M. Rogers, at the age of ten. Author's collection*

*The Eastern Point fort, from the 1871 sketchbook of Sarah Rogers. The government had turned the land back to Grandfather Niles in 1869, but the memory was fresh. Author's collection*

investment in seaside summer property which would hatch in its own good time, with good husbandry in the meanwhile. He herded his numerous brood (fifteen children, eventually, by three successive wives) aboard his sailboat, so the family story goes, like Noah embarked upon the flood, and took possession of the weathered farmhouse between the harbor beach and the freshwater pond that is separated from the sea on the other side by a membrane of sand; beach and pond now bear his name.

What could have possessed Thomas Niles — clean-cut and handsome in his youth, fearsomely bearded in his prime — to transplant his loved ones from the amenities of Boston to a distant and deserted semi-island several miles removed even from the crude necessities of a rough fishing port, a primitive saltwater farm of transcendental loveliness in the warm months, but wildly dramatic, desolate and galeswept during the cold? "I designed to make it my home, and I did so," he reflected with characteristic firmness in his twilight. "And I believed that I should be able here to pass the remainder of my days (being then well advanced into middle life) on an estate unsurpassed for beauty of situation, though then sterile and unimproved, engaged in the congenial pursuit of improving it and rendering it fertile, and believing that on my death my children would inherit in it a sure fortune by its steady enhancement in value, if I should not earlier have disposed of it to such advantage as to realize to them that fortune during my life."

A willful design nevertheless, but Thomas Niles was above all a man of business, and not famous for his sociability, either. The sole clue as to why he chose such a remote target for the rustication of himself and family may lie in the identity of the quite as extraordinary party who sold him the farm, John Perkins Cushing. Niles had transacted business with this great merchant of Boston on at least one earlier occasion of which there is record; that was ten years previously, when he sold Cushing two horses for $400 that the buyer thought might be worth $600, and received cash and cancellation of a $700 note against him, "for which," Cushing admitted to his diary, "I never expected to get anything."

Ku-Shing, as his Chinese admirers called him, had returned to Boston in 1831 after twenty-eight years representing so efficiently the mercantile interests in Canton of his Uncle Thomas Handasyd Perkins that at the age of forty-four he was rumored to be worth seven million. First, this most eligible bachelor in New England and perhaps all of America lost his singular distinction. Then he built an opulent mansion in Summer Street. And then (and here we must again rely on the account of Thomas Niles) Cushing "proposed to make a sea-side estate which should surpass in beauty of situation and in completeness of detail any other in the United States. For this, after careful examination of a great part of the coast of New England, he had finally selected Eastern Point as best adapted to his purpose."

During his exploration of 1606 the Chevalier de Champlain had sketched Eastern Point on his map of Le Beauport as "a tongue of plain ground, where there are saffrons, nut-trees and vines." The next visitor to describe the end of this low-lying peninsula, whose two and a half miles literally give Gloucester her great harbor, was that ubiquitous diarist, the Reverend William Bentley, who rode down from Salem in June of 1791 and was taken by his host, Daniel Rogers, on a tour of the farm. He recorded that "there is a delightful grove of Oaks, &c. within the point, to which the company resorts and enjoys a fine air in the warmest weather. The Farm is very rough, affords pasture, but there was no tillage land beyond the Pond towards the Point." Bentley was back in 1793 and complained that the Point road was so *horrible* that he returned to Gloucester on foot, "dreading to ride back through such dangerous passes."

Daniel Rogers died in 1800, and in 1830 his heirs sold the Eastern Point Farm, which then amounted to about three hundred acres, to Addison Plumer. The next year John Perkins Cushing returned to Boston from his China stint and in October of 1833 bought the farm from Plumer, and from George Clark another hundred-odd adjoining acres at the far end of the point, excepting the new lighthouse, for the aggregate sum of $4,175.

If it was Cushing's intention, as Thomas Niles claimed, to turn the Eastern Point Farm into the finest seaside estate in America, he apparently abandoned the idea almost immediately. Instead of North Shoreward, the following August he moved inland from Boston to Watertown, where he was in the process of accumulating two hundred acres, on the highest eminence of which he built a perfectly splendid country manor with all kinds of neo-Oriental overtones. For the rest of his life Colonel Perkins's nephew lavished his fortune on "Belmont," importing shiploads of flora from the world over and supervising every detail until his gardens were the horticultural wonder of the eastern United States. Three years before his death in 1862, portions of Watertown, Waltham and West Cambridge were incorporated and named Belmont in tribute to their grandest taxpayer.

As for his far more inspiring property at Eastern Point, John Cushing did little more than build a boundary wall of fieldstone that still stands between the harbor and the east shore of Brace Cove on the Atlantic. Indeed, as early as November of 1834, having just removed to Belmont, he was considering leasing out his great seagirt farm, which he did in 1836, not having set foot on it all the while. Evidently Eastern Point was too distant from Boston; for a vacation by the sea, like the rest of his clan, John Perkins Cushing preferred Nahant, where he put up his family at his uncle's hotel in the summer of 1836 and visited a half a dozen times — a two-hour trot from Watertown.

Whatever moved Thomas Niles to relieve "Ku-Shing" of the cares of absentee ownership that July of 1844, he set about with all the energy of the newly arrived gentleman farmer at the age of forty-seven, clearing and ploughing and fertilizing his acres with seaweed from his beaches, planting vegetables, orchards and shade trees, raising stock and cutting ice from the pond for the Gloucester and Boston markets.

The irascibility of Thomas Niles is family legend. Trespassers infuriated him; he ordered his adopted townsmen keep to their side of the Cushing Wall or face him in court. The antipathy was mutual, since Gloucester had always roamed the fields and woods and shores of the point, berrying, fishing, chowdering, gunning and making merry with neither let nor hindrance. The new owner put a stop to all that, even refusing his neighbor on the north, Isaac Patch, himself the eventual owner of 230 acres from harbor to sea, permission to continue harvesting seaweed — "sea manure" — from Niles Beach. Suits ensued, and appeals. The case of *Niles* versus *Patch* turned into a hornets' nest. Resentment mounted against the curmudgeon of Eastern Point. His barns burned mysteriously, and a farmhand was tried for arson. He shut off visitors to the lighthouse and expelled picnickers from his beaches. In the end he prevailed. After six years of acrimonious litigation the Massachusetts Supreme Court in 1859 ruled that Niles owned to the mean low water mark of Gloucester Harbor, that his land, roads and beaches were his private domain, securing for him and his heirs and generations of summer residents to come the exclusiveness he coveted as the key to his investment.

All this hard-won privacy at first didn't last very long. In 1863 the War Department seized fifty-three acres of the high ground of Eastern Point, piled up an earthen fort for the defense of Gloucester against Confederate gunboats, armed it with seven cannon and moved in a rollicking company of artillerymen. They remained until 1865, when the Confederacy collapsed. Farmer Niles had been grinding his teeth all this time and late that year filed a claim against his Uncle Sam for $64,980 in rent and damages.

During the course of presenting his case before the War Claims Commission in 1866 Niles persuaded several leading North Shore summer residents to testify to the spectacular rise in coastal property values and the potential of Eastern Point, if the United States would only dismantle its fort and evacuate. His witnesses agreed with grave complacency that most of the best available shore between Boston and Cape Ann had already been taken up and that Eastern Point was among the few promontories on the coast that jutted out sufficiently to benefit from the water-cooled southwester; indeed, it might even surpass Nahant as a watering place were it not for its distance from Boston, which none regarded as an immutable bar to development.

Finally the War Department gave in and returned his land to

Thomas Niles in 1869. Not until 1890, long after his death, did Congress pass a special act indemnifying his heirs, who by then had disposed of their inheritance, to the scaled-down tune of $6,050.

A terrible gale, perhaps a hurricane, in September 1846 cost Marblehead ten vessels and sixty-five of her men and boys, and her place of importance in the fishing industry. Gloucester was left un-rivaled, with a fleet of 127 schooners, and growing, and a busy waterfront that expanded rapidly around the inner harbor, giving rise to the village of East Gloucester, as differentiated from the rest of Eastern Point — a designation henceforth restricted to the Niles Farm.

The rest of the world first found out about East Gloucester's cool combination of rural ebb and tidal flow from one Joseph Kidder, a Boston druggist who in 1843 came with his family to board at the home of young Mrs. Judith Wonson on Wonson's Point, between Niles Beach and Rocky Neck. The Kidders brought their friends, and their friends brought theirs, and they overflowed across the road to Mrs. Mary Wonson's place, "The Fair View," which still offers a fair view of the harbor to its guests. Thus was founded the East Gloucester summer colony. "There were ducks and chickens raised on the place," wrote George Procter of Judy Wonson's fare, "to-gether with fresh vegetables, apples, pears and currants from the garden. John Bray, with his well known butcher's cart, with its choice assortment of meats, supplied the demands in this line. A cow supplied butter and cream. Lobsters and fish were plentiful, and the catching of the cunners furnished a never-ending pleasure in front of the rocks near the house. . . . The cooking was done by an open fire on the hearth, and there was one of the old style brick ovens which turned out delicious brown bread and beans, Indian pudding, pies and berry cakes. . . . There was an orchard of apple trees . . . surrounded by a white fence, with a row of currant bushes inside the fence. . . . A brook flowed through the meadow, and wild roses grew in profusion about the rocks in front of the house."

Gloucester suffered two distinct classes of summer visitors when the Boston people first started coming down in the 1840s — so his Grandmother Mansfield told Alfred Mansfield Brooks: "Boarders ate and slept under the same roof. Roomers went out for their meals, often so far as to have to be driven to and from at an extra expense of ten cents a round trip. This custom led to the local distinction between *boarders* and *hauled mealers,* all respectable people, but nobody except the natives who eked out a livelihood 'taking them in' at five to seven dollars a week thought of noticing them."

The extension of the Gloucester Branch of the Eastern Railroad in 1847 put the town in the business of swapping salt fish for summer folks. As the trade increased, the first strictly summer hotel, the Pavilion, opened on June 29, 1849, halfway along the town beach (Pavilion Beach ever since). A welcome sight from land or sea was this window on the harbor, set so amply astride the foundations of an enormous and most anomalous windmill of former days, wall to wall with the port's waterfront ropewalk, tiers of arcaded porches mounting to the roof, then up, up, to the glassed-in cupola, all topped off aloft with the fluttering, snapping house flag of the brothers John and Sidney Mason, builders and proprietors.

As the Masons had connections in New York and Philadelphia, they deemed it expedient to arrange not one, but two, opening dinners at their Pavilion. Professor Brooks's Grandmother Mansfield was invited to the first, "certainly not a select one, put on for the substantial citizens of the town, and not long afterwards to another very exclusive one given by the Masons for their out-of-town friends who had by that time about filled the house. This did not sit well locally, but little did the hosts care. She always felt it was a mistake and started a sort of social animosity between the 'natives' and 'summer visitors,' the former often making fun of the latter, who were not seldom disposed to look down their noses on their hosts."

All noses were on a level one August afternoon in 1853 when a large party of natives and Pavilion guests (and some "strangers," presumably gate-crashers) converged upon Eastern Point by carriage and boat on the surprising invitation of Mr. Thomas Niles, Esquire, who was making an unaccustomed effort to improve his public image. Back of the stone wharf near the quarry and the lighthouse was pitched a cool and spacious tent. On the beach below, an oven of flat stones had been assembled wherein clams and sweet corn tucked in blankets of seaweed exuded tantalizing clouds of steam. There were chowder and fried fish and other viands, singing and dancing to the clarion strains of Procter's Band, and speeches of appreciation for Mr. Niles. The host's purpose seemed to have been more than amply accomplished until several days later, when he declared heatedly through the newspaper that in offering the use of his property for the gala he had supposed its organizers understood it was to be a Dutch treat.

There was an open, easy elegance about the Pavilion, which, in the hyperbole of a female admirer the year it opened, was "an edifice of beautiful proportions, and is, in fact, the first specimen of architectural good taste ever seen in this place. Here under its very walls are daily performed swimming feats of incredible skill by young ladies who place their hands upon Old Ocean's mane familiarly."

The hotel was as irresistible to the brush of Gloucester's celebrated painter Fitz Hugh Lane as to the pen of one summering minstrel, who paid his carefree respects in *The Sea Breeze,* "a polka brillante composed and arranged for the piano forte by O. J. Shaw and cordially inscribed to his friends and companions THE BATHERS at Gloucester Beach, Summer of 1856," illustrated with an ingenuous lithograph of the Pavilion and the small schooner yacht *Sea Breeze* anchored off the beach amid disporting swimmers clutching Old Ocean's mane for dear life.

# 8

# Those First Yachts

PLEASURE BOATING ALONG THE NORTH SHORE MAY BE ASSUMED TO have originated with those light birchen canoes that the imagination of Alonzo Lewis set so gracefully swimming o'er the surface of the bright blue ocean, and it has ever since been the joy of anyone with access to anything that floats. Yachting, at the other extreme, was imported as an indulgence of royal governors, not all of whom had salt water in their veins; the seat of provincial power was temporarily at Salem in the summer of 1774, and Governor Thomas Gage, who was a general and not an admiral, spent his leisure hours cruising about Wenham Lake in a pleasure barge.

When William Bentley was settled as pastor of Salem's East Church right after the Revolution in 1784, "only two Sail Boats had any claim to the name when their construction was considered in regard to amusement." Seventeen years passed before a third was sufficiently yachtlike to draw his attention. The occasion was the fifteenth of June 1801, three months into the first administration of Thomas Jefferson: "Capt. G. Crowninshield junr carried me in his remarkably fast sailing Boat from Salem into Beverly Harbour. We made the whole course in 15 minutes & returned in 34, wind fresh at S.W. We made no tack in going, & one in Salem Harbour upon our return. I never did sail so much at my ease in any other boat."

George Crowninshield was a short and wiry bachelor of thirty-five; he had recently settled ashore to run the family's extensive business affairs after commanding various of its vessels in the world trade. The Crowninshields were ardent partisans of Mr. Jefferson (who made George's brother Jacob his Secretary of the Navy), and when George launched this fast sailer within a few days of the inauguration in March, he named her after the new President.

Captain Crowninshield was even faster ashore in his ornate waist-coat, his tasseled Hessian boots and his shaggy beaver hat, dashing through the streets of Salem in a bright yellow curricle. Dr. Bentley next sailed with the Crowninshields (Captain George, Sr., was his landlord) in the summer of 1803, one assumes in *Jefferson,* when he accompanied father and sons on a cruise of the Salem Bay islands in their "excellent boat . . . the most convenient and the best for sail-ing I have ever seen in this place." A month later he sailed to Cape Ann and back in this "noted boat," and three weeks after that, with brothers George, Jacob and Benjamin "in their fast sailing two Mast Boat & this was the first time that I ever was 15 miles from land"; they spoke a brig bound in from England whose crew "appeared surprised to find us in an open boat so far out in the Bay." This first North Shore yacht was thirty-six feet long and very burdensome by modern standards, displacing twenty-two tons. *Jefferson* is said to have been sloop-rigged originally and doubtless followed the lines of the small fishing vessels that were common on the coast.

Having loaned his name to the launching of the North Shore's first palpable yacht, President Jefferson gave a whole fleet of pleasure boats a mighty shove when he persuaded Congress in 1807 to adopt the Embargo Acts, by which he hoped to set America on a par at sea with England and France. Salem shipowners were reasonably con-scientious in foregoing their foreign trade, which left many the master and the mate on the beach with time on their hands. As Dr. Bentley observed the following August, "Since the embargo almost every person fond of sailing has purchased a sail boat & a great variety of experiments have been made upon the form of the boat & the manner of rigging, & these experiments have discovered great ingenuity with various success. . . . The Crowninshields, Derby's, Gardners, &c. & most of our enterprising Masters of Vessels have something of this kind they call their own & most of our Ship & boat builders & several of our townsmen who live at their ease." By September of 1808 the number of small pleasure boats in Salem and other North Shore harbors had "strangely multiplied . . . and upon every sudden gust some alarm is given." Two young men capsized in a squall and drowned in Marblehead Harbor, and another pair upset off Salem Neck. "The Seamen who are well qualified to navigate large vessels are found very inexpert in managing small craft & yet are often presumptuous from an ignorance of the principles on which dories with sail move."

The War of 1812 ended the yachting experiments of the seafaring class on the North Shore and enlisted little *Jefferson* in the privateering fleet of the Crowninshields, so overmanned that she looked to one spectator like "so many goslings on a tray." When his father died in 1815, George Crowninshield, Jr., retired from business altogether, as sons and heirs are sometimes wont to do under such circumstances, and devoted himself to spending their profits from the late war, no way more flamboyantly than on his latest enthusiasm, the hermaphrodite brig *Cleopatra's Barge,* eighty-three feet on the waterline and generally regarded as the first large private yacht built in America.

The *Barge* had all her owner's flair, $50,000 worth of it, which was a lot of money in those days. From afar she presented the profile of a warship, which was belied, as she hove into closer view, by her multicolored stripes on one side, and when she tacked, by a herringbone pattern on the other, all set off with colored rigging. The main saloon was nineteen by twenty feet, mahogany and bird's-eye maple, upholstered in red Genoese velvet and gold lace, with gilded mirrors, a chandelier, custom glassware, china and silver service. George Crowninshield launched the *Barge* from Retire Becket's stocks in 1816 and sailed her to the Mediterranean, where she was a sensation and visited by thousands of the curious. But he died suddenly on his return to Salem in 1817, and his gorgeous creation was sold to King Kamehameha as Hawaii's royal yacht, only to be wrecked by the royal sailors.

Except as the plaything of a Crowninshield, a *Cleopatra's Barge* was shockingly rich for Yankee sporting blood, and the opening concession to anything approaching yachtiness on the North Shore was not yielded up for another fifteen years, when Benjamin C. Clark, the young shipping magnate, located his summer cottage at Nahant in 1832 and built *Mermaid;* this small schooner was said to have been the first Boston-owned "yacht" to be adorned with that badge of degeneracy, a deck.

John Perkins Cushing had returned home from China with his fortune the year previous to *Mermaid*'s debut. Having more money than he knew what to do with, and having drowned his Calvinism in the Pearl River, which flowed past his Canton *hong,* Cushing got married, built a mansion in Boston, bought the Eastern Point Farm and Belmont, and then he, too, must have a yacht. His much younger cousin and protégé in business, Captain Robert Bennet Forbes, was also fresh from the China seas, where he had served the family interests to mutual advantage. Though not yet thirty but already gray ("I imagined myself approaching old age") and still "Black Ben" to his friends, Forbes was a master among mariners, having shipped before the mast at thirteen and assumed his first command at twenty. Cushing asked his cousin to oversee the construction of his fifty-eight-foot schooner yacht *Sylph* up the Mystic River at Medford during the winter of 1833.

*Sylph* was launched in the spring of 1834, and that summer Forbes and friends launched at Boston the Boat Club, with "no charter, no bylaws, no sailing directions, no flag, save the Stars and Stripes, and its only boats were row boats." Next spring the Forbes circle, most of whom were young Boston merchant-shipmasters cradled on the ocean wave (by which they had avoided being rocked to sleep at Harvard), bought the forty-foot, thirty-ton schooner *Dream* in New York and upgraded the Boat Club to the Dream Club, the first American yacht club on record.

Not satisfied with her performance, John Cushing had instructed the builder to cut *Sylph* in half and lengthen her by eight and a half feet that winter. This piece of Procrustean surgery made his yacht perceptibly swifter, which she proved on July 8, 1835, by winning an informal race from Boston to Nahant and back against the smaller *Dream* and the big new brigs *Henry Clay* and *Isidore,* though the owner thought the excessive rake of the masts gave her a weather helm. In another trial with *Dream,* whether this season or the following, *Sylph* did not come off so well, unless the account is apocryphal. This time Colonel Thomas Handasyd Perkins, Jr. (a dashing Beau Brummel dubbed "Shortarm Tom" by his intimates on account of his short right arm) and Captain Philip Dumaresq, who would be one of the great masters of the clippers, sailed *Dream* against *Sylph* around a buoy outside Boston Harbor; it was agreed that the crew of the lead schooner would drive a boathook into the buoy while going by, the runner-up to bring it back. *Dream* rounded first; Perkins hove his gaff home, and they finished ahead. Forbes and Cushing failed to retrieve this souvenir of defeat, and thereafter, whenever Shortarm Tom met Black Ben he hailed him: "Ben ahoy! Where is my boathook?"

At the end of July 1835, John Cushing, with his cousins, captains Forbes and William Sturgis, shipowner R. D. Shepherd (who had sold him the land for Belmont), Sam Cabot (Uncle Tom's serpent-sighting son-in-law) and Captain Daniel C. Bacon (another old China hand and Forbes's close friend and business partner) embarked in *Sylph* on a cruise around Cape Cod. Off Nantucket they fell in with the rather larger schooner yacht *Wave,* ninety-two feet, owned by John Cox Stevens, future founding commodore of the New York Yacht Club, "and got handsomely beaten by her," as Cushing noted in his diary. Near Woods Hole the tide carried them aground, and the owner, figuring his *Sylph* was a goner, sold her on the spot for a quarter of her cost to Forbes and Sam Cabot — a transaction that he did not note in his diary. But with help from a government cutter the wily Ben floated his prize. Homeward bound, they fell in again with *Wave* for a race down Vineyard Sound and were gaining when the rising wind decided Stevens to give it up and bear away for Tarpaulin Cove on the island of Naushon. Samuel Eliot Morison called this the first American yacht race of record, although one and possibly both of *Sylph*'s bouts with *Dream* might take the precedence.

*Sylph* was sold as a Boston Harbor pilot boat, and in 1837 Commodore Forbes, Captain Dan Bacon and William H. Boardman (called by one who knew him "as clever a specimen of human nature as ever sailed a boat in a stiff breeze") built the thirty-ton schooner *Breeze,* fifty-one feet long, doubling the fleet of the Dream Club. That summer they raced to Marblehead. *Dream* arrived first and anchored. *Breeze* came up and tied alongside. Forbes hospitably invited the rival crew into his more spacious cabin for lunch, and when they were below slipped aboard *Dream* and induced their cook to pass his guests' own food and wine over and down his forehatch. Upon the conclusion of this deception, *Breeze* cast off first and got under way. Forbes hoisted a well-drained champagne bottle (one of *Dream*'s) to his main gaff and maintained his lead back to Boston (so he claimed) by tossing empty bottles and strawberry boxes overboard, causing the still-hungry Dreamers, who had unwittingly shared their lunch, to heave to and pick up what they supposed, with by now astonishing naïveté, was good wine and good fruit.

That first American yacht club and most of its humorous commodore's fortune evaporated in the financial crisis of 1837, and Forbes returned to China to recoup. Yet, though the shore east of New York remained clubless for thirty more years, the building of the fast little schooners, which were merely modeled after the speedy pilot boats that raced out to meet incoming ships and put a pilot aboard, the informal matches got up over a friendly glass, and the boisterous good times had had their effect; the sport of yachting, as distinct in a vague sort of way from messing about in boats, had caught the imagination of a slowly growing number of those who could afford to buy, man and maintain their own private sailing vessels.

Robert Bennet Forbes was a superb sailor, where John Cox Stevens, the inventor-engineer-yachtsman, was merely first-rate, but when Stevens and friends celebrated the dawn of recovery from the

1837 depression by organizing the New York Yacht Club aboard his new schooner *Gimcrack,* anchored off the Battery on July 30, 1844, it stayed organized. A month later the New York squadron put in to Newport on its maiden cruise and rendezvoused with Captain Forbes in the chartered Boston pilot schooner *Belle* and Colonel William P. Winchester's sixty-seven-foot schooner yacht *Northern Light.* With David Sears of Nahant they were enlisted on the spot as the club's first New England members; thus was sanctioned the long and frequently amiable rivalry between North Shore and New York yachtsmen.

*Northern Light* rates more than passing notice. Colonel Winchester was a genial Watertown meatpacker, for whom a Boston suburb named itself when he presented it with $3,000. After Benjamin Clark replaced *Mermaid* with the twelve-ton schooner *Raven* in 1836, Winchester bought *Mermaid* and kept her until *Northern Light* was launched in '39. Designed and built by Louis Winde, a Danish naval architect who specialized in pilot boats at Boston, the *Light* was the *ne plus ultra* of yachting in Massachusetts Bay during her brief life (she was lost in the Straits of Magellan in 1850), reminiscent of the *Barge* for dash and derring-do. A crimson stripe slashed across the gleaming ebon of her topsides, her bends were varnished bright, and *Northern Light*'s crew of amateurs was uniformed by her convivial owner in white trousers, red shirts and straw hats encircled by red bands with flowing ends that were stitched with her name in gold; the standard ration before and abaft the mast was a brandy punch of no uncertain character, called "bimbo."

Quite typical of the small schooner yachts of this era, on the other hand, was *Nautilus,* built in 1842 for C. B. Pierce. She was thirty-two feet on deck, ten feet two inches wide, and drew six feet six. She had a sharp bow, marked sheer, a long keel, inside ballast, ten-inch bulwarks, a fourteen-inch cabin trunk, black topsides, the rest green. The cabin had standing room aft, settees, lockers, four berths, and a small galley forward. Typically, she was pilot-boat rigged. The method of measuring varied from builder to builder, as the yacht designer and historian William P. Stephens has pointed out, and many the rule-o'-thumb sloop was converted to a schooner in hopes of making her go faster, or vice versa, or lengthened as in the case of *Sylph,* and usually she wound up piloting or fishing anyway, "thus returning to her ancestors."

As the social nucleus of the summer North Shore, Nahant sheltered the greater share of yachts, including, besides Clark's *Raven,* hotelkeeper Phineas Drew's *Susan,* the quick little schooner *Avon,* owned by the Sears boys, David Sears's *Brenda,* J. H. Gray's *Cloud,* and the native Nahanter Jonathan Johnson's party schooner *Foam.* It was perhaps no coincidence, then, that two days after the New York Yacht Club ran its first regatta, the first such gathering of yachts ever held east of Cape Cod was sailed off Nahant on the afternoon of July 19, 1845, by eleven small schooners in a brisk southeasterly. The course was an acute triangle of twenty miles from off Ben Clark's namesake point, out around The Graves at the entrance of Boston Harbor, around Egg Rock in Nahant Bay and back to the start. The piazzas of the Nahant Hotel groaned under the weight of guests, the rocks and every height of land swarmed with the spread of spectators, and the sea along the course sighed to a burden of boats such as had never been seen offshore before.

The contestants were gunned off to a flying start from their moorings, sail up. Favored for the cup was *Cygnet,* largest of the fleet — nearly three times the burthen of *Nautilus, Avon, Neptune* and *Raven,* and owned by John E. Thayer, dean of the Long Wharf party boatmen of Boston — and she led all the way. The breeze freshened as the race progressed, and after the lead boats had hauled their wind under the lee of Egg Rock they boiled by East Point for the finish at a cracking nine knots. There, running a close third, was little *Raven* under the master hand of Benjamin C. Clark.

Naturally, with such a disparity among them, an attempt had been made to handicap the schooners, and *Raven* won the cup on time allowance. The result should have come as no surprise. Long, deep and sharp, *Raven* had carried her owner to victory, when she was new in 1836, over the fast New York sloop *Osceola* in a cele-

*Ben Clark's schooner yacht* Young Raven, *painting attributed to Clement Drew. Peabody Museum of Salem*

*Benjamin C. Clark. From*
Some Merchants and Sea
Captains of Old Boston

*Robert Bennet Forbes. From*
Personal Reminiscences

*John Perkins Cushing's schooner* Sylph, *first of the racing yachts. Peabody Museum of Salem*

*The Nahant regatta of July 19, 1845. Eastern Yacht Club*

brated race from Long Island to Halfway Rock off Marblehead and back, and since then she had reaped other laurels, which she bore, as an admirer had it, "gracefully in her beak." Her distinguished owner, whom James Homer considered the best amateur pilot on the North Shore, kept *Raven* for twenty years before he retired her for *Young Raven* in 1857. This was a long affair between a man and his boat, and she served him well. Homer wrote of a summer around 1840 when the sailboat *Tiger* "went over in a squall and sunk, with six young gentlemen, all of whom were, under Providence, miraculously saved by B. C. Clark, Esq. in the *Raven*. Well may that gentleman feel proud of his little craft and her exploits."

Clark got as good as he gave; he capsized himself one day sailing a smaller boat within a stone's throw of his own cottage but refused to be rescued by some passing Lynn yachtsmen and loyally awaited the arrival of the Nahant volunteers, who had launched their lifeboat from the station maintained at Joe's Beach by the Massachusetts Humane Society.

The New York Yacht Club's raked, 102-foot schooner *America,* built by a syndicate headed by Commodore Stevens, sailed across in 1851 and in the most important, if not the most exciting, race of the century beat Britain's best and brought home the Royal Yacht Squadron's Hundred Guineas Cup. *America*'s victory stunned Britannia and gave a further push to the already burgeoning interest in yachting on the East Coast of the United States, where there was money to spare as the fifties basked in the sun of prosperity, trying to ignore the gathering clouds of contention.

The alchemy by which George Steers, their schooner's designer, and the New York Yacht Club converted the Hundred Guineas Cup into the America's Cup deservedly and doubly reinforced New York's position as the yachting capital of the Western Hemisphere, because Steers was simultaneously introducing the first major innovation in American yacht design to the coast south of Cape Cod, namely the shoal draft centerboarder with a turn of speed that amazed the traditionalists. While the keel yachts modeled after the time-tested working types favored by Massachusetts yachtsmen were more happily adapted to the deeper harbors and the sea conditions east of the Cape, there was a lesson to be learned from the New York and Connecticut centerboard boats, initially the sloops: light displacement, under the right conditions, equaled speed. This catechism was administered in the summer of 1854, accompanied by a sound thrashing so that it would not be soon forgot — at least so we have it from the authoritative maritime historian and famous skipper of yachts and clipper ships, Captain Arthur H. Clark, who learned his splices on the Nahant boats of his father, Benjamin C. Clark.

It came about this way. The Napoleon of hotel proprietors, Paran Stevens, it seems, made a particular point of catering to yachts and yachtsmen when he reopened the refurbished Nahant Hotel in 1854 and attracted quite an influx, which included a certain half-decked centerboard sloop, the *James Ingersoll Day,* built by William Smith at Stonington, Connecticut. Though much the smaller, and without benefit of time allowance, the *Day* one day that summer beat the daylights out of the schooner *Surprise,* regarded by many as the fastest boat in Massachusetts Bay, in a race from Nahant to The Graves and back. Surprise indeed, and the more farseeing yachtsmen around Boston commenced to look askance at some of the old assumptions about long keels, inside ballast, displacement hulls and traditional rigs that had all been handed on from father to son without much question and had produced craft alike enough for suitably keen competition — until the appearance of the little sloop with the big name.

The lesson took about two years to sink in.

The first regatta to be held off Marblehead in 1852 had merely divided the entries over and under fourteen tons. The next such meet on the North Shore was so much less structured, if that were possible, as to verge on the chaotic. Gloucester, where fishermen's sons were weaned on brine, put on an extempore "regatta" in its own unique style on August 16, 1855, when fifteen boats simply tacked out the harbor and back. The Gloucester *Telegraph* thought the exercise "a very fine, yet rather singular scene, scarcely any two being rigged alike, or carrying the same amount of sail. . . . It would be difficult to state the winning boat, as no measures were taken to make due allowance for tonnage, nor any rules laid down for guidance, and as far as we can learn no judges were appointed to decide." No prizes, "and but few spectators, mostly chance ones, and but little interest was manifested on shore."

However, it all comes out of the hold, as the Gloucester saying goes. The fisheries were prospering, and a little fleet of local yachts reflected the fact. The second attempt at a regatta succeeded splendidly, for it seems to have been the best organized yet on the North Shore, a sweepstakes in four classes according to length of waterline, and time allowances between boats. Eighteen started off Pavilion Beach on September 3, 1858, and sailed outside Eastern Point over ocean courses, the shortest eight miles. Significantly, the most spirited match of the day was provided by the class of centerboard sloops led by Captain Robert Bennet Forbes, age fifty-four, at the tiller of his twenty-four-foot *Grace Darling,* which won eight dollars and "the commendations of all by her very superior performance."

Forbes must have been impressed by the *James Ingersoll Day* exhibition, because he had commissioned Smith of Stonington to build this centerboarder as a house present to himself when he moved his family into his new Manchester cottage the previous summer. The name was a characteristically Forbesian choice. Grace Darling was a noted heroine of the period, who braved a stormy sea in an open boat with her father, an English lighthouse keeper, to rescue survivors of a terrible wreck on the Farne Islands off the coast of Northumberland in 1838 and shared with him the gold medal of the Royal Humane Society. Her American admirer felt a kinship: in 1849 the steamship *Europa,* on which Forbes was a passenger for Liverpool, rammed and sank the barque *Charles Bartlett* in mid-Atlantic; Black Ben leaped into the ocean and helped save several survivors. The British gave him two medals, and on his return to Boston he was awarded a gold medal by the Massachusetts Humane Society, of which he was a leading light and trustee. *Facias ipse quod faciamus suades.*

*Grace Darling* was a very fast catboat when he got her, but not quite fast enough for Bennet Forbes, so he sailed her from Manchester one day in half a gale, through breaking seas over the bar between Tinker's Island and Marblehead Neck, and then threaded the needle of Shirley Gut to an East Boston yard to have her converted to a sloop rig. In the two or three seasons he had *Grace Darling,* Captain Forbes enjoyed a few brushes with the Burgess boys (and they were but boys then) off the Beverly shore in their *Cassie.* Like *Grace* (and probably inspired by her), *Cassie* was a centerboarder from the Smith yard with a cloud of sail, lead ballast and a small levee of sandbags for shifting weight to the weather rail. The Burgesses had been summering on Woodbury Point since 1858.

When the second Gloucester sweepstakes was run off on August 17, 1860, the owners of the three local centerboard sloops again suffered the seizure of the entrance fees by summer people "from up the line." This time the raiders were Franklin Burgess and his younger brother, Edward, who was twelve, in *Cassie.* Ned, who "always beat the rest of us," as his schoolmate Bill Lawrence of Nahant, the future Episcopal Bishop, admiringly admitted, never forgot that race. "We beat around the outer stake-boat so far ahead of the local boats that the patriotic keepers of the stake-boat cut her adrift, after we turned, so as to lessen the distance the other boats had to make!" Fishermen's tricks.

Captain Forbes returned to Stonington in 1859 and ordered the larger centerboarder *Scud* for himself and the keel sloop *Mist* for cousin John Cushing, both thirty feet on the waterline. Neither kept his boat more than a season or so; Cushing was seventy-two anyway and sold *Mist* to Francis E. Bacon.

On the sixth of July 1861, just as her new owner and *Mist* were embarking for a day of sailing on the bay, Captain Seth Simmons and a reporter for the Boston *Herald* identifying himself modestly as "E. B. H." clambered into a wicker basket. The lines were let go, the crowd huzzahed, and the hot-air balloon *Queen of the Air* ascended above Boston Common until, in a trice, "the horse cars crawled beneath us like flies." High over the harbor they floated on the wings of the southwesterly, and across the bluffs of Winthrop so far below, and then, as the bag cooled, the *Queen* began her regal descent, rather to the consternation of her passengers, who had counted (with supreme insouciance, considering the direction of the wind) on a dry landing.

There was Nahant, two miles off, just as Mr. Durant had viewed it with similar dismay in 1834. Below and all around, and rising up with alarming rapidity, the broad Atlantic. Ahead, the only two craft in sight, dead ahead in fact, a schooner and a sloop. The basket struck, scooped up a load of seawater, lifted as the breeze bore the bag along, surged above the waves with its soaked and gasping occupants for a couple of hundred yards, then dipped and dunked them again.

The *Queen of the Air* flirted thus with the watery element, alternately skipping, dipping and dunking for a mile or so, until Captain Simmons, with strength borne of the utmost desperation, hove himself up and opened the air valve a turn or two just as his runaway craft missed the sloop by a hair (it was *Mist,* of course, which had barely succeeded in luffing out of the way) and sailed into the fore rigging of the schooner *Atlantic,* bound down East. Simmons was hurled from the basket onto the deck, while E. B. H. splashed into the sea and was left astern. *Atlantic*'s crew immediately lowered away for him, but the boat swamped and dumped one of them overboard. They bailed their boat, cast off and rescued the fellow, while *Mist* came up on E. B. H. (who fortunately was a strong swimmer, for he was half a mile astern by now), plucked the newsman from the briny, gave him a change of clothes, chowder and champagne and set him ashore at Nahant with something to write about.

The *Queen of the Air,* having done her mischief for the day, worked clear of the schooner's rigging and soared off, "where she may still be going for all I know," as *Mist*'s Captain Bacon declared later.

Like hot-air ballooning, yachting was a bit touch-and-go along the North Shore in the years before the Civil War. There was not a yacht club on the coast, nor a proper yacht designer, few enough with the brass to call themselves yachtsmen, and fewer yachts with any claim to the name when their construction was considered in regard to amusement. And, as Captain Arthur Clark reflected back with a trace of yearning, "there was a great deal of sport and pleasure to it."

# PART TWO

# Colonization Completed

## 1865–1890

# 9

# Winthrop
## and the Little Wiggler

HAD FATE BEEN LESS BLIND TO HER CHARMS, THAT PART OF OLD CHELSEA called Winthrop might have vied with Nahant. The peninsular attractions of Pullen Point were appreciated by John Hancock and friends fifty years before Colonel Perkins built above Spouting Horn, but they fell under the blight of a pesthouse and then a war, and while Nahant's pastures succumbed to the croquet mallet and the Ice King's balm o' Gileads, Winthrop's breezy moor and marsh and beach and bluff remained the kingdom of the cows. Then one summer afternoon in 1845 destiny dealt a second chance for greatness, something it seldom does.

Judge Edward Greely Loring of Boston and his wife were gliding through Point Shirley Gut on the steamer, homeward bound from a stay at Nahant, and as they enjoyed the sight of the deserted Winthrop shore placidly passing before their eyes, the jurist ruminated on the pleasures of gunning along there when he was a young fellow. What a fine spot for a summer cottage, he remarked to Mrs. Loring. The judge was no doubt well aware, besides, that at that very moment his cousin, Charles Greely Loring, the "Squire," was getting settled in the first summer mansion at Beverly.

While Judge Loring was weighing the case, the scattering of country folks holding title to the remote reaches of Chelsea from Point of Pines to Point Shirley, between Saugus on the north and Malden to the west — old Rumney Marsh — seceded in 1846 from the seat of government at Ferry Village, which was far away and neglectful of their interests, and were incorporated as North Chelsea. Curiously enough, the new town had four times the area of suddenly shrunken old Chelsea and spread as far south of the parent to seaward as to the north of it.

As regarded his potential influence, Judge Loring probably considered the gain in local autonomy advantageous. The next year, he and friend George B. Emerson bought farmland and built their cottages on what is now Winthrop's Pleasant Street, looking across to Boston and the inshore islands of the harbor. Emerson was the first principal of English High School in the city and had a national influence in public education, besides being a cousin of Ralph Waldo Emerson. He was also an authority on the flora of Massachusetts, which accounts for the 1,500 trees he planted Tudor-fashion along the shore, not to mention the Emerson family's cherished "Love-making Tree," a pendant willow clutching in its languid embrace the secluded platform on which daughter Lucy gave her hand to the future Judge John Lowell.

Even as Judge Loring was rediscovering the Winthrop shore from the deck of the steamer, most of Point Shirley was being bought up by Joseph Warren Revere, son of the patriot, for his Revere Copper Company's smelter, on the rationale that the smoke and fumes would blow out to sea, most of them, and not bother anyone anyway but a few farmers. Soon after, Philip Farrington Dascomb built the Point Shirley House above the steamer wharf and only 125 yards from the copper works. Between these twin outposts of business and pleasure, Albert Richardson saw traffic enough in 1848 to start running a stage between Point Shirley and Maverick Square at the East Boston ferry terminal; this encouraged other summerers to join Loring and Emerson on the shore. Then in 1851 Boston took over the bridge linking Pullen Point to East Boston across Belle Isle Inlet and Breed's Island (Orient Heights) and abolished the tolls. Feeling quite independent now, the people in the south of North Chelsea seceded in 1852 and set up shop as the town of Winthrop. In 1854 the Eastern Railroad abandoned its water route to Boston in favor of the approach by land through Malden, which led to a reorganization and improvement of the East Boston ferry service that enabled Richardson to drive his omnibus on and then off to Scollay Square — ninety minutes and twenty-five cents from Point Shirley. By 1855 Winthrop had 407 summer cottagers from Boston.

If situating a restaurant in the shadow of a copper refinery on a distant and windy point of beach, an hour and a half from the source of custom, seems errant speculation on the part of Philip Farrington Dascomb, its purchase in 1850 by Orray Augustus Taft qualifies as arrant folly, tempered only slightly by the service of the omnibus, which could contain fifty-two passengers and swayed so sickeningly as it careened across the marshes that it tipped over at least once that is admitted of. However, Mr. Taft was a man to be reckoned with.

O. A. Taft learned the restaurant business from his father, the last landlord of Taft's Hotel, formerly the same Chelsea Hotel that had been leveled (with the hill it was standing on) during the previously noted deflowering of Ferry Village. The younger Taft's first preserved bill of fare after he took over the Point Shirley House, for August 9, 1850, offered eleven kinds of game birds at a stag dinner for forty-five; obviously O. A. had a loyal following at the Cornhill Coffee House, which he had been running, in Boston.

Next May the Point Shirley House burned to the ground. The neighbors were able to save nothing more than a few casks of liquor, as attested by various semiprostrate forms sprawled about the grounds in a contemporary newspaper illustration of the disaster. O. A. rebuilt at once. As Winthrop and the means of access to it grew, so did O. A.'s fame — his restaurant too, into a rambling, dormered building spread upon the shingle above the racing tide of Shirley Gut.

Challenge was as breath to Taft. A kerosene distillery moved out to the Point and added its vapors to the pall from the smeltery; he thrived on the mixture. When a hurricane bore down on the coast on September 8, 1869, O. A. was positively in his element. Vessels dragged anchor and drove ashore, roofs flew through the air, windows blew in, trees crashed to the ground, and at Point Shirley a party of gentlemen was midway through the bill of fare. Calmly and appreciatively the diners discussed the merits of the chowder and the fine points of the game as they stared out the windows at the boats bobbing in distress until the view was lost in sheets of rain and spray, and they congratulated each other on their snug situation while awaiting the *coup de maître,* a platter of upland plover being prepared by O. A. himself in his great kitchen.

Suddenly the tempest attacked the building as if to tear it from its foundations, and an awful crash shook the walls. All leaped from their seats. Mrs. Taft lifted her petticoat and ran to the kitchen. The main chimney had blown over through the skylight. Pots, pans, broken dishes, bricks and chunks of mortar covered the floor. In the midst of the ruins, ghastly in a rising cloud of dust, stood her husband, coated with soot, rain pouring down upon him through the shattered skylight. Triumphantly he held aloft his precious dish of upland plover.

"See!" he cried. "The birds are unhurt!"

Such was the spirit that soared above the slagpile the smelter had made of Point Shirley. Such was the devotion that maintained a garden of the palate where all around nothing green would grow in the presence of those noxious exhalations so poetically described in an 1868 tourist brochure (of Nahant, not Winthrop): "Over the Point often hangs a thick white smoke . . . which the sun sometimes touches so that it looks in the distance like a silver veil thrown over the land." Finally in 1869 the Revere Copper Company surrendered before the mounting resentment of its victims and departed, followed in two years by the malodorous kerosene distillery.

In time, Taft had forty-two dining rooms, and the world hammered at his doors. Summer weekends the town's streets were clogged with the carriages of the hopeful. Trains and steamers disgorged gourmets by the thousands. Battleships and private craft came to anchor, sending in boatloads of officers and yachtsmen. In perhaps his crowning coup, O. A. enticed from their regular haunt, the Parker House, for one or two dinners each summer the renowned Saturday Club (occasionally called the Atlantic Club) of Boston's lions of letters — Emerson, Holmes, Longfellow, Whittier, Hawthorne, Dana, Lowell and Motley, among others. When someone tagged them "The Mutual Admiration Society," Dr. Holmes countered: "If there was not a certain amount of 'mutual admiration' . . . it was a great pity, and implied a defect in the nature of men who were otherwise largely endowed."

Indeed Taft's was compared favorably with Delmonico's world-famous restaurant in New York. His fish and game list alone offered twenty-four varieties of seafood, from bonito "from the Gulf" to eels, turbot, sea trout, chicken halibut and mullet. At the ready were more than thirty species of birds, including five kinds of plover, two of curlew and four of snipe, various yellowlegs, godwit, peeps and duck, woodcock, rail and reed-birds from Delaware, willet from New Jersey, grouse from Illinois and owls "from the North." O. A. kept gunners and fishermen busy. From behind the rear end of a shotgun the supply of game looked limitless. Not, however, to Lynn's historian James Newhall. As early as 1865 Newhall deplored "the devastating hand of man" and "the success of the general conspiracy against nature" on the lower North Shore and condemned the slaughter of the shorebirds, which only a few years earlier had abounded on Nahant, a kill so nearly total that "he who would come hither for sea-fowling will be likely to find his only reward in that moral discipline which is the effect of disappointed expectation."

But the expectations of the lord of the Point Shirley House and his patrons would not brook disappointment. The day of the first base-ball game between Winthrop and Chelsea in 1882, the occupants of 1,500 horsedrawn vehicles jammed into Taft's and consumed more than one thousand wild birds. On August 17, 1883, O. A. staged a banquet that lasted from 2:45 in the afternoon until 7:30 that evening. He staked one thousand dollars on the spot to anyone present able to name an edible North American bird that he could not produce instantly, and had no takers. To top off the feast, he served each guest a hummingbird cooked to delectation and tucked into a walnut shell.

Winthrop did not go the way of Cold Roast Boston after all. There was no gold lining to that silver veil thrown over the land by

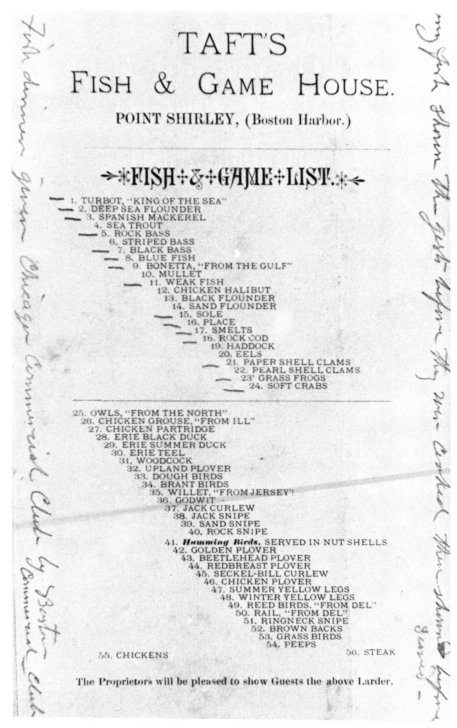

# TAFT'S
# FISH & GAME HOUSE.

### POINT SHIRLEY, (Boston Harbor.)

## →*FISH ÷ & ÷ GAME ÷ LIST.*←

1. TURBOT, "KING OF THE SEA"
2. DEEP SEA FLOUNDER
3. SPANISH MACKEREL
4. SEA TROUT
5. ROCK BASS
6. STRIPED BASS
7. BLACK BASS
8. BLUE FISH
9. BONETTA, "FROM THE GULF"
10. MULLET
11. WEAK FISH
12. CHICKEN HALIBUT
13. BLACK FLOUNDER
14. SAND FLOUNDER
15. SOLE
16. PLACE
17. SMELTS
18. ROCK COD
19. HADDOCK
20. EELS
21. PAPER SHELL CLAMS
22. PEARL SHELL CLAMS
23. GRASS FROGS
24. SOFT CRABS

25. OWLS, "FROM THE NORTH"
26. CHICKEN GROUSE, "FROM ILL"
27. CHICKEN PARTRIDGE
28. ERIE BLACK DUCK
29. ERIE SUMMER DUCK
30. ERIE TEEL
31. WOODCOCK
32. UPLAND PLOVER
33. DOUGH BIRDS
34. BRANT BIRDS
35. WILLET, "FROM JERSEY"
36. GODWIT
37. JACK CURLEW
38. JACK SNIPE
39. SAND SNIPE
40. ROCK SNIPE
41. *Humming Birds,* SERVED IN NUT SHELLS
42. GOLDEN PLOVER
43. BEETLEHEAD PLOVER
44. REDBREAST PLOVER
45. SECKEL-BILL CURLEW
46. CHICKEN PLOVER
47. SUMMER YELLOW LEGS
48. WINTER YELLOW LEGS
49. REED BIRDS, "FROM DEL"
50. RAIL, "FROM DEL"
51. RINGNECK SNIPE
52. BROWN BACKS
53. GRASS BIRDS
54. PEEPS

55. CHICKENS                                    56. STEAK

The Proprietors will be pleased to show Guests the above Larder.

*A corner of Mr. Taft's larder. Winthrop Public Library*

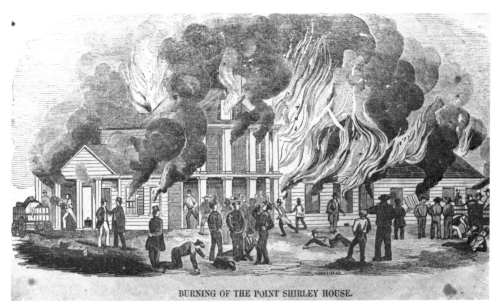

BURNING OF THE POINT SHIRLEY HOUSE.

*"Some casks of liquor," comments the caption in* Gleason's Pictorial Magazine *of June 28, 1851, "having been saved from the devouring elements, were almost as eagerly swallowed by the bystanders, who soon presented a sad appearance."*
Winthrop Improvement and Historical Association

*The copper smeltery casts its pall over Taft's in cut illustrating* Harper's Weekly *article of June 22, 1872, which noted that the proprietor "serves up his birds as affectionately as if they were his own children."* Winthrop Improvement and Historical Association and (inset) Winthrop Public Library

*The "Peanut Train" of the Boston, Winthrop and Shore Railroad poses with personnel about 1883 at Winthrop's Cottage Hill depot. Winthrop Improvement and Historical Association*

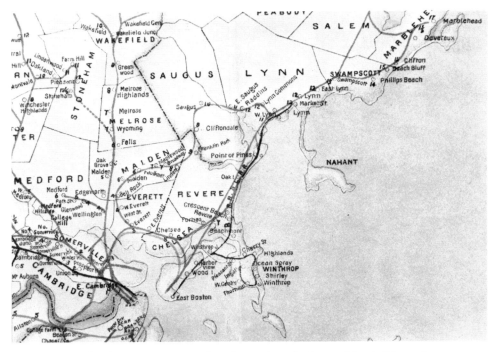

*The network of narrow-gauge railroads serving the lower North Shore, in a map of 1891. Essex Institute*

*Ocean Spray, view south toward Great Head, July 1876. Winthrop Public Library*

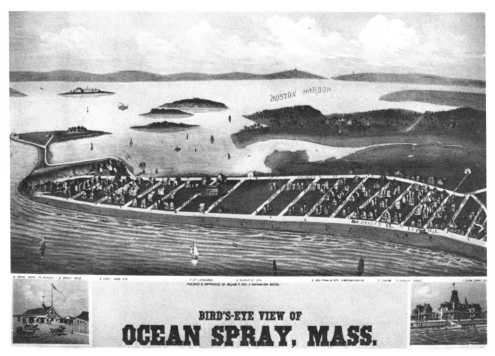

*Promoter's conception of Winthrop, late 1880s. Winthrop Public Library*

*Aphelion Club clambake, Great Head, 1886. Winthrop Improvement and Historical Association*

*Steam yacht* Ricochet *lies at her mooring off Sargent Street, about 1880. In back-ground is Governor's Island, today a runway for Logan Airport. Note oarsmen's derbies and galluses. Harry Whorf glass plate negative, from Winthrop Public Library*

the copper works. When ten years after the Civil War the pressure of the big city broke through the isolation of the old Chelsea shore, which had been bypassed by the Eastern Railroad, fashion too had passed it by. But that is not an end to it. Let Beacon Street perspire; the commonality of Boston simply sweated and would have their day, for the moment was at hand, and the man was Alpheus P. Blake.

Blake was Pied Piper and Johnny Appleseed rolled into one, with the hand of a Paul Bunyan and the tongue of a Messiah, a tall, spare speculator who started as a poor boy from New Hampshire and made his first fortune developing the Hyde Park section of Boston's Dorchester. Looking for richer satellites to bring within the orbit of the city, he lit upon this bypassed, population-barren territory of the lower North Shore. Around 1871, the year North Chelsea became Revere, A. P. Blake formed the Boston Land Company, bought up a thousand acres of East Boston, Winthrop and Revere, and with the boldness of a Vanderbilt conceived of their development as a great recreational and residential region to be fed from Boston and Lynn by a cheap-to-build, cheap-to-run and cheap-to-ride narrow-gauge railroad.

The time was ripe for taking on the Eastern Railroad, which had disdained any extension of branch service into this unprofitable region on the sea side of its main line. Moreover, the road was embroiled in a "Depot War" with Lynn over the inadequacy of its Central Square station and haughtily refused to run trains on Sunday, leaving travelers to contend for seats aboard an ancient stage that made one round trip between Salem and Boston. To complete its villainous image, Eastern had suffered a setback in public confidence from which it never really recovered; this was the infamous Revere Disaster on the foggy evening of August 26, 1871, when the Bangor Express plowed full speed into the rear of a Beverly local at the Revere station, killing twenty-nine and injuring fifty-seven, all because of chaotic dispatching compounded by the road's inadequate double-tracking and the outrageous refusal of the superintendent to make use of the telegraph between stations.

Lynn's smoldering dissatisfaction with the Eastern first flared up in 1861 in the form of the Lynn and Boston Street Railway, a horse-car line its founders trusted would "prove no small regulator of the freaks and follies of the great steam corporation." The railroad of course resisted the reinstallation of Dobbin on rival tracks as furiously as the Eastern Stage Company had battled *its* incursions a generation before. But the horsecars had been the darlings of Boston for five years, and in 1861 the first of these pleasant anomalies to appear in Essex County was clattering along the Salem Pike between Lynn and Winnisimmet Ferry, soon all the way over Chelsea Bridge to Scollay Square.

The operators of the Lynn and Boston sensed the recreational possibilities of great Chelsea Beach and extended a branch track to a restaurant above the sands, whose fame before long rested on its reputation as a liquor nuisance. They also offered to run tracks along Long Beach to Nahant. Cold Roast expectedly turned a cold shoulder, causing Mrs. Tudor to start up her private "barge" over the beach to Maolis Gardens. Nahanters remained frigid to any and all proposed arteries of influx. Repeatedly they spurned the horsecars, and a steam railroad, and they held off even the electric trolleys until 1903.

Its first year, the sixty-one horses of the Lynn and Boston hauled twenty-one cars and 253,447 passengers 132,310 miles at seven miles an hour along twelve miles of track and contributed $132.41 worth of manure. The larger cars carried a conductor on a rear platform; the smaller, platformless, were called "bobtails." Long or short, they rattled about their business on absurdly abbreviated wheelbases that gave them an especially teetery look when loaded with portly gents hung with ponderous watch chains, headed for office, factory or beer parlor. The operators got the better of temporarily immovable obstacles by driving off the track and around them. Winters along the steppelike Lynn and Revere marshes, the driver huddled up front against the arctic blast, nose dripping, reins to the miserable team in one mittened hand, brake grasped in the other, while inside, the passengers froze or roasted according to their distance from the salamander stove that irregularly ignited the nicotine-stained straw on the floor and supplied coals to thaw out frozen switches. But then came spring, and the fancy-painted open cars with their running boards were wheeled out of hibernation. Up rolled the curtains, and it was off to Chelsea Beach, with the sea breeze blowing through, all joy and jollity.

Nevertheless, Alpheus P. Blake had a vision, and bobtails hauled by plodding nags were not part of it. He looked to bring the Boston Land Company's thousand acres within commuting time of Boston, and to transport sweltering Bostonians by the tens of thousands to the beach for a few hours of relief. On April 8, 1872, the Boston, Revere Beach and Lynn Railroad was organized. Blake's equation: light roadbed and light, three-foot track, plus light rolling stock, low cost, low maintenance and low fares, multiplied by high volume, equals glorious dividends.

Construction moved rapidly along the eight miles from Lynn across the marshes, on trestles over the Saugus River and along the Point of Pines and the great beach within reach of the spray, to Beachmont, across more marsh past Belle Isle Inlet to Orient Heights, thence on fill and trestles to Harbor View, Wood Island and Jeffries Point, where the tracks shot through a 400-foot brick tunnel to the company's East Boston ferry slip for the passage on its steamers of four-fifths of a mile across Boston Harbor to Rowe's Wharf on Atlantic Avenue at the foot of Broad Street. Every challenge was met and conquered. Along the crest of the beach, according to one account, the sand "kept sinking under the ties and what was infinitely worse, getting into the workers' beer. This caused a two-day strike until the situation was remedied." When a Revere crowd, grumbling "We don't want all the riffraff of Boston at our back doors," blocked the link-up of the two work gangs on the Point of Pines, the boss snuck his men out that night and laid the rails before dawn.

On its first day, July 29, 1875, the Narrow Gauge carried 1,078 passengers — the opening freshet of the flood to come. The slim coaches were elegantly appointed (seats in plush, with silver-plated mountings), some closed, some open after the manner of the summer horsecars. They flew across the marsh and above the seething surf behind *Orion, Pegasus* and *Jupiter,* the sturdy little locomotives in black and gleaming brass with their cyclopean lanterns, hayrake cowcatchers and bulbous funnels, delivered for $7,000 apiece. The entire "Little Wiggler" was completed within its capitalization of $350,000, including the ferries *Oriole* and *Union* — all this in a period when railroad construction had been almost halted by the depression following the financial panic of 1873.

The impact on Revere (formerly Chelsea) Beach was explosive. Blake had tapped wells of yearning, had drilled a summer safety valve into the simmering subterranean frustrations of a mass of city people, and had run an outlet, round trip twenty cents, to the sea.

Hanging off to the southeast of the direct new line to the beach, Winthrop was at first circumvented by the Narrow Gauge, a slight for which the citizens soon enough were grateful. At Winthrop Junction in Orient Heights the destinies of the sister towns divided. With pounding pistons and screaming steam the beach train sped passengers northeast from Boston faster than diversions could be devised, eateries erected or bars stocked. For Revere was wet. By contrast, the horsecars of the financially wobbly Winthrop Railroad Company had since 1873 been dawdling their wobbly way from the East Boston ferry to Winthrop Junction and then southeast across the Belle Isle Bridge past deserted Winthrop Beach to Point Shirley, Taft's and the steamer wharf. Winthrop, if not entirely dry, was moving in that direction.

During a downpour on the Fourth of July 1874, while the Narrow Gauge was still abuilding, Mr. George E. Woodman set out on foot from the horsecar station to explore the shore road to Point Shirley and came upon the grand expanse of Winthrop Beach, broken only by a solitary fisherman's house. He hurried home and returned with a three-family tent colony under the banner "Atlantic Wave." The superintendent of the horse railroad at the time was a former Union Army surgeon, Dr. Samuel Ingalls. An operator in more ways than one, Dr. Ingalls regarded the tents and listened to the distant sounds of spikes being driven up and down the Narrow Gauge's right-of-way, and purchased fifty-five acres of Winthrop Beach. "Ocean Spray" he christened his investment and in 1875 commenced to parcel it out at two cents a foot (shortly up to eight cents), insisting upon a no-liquor clause in each and every deed with the admonition that "there shall be one seagirt resort where the fiend of the still shall not hold court."

Trim summer cottages sprouted along the bank above Winthrop Beach, though not much else, for it was all gravel, "where the ocean sports at will, sometimes in its rude mood trespassing on front yards, spoiling flower-beds, and hanging sea-weeds on the fences." In its windows Ocean Spray hung red and green lanterns the evening of its third anniversary clambake in August of 1878, and ten thousand turned up to hear the Winthrop Brass Band try out its brand new stand.

Ten thousand. Quite beyond the capacity of the Boston steamers that touched at Point Shirley and of Winthrop's moribund horse railroad, but not of an offshoot of the Little Wiggler at Winthrop Junction, just entering service that spring, nicknamed "The Peanut Train." This was the Boston, Winthrop and Point Shirley Railroad, whose narrow-gauge tracks, being nothing more than flimsy angle iron on wood stringers, demonstrated an annoying buoyancy when extra high-course tides flooded the marsh. When safely aground, the Peanut Train tooted through Magee's Corner and behind Ocean Spray the length of Winthrop Beach to Great, or Winthrop, Head. Near the Head at St. Leonard's the BW&PS (Dr. Ingalls was an owner) installed a depot-hotel. Thus came into being Winthrop's first true rail service.

Most of Great Head was the domain of the Tewksburys, whose weathered homes soon stood like boulders above a snowdrift of tents. When shingles replaced canvas in the early 1880s the Great Head subdivision emerged from anonymity as Cottage Hill, while over on the Boston Harbor shore, east of Cottage Park, shone Sunnyside, Judge Loring's colony of 1847, and Woodside Park behind it. Thomas A. Edison was a houseguest at Woodside in the summer of 1885 and created a stir at the drugstore one day when young Billie Stover was unable to mix a compound he wanted and The Wizard stepped behind the counter and stirred it up himself. Sunnyside's sunniest were members of the Vokes family of English comedians, who had an interest in the Vokes Bijou Theatre in Boston. At Ocean Spray the wenching, wassailing, multimarried Boston-born comic Nathaniel C. Goodwin, Jr., slipped in past the censorious eye of Dr. Sam Ingalls, possibly getting a laugh from the description of the colony in *King's Handbook of Boston Harbor* as "peculiarly homogeneous and mildly evangelical, with every evening devoted to some form of associated pleasure, musicales, square dances, or chapel-going, and ending early, so that by ten o'clock nearly all the house-lamps are out. . . . [Winthrop] is still remarkably free from the foreign element, and consequently enjoys almost a complete immunity from pauperism and crime. Liquor is legally banished from its borders, a fact to which the delightful peacefulness and decorum of the beach villages may be attributed. Bibulous roisterers find a woefully dry country southeast of Revere Beach, and make no second visits there."

The Narrow Gauge was the making of Winthrop as a resort for Boston. Boston was its unmaking. In 1888 the railroad looped the town with more than thirty summer trains a day, augmented by an hourly steamer schedule. The cottagers streamed in, and many remained the year round, 2,700 in 1890, 6,000 by 1900, when only half the houses were closed for the winter. The construction of the seawalls and boulevard of the Winthrop Shore Reservation that year quarantined Winthrop Beach from commercialization, for most of the hotels, never numerous, were gone by then, while the unfinished hiatus with the Revere Beach Parkway behind Short Beach — the frequently impassable "Missing Link" — discouraged automobile invasion by roisterers until its completion in 1922. Winthrop people with long memories of the smelter and the kerosene distillery manned the barricades against new industry. At the end of its yardwide lifeline to Boston, the town slipped cottage by cottage into suburbia.

Once so impossibly distant from the city by land, Winthrop in the

1920s began to wonder if it was rather too close by sea. A rival peninsula, called by its creators the Boston Municipal Airport, crept out from East Boston into the harbor, drying up the waters that had always laved the southwesterly on its way to cool the brow of Pullen Point. As Boston grew, so did its flying field, into the Logan International Airport. Came the jet age. The ever-lengthening runways fingered within 250 yards of that shore where Judge Loring had planted his summer cottage and George Emerson his trees. Belle Isle Inlet and its flats were partially filled for the Suffolk Downs racetrack and the million-gallon silos of that wry euphemism, the "Oil Farm." The debris from all this filling ruined Winthrop's salt marshes and shoaled its harbor and the channel of Shirley Gut. Not that it mattered; the excursion steamers were long gone, and during World War II the army built a causeway across to Deer Island, where Boston maintained its House of Correction.

Off the penal island the Metropolitan District Commission dumped the combined sewage of forty-one communities; the vapors peeled the paint from Winthrop's cottages. The fumes of oxidized kerosene from the jet aircraft screaming over the rooftops drifted down on Boston's first resort, a small community that had expelled a kerosene distillery and a copper smelter in the days when it was possible to deal with such nuisances and to keep the bird population under control with the efficiency of an Orray Augustus Taft.

# Revere Beach
# Is the Place to Go

A TORRENT OF SUPERHEATED BOSTONIANS BOILED ALONG THE TRACKS OF
the Boston, Revere Beach and Lynn Railroad that opening summer
of 1875 and spilled across Beachmont, its first outlet on the four
miles of the beach. The Narrow Gauge had been created by the
Boston Land Company expressly for the purpose of populating
the thousand remote acres along and behind the beach, which it
had gathered in on speculation from owners all too eager to unload.
Overnight the slopes of Beachmont blossomed with a colorful crop
of tents sown, and soon to be reaped, by the savvy salesmen for
Alpheus P. Blake's syndicate.

The company three years earlier had picked up 160 acres of the
Sale family farm and marsh at Beachmont for $23,000. From its
summit, Blake and his lieutenants could survey the rest of their
promised land, stretching north in a carefree arc of shining sand and
surf, mile after practically deserted mile to the Point of Pines, shimmering in the distance. The only way into Beachmont had been over
a carriage road from the town center. Came the Narrow Gauge, and
suddenly this wild and windy saltwater farm was a ten-cent train
and ferry ride from downtown Boston. The first summer of the
railroad the land company auctioned off lots at two and a half cents
a foot and threw in a five-year pass to every buyer who promised to
build. Tents by the score whitened the slopes above the shore. Two
thousand came each season to rough it on the fields of Beachmont.

Within eight years the land was up to fifteen cents a foot and Beachmont had 173 dwellings, three more than all of Revere in 1871.

The next influx came half a mile farther on at Crescent Beach, the sharp curve with which Revere Beach departs from Roughan's Point. Here at the foot of Beach Street the railroad built the New Pavilion Hotel on the site of the old, which had been moved a quarter mile south near the Cove House, a weathered oasis of chowder and rum. The New Pavilion doubled as the depot by spanning the tracks with galleries held up by four towers and embraced the trains for seven years before it was moved a few feet closer to the ocean (and France) as the Vue de l'Eau (pronounced *voodle-oo*).

After puffing out of the hotel the Little Wiggler embarked in earnest upon Revere Beach, which to the end of the Point of Pines is nothing more than a barrier reef of sand hove up out of Broad Sound by wave and current. Above the tide a string of summer shanties, bath shacks and bistros clung to the windy dunes as if tossed overboard disdainfully by the passing train. Where Revere Street died out in the sand the horse railway's Railroad House slaked the thirst, abetted by the Atlantic House, the Robinson Crusoe House, and, a few hundred yards on the beach beyond, the Rockaway House.

Surrounded by salt marsh midway behind Revere Beach were the twenty-three acres of Oak Island, the next stop on the Narrow Gauge. Being across the railroad tracks from the beach and the mainstream of humanity, Oak Island rapidly developed as an outing refuge for social clubs and ethnic fraternal organizations. Its damp, wooded western half is said by Benjamin Shurtleff, Revere's historian, to have yielded nearly four hundred species of flora, more than any other marsh island on the Massachusetts and New Hampshire coast, and until World War II it was still "making a last stand against the encroachments of an ever increasing population, and the destructive results to the native flora which necessarily attend it."

Entering the isthmus between the Pines River and the ocean, the

Narrow Gauge dropped unaccustomed prosperity on the bleached piazza of the Neptune House, next to the oldest of the beach hotels in both time and place, and chugged on, hugging the dune. The roadbed broadened into the Point of Pines, the mile-long spit of sand and pitch pine that brings Revere Beach to an end in the Saugus River; here the pint-sized train paused at the Ocean House, the beach's oldest and most remote, before heading with a hiss of steam, clanking driver wheels and a couple of long toots on the whistle for the trestle bridge and Lynn.

Before the advent of the Wiggler, the Ocean House was the solitary habitation on the Point of Pines. The first proprietor was Solomon Hayes, a New Hampshireman who opened it for business in 1834 as the original Robinson Crusoe House, described by Newhall as "a sort of public house, where scant accommodations could be had; a house not sustaining the most unblemished reputation, but perhaps as good as is usually found in retired places near large cities."

The Boston, Revere Beach and Lynn Railroad had been irrigating the Point of Pines for six years when suddenly, and lushly, the desert bloomed. Watered by a financial cloudburst of half a million dollars from Lee, Higginson and Company (this was 1881, the year Major Henry Lee Higginson founded the Boston Symphony Orchestra), the Chelsea Beach Company bought the prime 200 acres of the Pines, and the Ocean House, which was refurbished and renamed The Goodwood. Immediately the company began construction of The Pines, a resort hotel of five stories in the Queen Anne style just becoming popular, three hundred feet long, a hundred wide, girdled by a thirty-two-foot veranda, containing three hundred chambers and two dining rooms with a capacity of two thousand, advertised as the biggest on the New England coast. Simultaneously there arose a steamboat wharf, a racetrack, and a bandstand illuminated by 182 gaslights in white globes. The fuel for these, and a thousand other jets upon a thousand iron arches that leaped across the landscaped walks (and innumerable more in the rooms and airy porches of their complex), and the energy for the novel electric lights interspersed among them, were provided by the owners from their own gashouse and generating plant.

Like water they spent the money of Messrs. Lee, Higginson. They built bathhouses and boathouses, cottages and a café, and painted every last roof red, from which they descended to the brighter colors; they planted lush lawns and trees and shrubs and beds of flowers, pitched a striped tent, festooned Chinese lanterns everywhere overhead, stocked an arsenal of fireworks, hired the Germania Band and opened in time for the Fourth of July 1881. And the city came, by boat, by bicycle and by buggy, atop the swaying barge, crowding the rails of the steamers, stuffing into the horsecars and overflowing even the Narrow Gauge into the capacious coaches of the Eastern Railroad, which that summer belatedly bid for a piece of the beach trade with a branch leaving the main line at Oak Island, running above the sands through the Pines and across the Pines River at Saugus River Junction. That first season sixty-two trains a day each way stopped at the Pines station. Every evening, between dissolving stereopticon views of far-off lands, departure times were flashed on the screen. Twelve thousand heard the first concert of the Germania Band. Twenty thousand packed onto the Pines for Lynn Day, featuring a five-mile foot race from Central Square. One hectic Sunday the Narrow Gauge alone carried 16,321 passengers.

Three miles down the beach, in the meanwhile, the excursion steamer *John Sylvester* eased into the Great Ocean Pier with a thousand guests on its forty-five-minute inaugural voyage from Foster's Wharf at Boston to what was claimed by the Boston Pier and Steamboat Company to be the longest dock in America. The merits of a steamship connection with booming Crescent Beach and Beachmont had been obvious enough. But there was a problem: the slope of the beach kept all passenger vessels at bay for a third of a mile out. The solution was the Great Ocean Pier, thrust 1,700 feet into Broad Sound from Roughan's Point over Cherry Island Bar. Two thousand piles were secured in wooden caissons filled with mud and stones on the underlying ledge; a worn-out barge was loaded with rock and sunk as the foundation of the steamboat terminal. While the pier proper was twenty-two feet wide and roofed over, dancehalls bulged midway and at the outer end by the terminal, high above the sea where the breezes played, splashed with gay colors and open to a view of the moon rising above a shapely neckline. Shoreside hulked a capacious, twin-towered café. The *John Sylvester* and *Eliza Hancox* made eight round trips daily from Boston.

The Great Ocean Pier wanted only rail service to the entrance, and this was supplied in time for the grand opening by the ubiquitous Alpheus P. Blake, who obligingly organized the standard-gauge Eastern Junction, Broad Sound Pier and Point Shirley Rail-road, known to some as "The Alphabet Road," to others as "The Short Road with the Long Name," connecting with the Eastern at Revere (Eastern) Junction and steaming along behind Crescent Beach to the Ocean Pier café.

Blake, as usual, had a grand strategy, and soon it unfolded. Northward he extended the Alphabet Road above the beach to the Point of Pines, and southward over the right-of-way of the narrow-gauge Boston, Winthrop and Point Shirley (by merely adding a third rail) to the Point Shirley wharf, where it met the Boston steamers *Baltimore* and *Philadelphia*. In 1883 the EJBSP&PS merged with the Peanut Train (BW&PS) as the Boston, Winthrop and Shore railroad (BW&S) and was leased three years later by Blake's Little Wiggler, the Narrow Gauge (BRB&L). The Eastern (ER), meanwhile, succumbed at last and was leased by the Boston and Maine (B&M) in 1884, absorbed by it in 1890. Next year the Narrow Gauge won the alphabet marathon by doing likewise to the BW&S and ruled the rails from Point to Point.

The concurrent opening of The Pines and the Great Ocean Pier the summer of 1881 rocketed Revere Beach into the popular fancy with bursts and blasts of fireworks and brass that outblazed and outblared, and outdrew beyond any comparison, the old-fashioned amusements across Boston Bay at Hull's Nantasket Beach.

Nantasket was, in fact, much the senior resort. Its sidewheel paddle steamers had been shuttling excursionists from Boston for half a century. The Rockland House rose above the beach there in 1854, the Atlantic House in 1877; they expanded ten times over and were joined in 1879 by the Nantasket Hotel; and other arks were in the works. To supplement the steamers, the Nantasket Beach Railroad pushed out in the seventies from Nantasket Junction as an offshoot of the South Shore branch of the Old Colony Railroad and ran the length of the beach to Pemberton at the end of Hull. Except for gambling and drinking in the hotels, the fun and games at Nantasket were tame and couldn't hold a candle, certainly not a Roman one, to the garish splendors of The Pier and The Pines, while the Nantasket steamship and rail service were no match at all for the speed and convenience of Blake's brilliant stroke, the Narrow Gauge.

Charles H. Thayer, genius of the extravagant, ran the amusement park at the Point of Pines. He opened in 1881 with two set fireworks pieces anchored off the beach, representing the Union and Confederate ironclads *Monitor* and *Merrimac;* their no-win duel of the Civil War was still fresh in the minds of older spectators and a thrilling episode of recent history to the youngsters. Young and old gaped at the crude silhouettes exchanging flaming trajectories of bombs which exploded in showers of stars, casting water, beach and watchers in the eerie light and drifting smoke of re-created battle.

Thousands were drawn to these evening spectacles, to munch popcorn from wheeled stands lit by the flicker of torches, to guzzle beer and absorb the sonorities of the Germania Band that flourished and flowed forth on all sides into the night from its gas-illuminated bandstand. Thayer had latched on to a sure-fire draw, all right. Night after night of his second season the sky over the Pines was a screaming, hissing, thumping, thudding, spectral blaze of fire balloons releasing rockets, stars and serpents from on high. One battery discharged five thousand stars in a continuous fusillade that culminated in a mushrooming bouquet of a thousand rockets. Comic monsters leered luridly out of the darkness. Mr. Barnum's circus paraded by in exploding caricature (the Big Top was in Lynn in

July, featuring Jumbo the elephant, attendance twenty-five thousand). In climax Admiral Farragut's fleet hove up under full sail and reduced the fort at New Orleans in a manner most satisfactory to the fervid fans who packed into the grandstand at the Pines racetrack for the event.

Hardly had this latest triumph opened when news arrived of the British fleet's bombardment of Alexandria on July 11 in retaliation for a massacre of Europeans. In a trice Thayer exchanged Louisiana for Egypt, Farragut for Sir Beauchamp Seymour, and, the more to personalize the news of the month if not the hour, constructed a mammoth portrait of the supposed villain in the affair, the Egyptian war minister Arabi Pasha — all this against a running bill of round upon round of band concerts, swimming and rowing races, Wild West shows and, one night, the blowing up of a derelict ship offshore.

Summer's spectacle of 1883 at The Pines was a reenactment of the Civil War battle for Roanoke Island under the supervision of the Lynn post of the Grand Army of the Republic, fought by a thousand uniformed veterans armed with muskets, sixteen fieldpieces and unlimited stores of black powder and red fire, to the delight of twenty-five thousand who witnessed the sham siege on the banks of the Pines River. Boston had never seen the like of it, nor had the Chelsea Beach Company, which the next year had to admit it was broke, in large measure due to the cost of Thayer's spectacles and to the fact that, unlike the usual amusement park created and owned by a horsecar company as a passenger promotion, the management got no cut of the fares.

The company was reorganized. (Charles Thayer landed on his feet, of course.) Baldwin's Boston Cadet Band was engaged and played before standing-room crowds so ringingly that after eight seasons the leader bought out his employers. In 1885 The Pines presented a six-day music festival that drew 108,000 riders on the Narrow Gauge; on the evening of August 12 it touched off "Five Miles of Fire," a thoroughly publicized illumination of the entire beach by hundreds of bonfires, fireworks, colored fire and lanterns, scored for

*The Great Ocean Pier from Beachmont, about 1883.*

*H. T. Wing photo, from Henry L. Nicolas*

*Advertising card telescopes the pier's great length. Peter McCauley collection*

*William Andrews embarks from Revere Beach June 18, 1888, on solo attempt to cross the Atlantic in his twelve-foot, lateen-rigged sloop,* Dark Secret. *Atkins Higgins photo, from Doris Cunningham*

*All aboard for Revere Beach on the Lynn and Boston horsecar. Revere Public Library*

*Pines Hotel, early 1880s. Madeline Berlo Rhea*

*Point of Pines poster, 1880s. Boston Public Library, Print Department*

eleven bands and avidly enjoyed by forty thousand pyrophiles. Show-
man Thayer came up with Revere Beach's first figure-eight roller
coaster. (He got his inspiration from a "jolly-go-round" at Coney
Island, where he had been snooping about for ideas.) The 500-foot
ride took eighteen seconds and cost a nickel. "A fool and his money
are soon parted," one passenger said, "but that is the quickest parting
I ever experienced. A schooner of beer would have lasted longer."

Combining the pageantry of a sham battle with the pyrotechnic
props of the set pieces, Thayer in 1886 gave the world the "pyrorama" in a repeat of his *Monitor-Merrimac* encounter, this time on
dry land. Concealed crews moved the adversaries around the racetrack past a fort and lighthouse; other wooden warships stood off in
the distance, while a cast of live soldiers and sailors dashed about
under a fury of rockets, chemical fire, stars and bombs. It was a
great hit. Over the next three seasons Thayer's old Battle of New
Orleans was given the pyrorama treatment; then came "The Fall of
Tunis," and in 1889 "The Apaches," allegedly staged with real
Indians. The Narrow Gauge ran pyrorama specials to The Pines, and
Pyrorama Parties were the rage. Thayer imported a Coney Island–
type "Carousel," installed soda pop pavilions for those "who never
take suthin'" and produced an eight-day music festival starring
Liberati, the Italian cornetist, with Baldwin's Band; Baldwin pre-
sented his soloist with a Thirty-second Degree Masonic charm, and
the grateful management presented Baldwin with a diamond ring.

For less than fifty cents, the Boston *Daily Record* advised readers,
you could get out to The Pines from the city, hear the music, eat and
return, "probably a happier man for the trip than the man of wealth
who makes a tour to Saratoga and wears himself and a $50 bill quite
out."

Entertainment at the Great Ocean Pier was pitched to the younger
set, which accounts for the metamorphosis in 1883 of one of the
dancehalls into a roller skating rink toasted by the management as
the largest in the world: a quarter of a mile around, with twin bands
playing the same music at both ends. The Revere *Journal* suggested

that youthful skaters temper their zeal in view of the national crusade of the moralists of America against the sport, which was regarded when it came into vogue as a healthy offset to the dancing craze, since "the familiarities of the waltz and polka seemed impossible on the tricksy rollers. . . . But skillful skaters soon learned in effect to waltz and swing." Such mild reaction was not shared by one reader who warned against the evils of "companion skating," the opportunities it provided for uninterrupted flirting, and boldness and familiarity between the sexes, and its immoral influence on children placed in "association with those older than themselves of all grades of society, and even the hoodlums, which on account of its cheapness [admission fifteen cents] are accessible to its surface."

The owners of Oak Island Grove had a finger to the wind too, and as The Pier did, turned their dance emporium into a roller rink. With a new and larger ballroom, bowling alleys, shooting galleries, swings, flying horses, roller coaster (straight grade, half as fast as the figure eight at The Pines), boats, menagerie and aviary, Oak Island catered to blue-collar outings. During a typical midsummer week in 1881 it was visited by picnicking members of the Boston YMCA and their girls, the Daughters of Rebecca, the Olive Branch Lodge of Odd Ladies, the Celtic Association of Lowell, the Lawrence Irish Benevolent Society (several senior members danced the jig as it should be danced) and a party of eighteen Scandinavians who arrived by barge. The Hibernians converged on the grove, and the Scottish clans; and in the summer of 1888 the National Irish Association, eight thousand strong, piled in for a baseball game and a bicycle race, hurling matches, and horseracing on the beach. Even polo and cricket were occasional attractions.

Fifteen thousand packed the Oak Island park to cheer on four champion European horsemen clad in armor, whacking away at each other with broadswords (a vogue then current) for a $1,500 purse put up by the hotelmen. By way of contrast, two prizefighters mixed it up for five hours and seventy-two rounds to a draw behind the blackened windows of the guarded, crowded stable of the Atlantic House, while an equally clandestine match with soft gloves at the Ocean Pier in September 1886 between Paddy Walsh and Jack Maglone lasted but eight rounds, no blood drawn, and was considered a tame affair by the disappointed spectators.

The novel electric lighting supplied by its generator was so popular at The Pines that in 1884 the North Shore Company was organized to extend it to the rest of the beach, and five years later to the whole town. From across the Pines River, James Newhall thought it an impressive sight. "The Point of Pines," he wrote, "with its groves and its spacious and tasty architectural erections, now presents a remarkably picturesque appearance as viewed from the heights of Lynn. And when at evening the grounds are aglow with the brilliant electric lights, sharply defining the swaying branches and lightly gilding the ocean swells, and the capacious houses are illuminated, story above story, the scene is very striking — almost fairy-like when is added the softened music of the band floating over the intervening waters."

Amusement parks and inventors had a mutual affinity: one was ever on the watch for the crowd-catcher, and the other for the crowd. When power was extended beyond the Pines, Leo Daft, a pioneer in the development of electric street railways, was there. None was yet in practical use anywhere, but its originator installed a demonstration line in 1884 and next year, in advance of the Fourth, had the diminutive Daft Electric Railway (the squat, square engine took its power from a third rail) whirling along carrying curious beachgoers on a half-mile run between the soda pavilion and the Pines steamer landing. Another twist in the novelty was, as the Revere *Journal* reported, "bathing by the electric light at the Vue de l'Eau."

Even more so by the day's revealing light, sea bathing, more surely than any amount of studied social satire, had the effect of loosening the grip of Victorian convention on its victims. How could one but be amused by it all?

Preparing for the water, ladies divested themselves (never "undressed") of the swaths of mysterious funereal raiment, button shoes, layers of corsets, petticoats and unmentionables, billowing blouses, mushrooming hats and black parasols that were *de rigueur* on dry land, in exchange for pendulous flannel or woolen dresses, bloomers, long stockings and floppy oilcloth caps. The gents were hardly better off, stepping out of the stifling haberdashery in which they were imprisoned by fashion into what looked like one-piece pajamas or woolen union suits and the inevitable oilcloth caps. These harlequin outfits were commonly rented catch-as-catch-can from bathhouse operators. They were by nature and necessity so loose-fitting and at the same time so relatively airtight, in spite of moth holes, that in the water they exhibited "the tendency to billow out like half submerged balloons, giving the general appearance of blue cabbages floating wrong side up," according to an eyewitness description. The phenomenon may account for the Revere *Journal*'s report that "a man reading a newspaper, while floating on his back in the water at Crescent Beach on Wednesday afternoon attracted much attention."

Getting in and out of your bathing costume was a complicated and protracted procedure requiring the privacy of a bathhouse, whether you were a day-tripper or staying at a hotel. (A hotel guest padding across the lobby, dry or dripping, would have been subject to summary expulsion, if such a performance were not so utterly unthinkable.) At Revere Beach in the late 1880s you could pay your money and take your pick, judging from the advice in a guidebook that "the elegant bathrooms are free from the objections of many other bath-houses on the beach, being retired and free from the curious gaze of strangers." For the ultrasensitive, across from Oak Island a Lynn man operated a wheeled bathing car that he moved up and down on portable tracks with the tide, thus affording his custom the minimum of public exposure — the latest refinement in the bathing machine introduced sixty years earlier by the Nahant Hotel.

The overweight and the overage (who should have known better), preponderantly female, were the easiest marks of the beach wag. There were the usual vaudeville gags (only too true) about the

matrons losing their dentures in the surf and going dinnerless while
small grandsons waited for the tide to retreat. And the idle press
made much of such items as the elderly and absentminded lady who
permitted the incoming tide to strand her on a bathing raft. Ingenious chivalry dragged a settee down the beach and floated it out;
the transfer was made at sea, the lady in distress was lashed securely
and "towed in by her preservers as nicely as a man of war by a
government tug."

Revere Beach from the first Roman candle was geared to fun, not
fashion, not excluding the year-rounders. "The gentlemen of
Beachmont," snickered its correspondent in the Revere *Journal* of
March 7, 1885, "are the subject of mirth among the neighbors this
week. Last Sunday they arrayed themselves in their old clothes and
big rubber boots, and taking their clamming implements sallied
forth in the morning to capture the succulent bivalve. They forgot,
however, to consult the almanac, and the time chosen for the expedi-
tion was just at high tide, when the clam flats were under several
feet of water."

By the mid-eighties the flood let loose by Alpheus Blake and his
Narrow Gauge was quite unrestrained except at the company-con-
trolled Point of Pines. It presented Revere with serious but only
vaguely appreciated problems. At Beachmont the cottages crowded
thick upon one another, and tenters still clung to the slopes and
fields overlooking Broad Sound, often presenting the passerby with
an elaborately contrived contrast between the simple white canvas
domicile and its contents and appurtenances. Many were decked
with wooden floors and furnished with rugs, settees, chairs, afghans
and beds behind gossamer barricades of mosquito netting. Arranged
about were the folding floor screens, Japanese fans, Indian baskets,
kaleidoscopic hangings, sentimental engravings and other doodads
of the period. Not infrequently the family servant or local hired girl
was set up in a separate cook tent. Tenters tended to aggregate. One
of the first on the beach, Mr. A. A. Persons of Woburn, was known
up and down as "The Happy Man." He returned for the 1885 season

to his usual stakes below Oak Island to find that his fellow campers from Melrose had organized as "Happymansville" and elected him mayor.

Not all the "tents" were of cloth however. A growing number were "cots" (a euphemism for shanties), and as the 1890s approached they were shouldered and elbowed along the beach amongst cheap bathhouses, eateries, bars, beer joints (the nickel beer was everywhere to be had, the thirst for it maintained with handfuls of famous "Revere Beach Chips," the potato chip said to have been invented by café owner George Sleeper), galleries and arcades. The crowding was closest at Crescent Beach and Beachmont, whose residents in 1887 were assured by a sanitation expert that a fifteen-inch sewer pipe carried to the end of the Great Ocean Pier would solve any problems along that line to which they were privy and be no "detriment" to bathers.

Within a dozen years of Revere's penetration by the Narrow Gauge the fears of the citizens that the railroad was an iron horse of Troy for the riffraff of Boston had proved out. Hundreds of thousands of innocents — and many times the usual per capita of pickpockets, confidence men, fancy ladies, roughs and hoodlums — swarmed off the trains, horsecars, steamboats and every variety of private conveyance to seek their pleasure, ply their trades and get their kicks, and the pragmatic proprietors of Boston's Coney Island were not backward in accommodating them. The increasingly sophisticated and naughty beach wagged the country town. A few of Revere's staunch old residents who had occupied the land when human footprints on the sands were objects of curiosity saw the dangers lurking inside the bonanza, wondered if a devil's compact had not been made and tried to check the unbridled sale of liquor; but year after year through the 1880s, overwhelmed by the threats and blandishments of the hotelmen who ruled the beach, their townsmen voted for licenses.

One July day in 1884 eight young drunks pulled up in an express wagon outside a photo gallery at Crescent Beach and demanded to have their pictures taken. When the two owners tried to bar them at the door, they pushed in, beat them up and assaulted the assistant, Miss Maggie O'Neil, who "although of slight build, was active and full of pluck, cutting the face of one assailant with stones which she threw with unusual precision." The ruffians broke the windows of the shop, smashed the camera and drove off. No one in the crowd outside came to the assistance of the victims, and there were no policemen around.

A couple of years later the Revere police chief was suspended after he boarded a horsecar while drunk, knocked the conductor into the street and struck a woman passenger when she declined to give up her seat to him.

A thrill a minute. That was Revere Beach for you, right from the word go.

# 11

# Marblehead Succumbs as Swampscott Hums

ON A SUNDAY MORNING EARLY IN THEIR CLASSIC CRUISE DOWN EAST the summer of 1858, that ever-curious, ever-amused newspaperman Robert Carter and his curious, amusing companions sailed *Helen* into the long and rockbound harbor of Marblehead. They dropped anchor and rowed across to inspect the Neck, the port's partially protecting promontory, which they found to be nothing more nor less than a breezy pasture.

After a swim the argonauts made for the shade of a stand of elms above the water, lit their cigars and contemplated a prospect which the imaginative Carter thought could have no rival between Rio de Janeiro and Bar Harbor, their destination on the Maine coast. A magnificent harbor, as they could see, quite safe against all winds save from the northeast, as they had been informed — and as was demonstrated in a few hours when a violent thunderstorm from that quarter almost hove their sloop upon the rocks.

Not exactly a friendly harbor. "We went ashore to take a look at the town, which has always been reputed one of the queerest places in New England," wrote Carter, a New Yorker. The streets were as narrow and twisted as the inhabitants, with their queer harbor, queer talk, queer dress, queer ways and queer notions. "The people were formerly the most uncivilized in New England," the journalist had been told (Dr. Bentley, who knew them better, and earlier, was less tolerant and called Marbleheaders "as profane, intemperate, & ungoverned as any people on the Continent") — "and the boys so rude and turbulent as to be a terror to strangers, whom they were accustomed to stone, or, as they themselves expressed it, to *rock*, for amusement. But of late years the place has much improved." Carter did not venture to explain how or why Marblehead had improved, and his parting compliment implies that the visiting yachtsmen from *Helen* escaped a rocking (or "squaeling," as some 'Headers called it) for reasons unknown to them but for which they were grateful.

The fact is that creeping civilization had so weakened the independent fiber of the town since fishing gave way to such lubberish pursuits as shoemaking that mainland Marblehead would be able to hold off the summer invasion of the *strangers* for only another ten years, until after the Civil War. Sneaking up by sea, strangers had already succeeded in capturing the town's little Cat Island, a mile northeast of the Neck, without so much as a rocking. When earlier aliens built a smallpox inoculation hospital on Cat — from Robert Catta, the first owner — Island back in 1774, 'Headers knew what to do: they rowed out and burned it down. Now they just grumbled when the Salem Steamboat Company, organized for the express purpose, bought Cat's fifteen scrabbly acres in 1851 as a holiday resort for millworkers from Lowell.

Actually, the acquisition of Cat Island was part of a larger and rather ingenious speculation. The previous summer the same strangers started the Salem and Lowell Railroad in the opening seance of a quixotic dream with which they were possessed of restoring Salem's lost commerce as the port for the fast-growing inland textile city. The offshore resort was to be an attraction for passenger traffic. They changed the name to Lowell Island and built the Lowell Island House, with a hundred rooms, dining hall and bowling alley. A thousand Lowell people were entrained to Salem on the new railway for the opening in August 1851, then shuttled by steamer to the island for a mass picnic.

Fishing, sailing, sea bathing and the inevitable divine services that mill owners supposed were uplifting for those faceless employes called "operatives" were high among the attractions. Spirits were not, and indeed were banned, with the result, as the management rejoiced, that "rowdies have taken a disgust at Lowell Island because they can find no intoxicating liquor there. Their absence will not lessen the satisfactions of decent people with the place." The novelty of the first full season of 1852 was a regatta of eleven boats sailed over a course of nine miles, Marblehead's first such contest. The summer ended with a dance lasting until three in the morning — "the music was by the celebrated Germania Serenade Band of Boston and was remarkably chaste and beautiful. Unanimous expression in reference to the Ball was of unalloyed delight."

Salem disappointed its promoters as Lowell's port. The railroad only limped along, and in 1857 the steamboat company was forced to sell the island to Colonel Gorham L. Pollard of Lowell, who renamed it after himself and ran the hotel until 1869, when a Boston man bought him out. Cat Island it was again, until in 1878 it fell into the hands of Samuel B. Rindge, a merchant-banker of Cambridge, whose son, philanthropist Frederick Hastings Rindge, converted the hotel into the Children's Island Sanatorium, fulfilling Cat Island's therapeutic destiny, wrenched from it by Marbleheaders fearful of the pox so near their shore. For sixty years the sanatorium did its good work, until funds ran out in 1946. But Cat Island had more lives, and its sixth is as the Marblehead YMCA's summer camp for children.

Defining the Neck as part of mainland Marblehead stretches the point because in the days before its "discovery," like Nahant and Gloucester's Rocky Neck, at high tide it was an island and quite impossible to gain dry-shod across the sandy isthmus, sometimes called Riverhead Beach, at the head of the harbor. The natural insularity of its three hundred acres was reinforced by the cultivated reclusion of the villagers, whose reaction when the late Jesse Blanchard's executors tried to auction off his 130-acre farm there for a summer resort in 1835 can best be imagined. A summer resort at

Marblehead! The executors advertised that the ocean view equaled Nahant's: "To the sportsman and angler it presents the greatest of facilities for the prosecution of their sports. In the summer season, pearch and tautog are caught from the rocks in abundance; plovers and curlews abound in the pastures. Persons disposed to obtain summer residences will find, in the Neck, capabilities equal to those of Nahant, with the additional conveniences of being nearer Marblehead and Salem. . . . A Public House might be erected here, which would make the Neck a fashionable resort for people from all quarters, as soon as the beauty of its situation and its other attractions became more generally known."

The enterprising executors were thirty years ahead of their time. No resort-minded bidders took the bait, and Ephraim Brown added the Blanchard farm to his other holdings on the Neck until he had 240 acres under cultivation and was marketing produce as far away as New York.

Not until the ending of the Civil War released a surge of yearning for fresh air and good times was Marblehead breached, and then not from Boston, the expected quarter, but by Lowell, captor of Cat Island, with reinforcements from neighboring Nashua over the line in New Hampshire, and Peabody. The strangers struck almost simultaneously along the portion of the coast of Marblehead next to Swampscott always known as the Farms, now frequently called Clifton, and on the harbor shore of the Neck.

Supposedly Clifton was named for the Clifton House, Marblehead's first small summer hotel, built by Benjamin P. Ware on the water side of his farm in 1846, the year before his marriage to Hannah Clifton of Salem. Ware was a sturdy son of the soil (not Marblehead's but Salem's, to his disadvantage locally), who with his father and brother brought back to life the farmed-out Hinkley farm they had acquired in 1831. Being a stranger himself, Ben Ware was not heir to the native suspicion of the outside world. Quite the opposite; he welcomed out-of-towners to his Clifton House, and their cash, so heartily, and pushed so energetically for Marblehead's future as a resort, that he incurred, in the carefully chosen words of one admirer, "many criticisms of doubt expressed by short-sighted and narrow-minded men."

The year after Ware opened the Clifton House, the Marblehead and Lynn Branch Railroad Company was incorporated to run tracks along the shore from Marblehead to connect with the Eastern at Swampscott. This would have turned the Ware farm into a gold-field of which the Clifton House was no doubt built in anticipation, but the attempt failed for insufficient capital. Almost twenty years passed before the shore line proposal was revived by Marblehead interests that wanted a more direct communication with Boston than over the existing branch, which backtracked through Salem. However, Swampscott, looking to itself, countered with a rival effort to get the county to push a shore boulevard through its own poten-tially rich seaside, stopping at the Marblehead line. Ben Ware was behind the railroad scheme, or an extension of the boulevard through his adopted town — he didn't really care which — and it was at this juncture, around 1866, that people from nearby Peabody discovered Clifton (with his prompting) and pitched the tents of their Peabody Camp.

All this road-and-railroad agitation, coming on a wave of postwar euphoria, reached out and shook up even the proprietors of Marble-head Neck. After Farmer Ephraim Brown's passing in 1861 the heft of his acreage was leased by his trustees to Martin Ham. In the summer of 1866 Farmer Ham sublet patches of shore on the ocean side of the Neck opposite Tinker's Island to campers from Lowell and Lawrence and rented a shanty near the head of the harbor to a group of men from Nashua. The next spring, on the initiative of Judge Thomas Pearson, the Nashua crowd bought a small lot on the harbor from John Gregory, divided it six ways, framed cottages and barns in New Hampshire, brought them down to Marblehead, as-sembled them and moved their families into the first permanent summer houses on the Neck on the Fourth of July 1867. Theirs were the only buildings on the entire peninsula from the Ham farmhouse by the beach to the lighthouse at the entrance to Marblehead Har-bor. "We then had to open three gates before we could get at our houses," recalled Judge Pearson, "and then it was through much faultfinding we could pass at all."

Perhaps one need look no farther than a mile offshore to Cat (Lowell) Island for the route by which the fault-found inlanders came upon the inhospitable gates of Marblehead Neck. Whatever the agency of their discovery, the breezy Neck drew them to its shores under the same atmospheric conditions that a few years earlier had driven off an ancient female native, who in frustration finally moved across the harbor to town because "I wish to die sometime, and people never die on the Neck, it's too healthy there."

Judge Pearson succumbed to nostalgia when he thought back, only ten years after he planted his colony, how "it was no uncommon sight on Sunday evening, in 1869, to count between fifty and seventy-five dories on the Nashua shore. Those were the most enjoyable days for rest and fun which the settlement has ever known. White vest and neck ties, silk hats and kid gloves, trailing dresses, Valenciennes laces, button gloves, and high heeled shoes, banged hair (except what the wind banged), were laid aside and tried to be forgotten in the universal desire to be happy and make everybody else happy on the whole Neck — a sigh for the good old times!"

The tenting craze, which would soon spread to Beachmont and Ocean Spray, had given the ocean shore of Marblehead Neck by 1870 "the appearance of an encampment of a small army," with the familiar wooden floors, rococo furnishings, cooking tents and domestic tents, and tents combined with cottages. But the appearance only. This fresh, newly discovered summer life on the charming shores of the farm, with the broad blue bay to seaward, the harbor so full of interest to the inlander, and the queer, twisted village across from it, brought a new light to the lives of the summers after the dark tunnel of the long war — and a happy release from the Victorian restraint of the city. It has also been suggested that the rush to Marblehead, as to elsewhere on the North Shore, was quite as much the escape of the affluent, from the encroachments of industrialization and immigration on their way of life, to a secure Protestant coastal bastion.

When the first road to the mainland was built over Riverhead Beach in 1870 the Hams converted their place nearby into Riverhead House, later the Atlantic House of fish dinner fame; but even after the first horse-drawn barges began running between the Neck and the railroad depot, dories remained the pleasanter way of getting across the harbor. It was a free life out on the Neck, scrambling over the ledges, rambling the fields, swimming and rowing. Blue flannel shirts were the passion, wrote a visitor — "the booths and cozy little shanties are in full bloom, dainty city damsels may be seen bereft of fashion's folly and conducting themselves in a manner that would shock the sensitive nerves of a sojourner at Newport or Saratoga; and stiff and stern pater familias frees himself entirely from the meshes of his ledger and bank account, and roams about the Neck, revelling in the freedom he encounters at every step."

Bewhiskered Ben Ware's espousal of "modern ideas" was half vindicated with the completion of the Swampscott section of Atlantic Avenue in 1870 and its grudging extension by Marblehead through Clifton and Devereux to the center soon after. His triumph was complete when the Eastern Railroad opened its shore branch between the two towns in 1873, escalating the boom in summer property set off by the road and more than repaying the adjoining landowners, who had agreed to foot the bill for the depots at Phillips Beach, Beach Bluff, Clifton and Devereux. The prophet was of course unhonored by the general run of his townsmen, who during the bitterest rounds of the fight against his modern ideas had raised the cry "Be-ware B. Ware!" and muttered on the street corners that "the first thing you know you'll go down town and meet someone you don't know." When it reached the point where Ware would emerge from church to find insults daubed on his carriage, he coolly transferred his ablutions to Lynn.

Atlantic Avenue made Swampscott *the* late afternoon promenade for the smart turnouts of the North Shore. The Boston *Times* reported that it was "graded to perfection, broad and hard, while its recent extension to Marblehead gives a glorious ride of nine miles,

*Quiet elegance was the mark of the first new Ocean House above Swampscott's Whale Beach, photographed in 1880. Two seasons later it burned to the ground. Lynn Historical Society*

*Lincoln House Point from Blaney Beach, Swampscott, about 1880. Nahant makes out in the distance. Lynn Historical Society*

*"Strodehurst," of forty rooms, was Charles W. Galloupe's response to the fires that leveled his two earlier summer mansions on Phillips Point, Swampscott.* History of Essex County

*A summer sitting room in James Little's "Blythewood," Little's Point, Swampscott.*
*Essex Institute*

*Early yacht yard above Skinner's Head, looking up Marblehead Harbor, 1887.*
*Essex Institute*

*Benjamin P. Ware.*
History of Essex County

*The Island House in its prime, probably 1860s, was nearly as big as Cat Island.*
*From "History of Catta Island off Marblehead," by Richard W. Searle*

*Marblehead Neck and the upper ferry landing, from near the Eastern Yacht Club, about 1890. Essex Institute*

*Sailing yachts have already captured Marblehead Harbor in 1887 as the catboat ferry takes on passengers for town at the post office landing on the Neck. Essex Institute*

with a sea view all the way on one side and the groves and highly cultivated farms all about." As much elegance and as great diversity in horses and vehicles as could be seen anywhere, wrote James Newhall — "the gay nag pranced with the lordly equipage, and the rawboned roadster with his rattling gig" — and estimated that Swampscott was host to eleven thousand visitors during the summer of 1872.

The host at the old Swampscott Tavern, S. H. Wardwell, had regarded with approval the swelling rush of summer travel and traffic past his door and bought the Marshall House near the end of Fishing Point to increase his trade. Adjoining, on the very tip of the Point, he built and opened the Lincoln House, named for the President, in 1864, the year the Ocean House happened to burn to the ground on Phillips Point. S. H.'s brother, E. N., then bought the Beach House, moved it from Phillips Point to Whale Beach and renamed *it* the Ocean House. After a few years E. N. sold out and joined S. H. in the management of the Lincoln House, which doubled and tripled in size though the Wardwells stuck to their claim that since it was "completely removed from the rush of travel and traffic . . . its worst disturbing sounds are the rattle of dory oars against thole pins, or the whirring of halliard blocks as the fishermen round up to their holding ground in the lee of Dread Ledge."

Rather less than catastrophically, the new Ocean House followed the fate of the old and burned down in 1882, only a year after its purchase by R. W. Carter of Boston, who in 1884 rebuilt and reopened a *new* new Ocean House, which he called the New Ocean House. This raised the room count in the town's sixteen summer hostelries, large and small, to six hundred and made Swampscott the North Shore's leading hotel resort of the day. By the turn of the century the New Ocean House, which might better have been named the Phoenix, was one of the grand spas of the New England coast. And so it remained until the middle of this century, when it, too, met its fiery fate.

Like dominoes, one after another of those highly cultivated farms along the shore from Fishing Point in Swampscott to Marblehead's Peach's Point tumbled onto the market in the decade after the Civil

War, in speculative anticipation of the ending of the shore's isolation or as a consequence of it.

After the first Ocean House fire on Phillips Point in 1864, Charles W. Galloupe and three associates bought the twenty acres of the grounds and subdivided, Galloupe taking the commanding share for his elegant summer mansion. Galloupe's Point, as the western bluff of Phillips Point became known, was obviously jinxed; his "Bay View Cottage" went up in flames in 1876 for a $60,000 loss, and in four more years his "Summit Villa" was in ashes too.

Over in Marblehead, with Atlantic Avenue and the railroad headed right for the heart of them, the Horace Ware estate at Clifton and the 110 acres of the George A. Smith farm in Devereux surrendered to subdivision in 1870. Francis B. Crowninshield sniffed the trend and, with the sixth sense that had concentrated so much of Salem's wealth in his family's hands, bought most of Peach's Point on Marblehead's northeast shore for $9,500 in 1871. F. B. built his own summer cottage the next year on this rocky pasture first occupied by the fisherman-settler John Peach, then one for his son Benjamin (who in 1875 gathered in most of the rest of the point for another $21,000) and before he died in 1876 a third for his daughter, Mrs. Josiah Bradlee. Benjamin tightened the Crowninshield grip with four more, plus a stable for the family compound and water tanks up on Pitman Hill.

A small but dramatically situated leftover portion of Peach's Point somehow slipped through the grasp of the Crowninshields and into the hands of Samuel Rindge in 1880, two years after the Cambridge banker bought Cat Island, which he decided was not to his taste. (They sold another in 1899 to Miss Evelina du Pont, whose niece Louise married Francis B. Crowninshield and became, in time, quite literally the *grandest dame* in North Shore history.) After the Rindges moved to California to enjoy the proceeds of their speculation in some of the land on which Los Angeles was built, they continued to return to Peach's Point summers until abruptly one day they walked away forever, "leaving the house as if they were merely going out to tea," according to one version.

James J. H. Gregory, Marblehead's homegrown Seed King and

father of the "Mother Hubbard Squash," erected the first large cottage on Naugus Head, facing Winter Island across Salem Harbor, in 1876. President Garfield, it is said, reluctantly declined Mr. Gregory's invitation to make the place his summer White House in 1881; had he accepted, he might have avoided that fatal bullet from the revolver of Charles J. Guiteau in the Washington railroad station on July 2. From the Seed King's benign spadework sprouted a tent and cottage colony and a popular picnic, dance and band concert spot, Naugus Head Grove.

The most far-reaching effect of the reality of Atlantic Avenue and the prospect of Eastern Railroad's Swampscott branch was the decision of the trustees to sell the 230 acres of the Ephraim Brown farm, with its two miles of coast. Thus was one of the North Shore's three most dramatic peninsulas auctioned off on January 11, 1872, to the Marblehead Great Neck Land Company for $250,000. The deal decided the railroad to go ahead with the shore line to Marblehead. After thirty-seven years the aspirations of Jesse Blanchard's farseeing executors to rivalry with Nahant seemed about to be fulfilled.

Four of the eleven shareholders in the land company, incidentally, already shared a common interest in the theatre as well: the actor Junius Brutus Booth was a summer resident of Manchester and manager of the Boston Theatre; Benjamin W. Thayer was his Manchester neighbor and co-owner of the theatre with the third investor, Orlando Tompkins; the fourth was the well-known English actor E. A. Sothern, who made Lord Dundreary the classic silly ass of the British upper classes in *Our American Cousin,* the play Abraham Lincoln was watching when one of Booth's actor brothers leaped into his box and shot the President. (Sothern was not in the production at the time.)

The new owners of the Neck built Ocean Avenue, laid out 250 lots ranging from a half to two acres and suggested pointedly to the lessees of the Lowell Camp, who had been enjoying some of their best ocean frontage courtesy of Farmer Ham, that they buy or begone. A few paid up and improved their cottages, but the majority pulled up and the next season, 1873, set up a refugee camp of sorts at Juniper Point on Salem Neck.

Hard times in the wake of the financial panic of 1873 dogged the overextended promoters of Marblehead Neck. Land sales fell off, and in 1878 came the inevitable foreclosure and reversion of the balance of the farm to the Brown estate. The trustees completed the circumferential avenue, added connecting roads and resumed land offerings, with reserve clauses guaranteeing right of public (meaning Neck residents) access to water frontage. This Neck clubbiness went back to 1866 when Judge Pearson and his Nashua friends prevailed on a Congregational divine from upstate New York who was camping with his family to hold a Sunday service in a large "boarding-house tent," as the judge called it. About fifty summer people brought their chairs and dropped three dollars and eight cents in the hat passed by His Honor after a "very well written, earnest, Christian sermon." They made do here and there until 1876, when the Marblehead Neck Hall Association was organized to build a hall for socials and to observe the Sabbath, a practice Judge Pearson was certain "contributed largely to warding off the spirit of Sunday desecration and lawlessness, which was too often indulged in on that day, and tending toward a more quiet Christian observance of it by the temporary dwellers by the sea."

By 1880 there were seventy summer cottages on the Neck; like those on the Marblehead mainland, they were singularly unpretentious. According to one contemporary judgment, none but a handful of the most recently built could rival the summer architecture of Swampscott and Cape Ann for splendor — the reason being that people who selected *Marblehead,* wealthy and cultured as many were, came for recreation and rest, not for show.

The new Neckers had chosen to be in a world of their own, and it was perhaps their wish to be as different from Marblehead, which was different enough itself, that motivated a rather humorless campaign to rename the Neck "Manataug," which some summer pedant claimed the Indians had called the place. The old 'Headers naturally would have nothing to do with such pretentious nonsense. Assuredly it was the desire of the Neckers to have the best of *both* worlds that motivated Captain A. Allen Pitman to launch trans-harbor service across to the town in the summer of 1880 with the steam ferry *Lillie May*. His landing was not far from the depot, and he made twelve round trips, which gave Captain Pitman twenty-four opportunities a day, of which he evidently took advantage, to inflict his infamous two-liner on his captive passengers:

City feller: "Say, does this train stop in Marblehead?"

Conductor: "Wal, if it don't there's gonna be one helluva splash."

After only three seasons of quips and trips, Captain Pitman mercifully gave up on both and turned the run over to Philip B. Tucker, who had been ferrying the harbor with a string of dories and sailboats for years and now continued with steam.

The single event that only fifteen years after its settlement crystallized the character of the Neck and to a great degree charted the future course of the town was the decision of the Eastern Yacht Club to locate permanently at Marblehead. Almost since its inception in 1870 the club had been the largest and richest in New England, and the construction of its first clubhouse midway on the harbor shore of the Neck in 1881 established Marblehead as the yachting center of the Northeast. Next year a hotel of eighty rooms, named the Nanapashemet after a North Shore Indian sagamore as if in vengeance for the rebuff of Manataug, was built high on an ocean bluff across from the new clubhouse, probably as a support facility. Before the decade was out, the Corinthian and Pleon yacht clubs had arisen for boats too small and sailors too young for Eastern; Marblehead sloops had retained the America's Cup three times running, and the queer old town was on the map.

The trouble was that Benjamin P. Ware, who had done so much for Marblehead, was now doing his damnedest to undo it all by *changing* the map. The earth started shaking in the fall of 1884 when Ware led an agitation to break off the Neck, part of Devereux and all of Clifton from Marblehead, and Beach Bluff and Phillips Beach from Swampscott, and make a new town of them. To that end he and his co-secessionists put in twin petitions to the state legislature. The shore was in an uproar, and the alarm was revived: "Be-ware B. Ware!"

Ben Ware, with his modern ideas for the Farms, pushing for Atlantic Avenue and the shore branch of the railroad, had succeeded too well. New summer cottages were rising one beside and behind another, along with boardinghouses and several hotels, of which Ware's Clifton House, now managed by his son and namesake, was not the least, for he could take in 125 guests, feed them from his own large vegetable garden and fruit farm and herd of thoroughbred Ayrshires, and divert them with riding, billiards, bowling, croquet, baseball, picnics, bathing and boating.

Look, the petitioners exclaimed, what we have done for our respective towns! And look, they complained, at what is being done to us! In return for carrying twenty-four percent of the tax load, in the case of Marblehead, they got back one percent in services in the form of scant fire protection, hardly any policing, very little road work, but with so much more than their share of liquor licenses and resort permits that "the roads and stores are infested with disorderly persons, who frighten ladies, children and the timid with unrestrained ribaldry."

Not much was said by the secessionists about tax-dodging, an issue which was coming to the fore with the public revelation that many a wealthy Bostonian was ducking high city taxes by claiming for his legal residence his summer home on the North Shore, where the taxes were low. The recent invasion of the horsecars was likewise soft-pedaled by the petitioners. The Lynn and Boston Street Railroad had extended service to Swampscott every fifteen minutes in 1881, and then on to Marblehead in June of 1884, a few months before the secession movement surfaced, and with startling results, conveying as many as three thousand passengers a day. A few weeks later the Naumkeag Street Railway started running *its* horsecars off for Marblehead.

Would the developing shore from Phillips Point to Marblehead Neck be trampled by the thundering herd, dumped off the bobtails before every private gate at five cents a head? There was a popular ditty going the rounds already:

*Hail! today cheap transportation*
*Comes in triumph to our station;*
*Bearing in its train the story*
*Anti-monopoly, the people's glory!*
*Roll it along, through all the town,*
*The people's right — cheap transportation!*
*See the people come to meet us!*
*At the station many greet us!*
*All take seats with exultation.*
*Glory in cheap transportation.*

As far as Marblehead was concerned, the proposed amputation would give the new town most of the parent's area and seven of its thirteen miles of coastline. Injury enough. The insult, which the town fathers carefully brought to the notice of the legislature's committee on towns during the hearings in 1885, was enough to kill the proposition outright: while the Farms and the Neck accounted for $1,000,000 (a figure inflated by double, claimed the petitioners) of Marblehead's $3,270,000 real estate valuation, only sixty-one of the 1,930 registered voters resided in the area in dispute, and but nineteen of 1,405 pupils attended the Farms school. Ben Ware and his cabal tried to revive their secession in 1886, but the steam had gone out of it.

This time around, 'Headers were dead right in bewaring Ben Ware. They could ill have afforded the loss of the cream of their summer colony. On Christmas Day, 1888, a fire swept through the town center. It destroyed fifty buildings, including a number of the new shoe factories. Two thousand were put out of work. A comeback was attempted, but many of the unemployed had been forced to leave town for other work, and the disaster was the death knell of Marblehead's shoe industry, just as the terrible gale of 1846, which took ten vessels and sixty-five crew members and decimated the fleet, had been the beginning of the end of its fishing industry.

As the 1880s closed, population dropped to the lowest level since the September gale, and the proud and independent citizens of old

Marblehead turned to a future quite largely dependent upon the foibles of the summer strangers and the fortunes of those whose fleets of shining yachts had captured their harbor, let it blow no'theast till the skylight dripped on the backgammon board and be damned.

# 12

# Yachting Gets Serious

YACHTING WAS ONE OF THE LESSER CASUALTIES OF THE CIVIL WAR, which all the while fertilized old fortunes and seeded new ones. When it was all over there were dollars to be spent, yachts to be built, oceans to cross. The peaceful summer of 1866 Captain Arthur H. Clark took a crew of professionals and amateurs, which included Henry Wadsworth Longfellow's son Charley, in Uncle Tom Appleton's forty-eight-foot sloop *Alice* on a precedent-making, record-breaking sail from Nahant to England in the smashing time of nineteen days. That December James Gordon Bennett, Jr.'s schooner *Henrietta* copped a $90,000 stake from *Fleetwing* and *Vesta* in a daring winter race to Cowes under the burgees of the New York Yacht Club.

Before the year was over the Boston Yacht Club had materialized out of this postwar burst of yachting excitement. Although the club was the first in Massachusetts Bay since the Dreamers, its North Shore members fretted from the start over the distance of the station at City Point, South Boston, from their piazzas. After a couple of years, in the jaundiced view of one, "the only results of the organization were the comfortable social gatherings which were afforded at the elegantly furnished rooms of the club, on the corner of Tremont Street and Pemberton Square."

Perhaps not quite the only results, because impatient Beverly sailors activated the "Essex County Squadron" for impromptu sweepstakes off Marblehead in 1868 and 1869; eight of the Squadron's sixteen member schooners and sloops were based at Beverly, four at Swampscott, two at Manchester and one each at Gloucester and Nahant. By now upwards of fifty substantial pleasure craft were afloat in Boston Bay. "Iron rigging had replaced hemp," wrote Edward Burgess, "iron-strapped blocks replaced the old rope-strapped pattern, decks and spars were no longer painted, yachts were fitted for cruising, and yachting began to be a recognized sport."

The racing cauldron stirred up by the Essex County Squadron boiled over into a cabalistic session of Boston Yacht Club dissidents on the evening of March 5, 1870. Meeting furtively at the Park Street home of John Heard, these disloyalists created the Eastern Yacht Club, as noted in the previous chapter, and elected their host their commodore, Franklin Burgess their vice commodore. Heard was a nephew of Augustine Heard, the China merchant. For some years before his return to the States and his settlement for the summer on Ober's Point east of Beverly Cove, Commodore Heard had been the family firm's managing partner in Canton, where he owned and raced yachts, probably from the Canton Regatta Club, started by Bostonians on the Pearl River in 1837. In no time Eastern had a roster of eighty, a set of bylaws providing for the election of new members by six yacht owners and five non-owners and the rejection of candidates by five blackballs, sailing regulations, a uniform and a burgee . . . but no fixed home. So a room was hired on India Wharf in Boston for convivial purposes.

Eastern beat out the Lynn Yacht Club as the first on the North Shore by only two days. The yachtsmen of the shoe city organized on March 7, 1870, and actually went on to sail the North Shore's first club regatta with a fleet of fourteen over a seven-mile course on June 17. A year to the day later they dedicated their clubhouse on Beach Street. In July 1872 the Lynn squadron cruised east for the first time and competed in the first "Shoe Manufacturers' Race" for cash prizes. Their pride was the forty-foot sloop *Lillie,* built in 1871 by a syndicate calling itself "The Twelve Apostles."

Lynn was strictly a local club, while Eastern was Boston money and North Shore. It, too, sent fourteen yachts to the starting line of its first regatta on July 12, twenty-five days after Lynn's. But the course was forty miles from Marblehead Rock to Minot's Ledge and return, and the fleet was convoyed by a steamer laden with flag officers, ladies and musicians. At the end of the month the Easterners headed east to Mt. Desert Island for a fortnight's cruise, and by the end of the season there were sixteen schooners, nine sloops and one steam yacht in the squadron; the steamer, *Minnehaha,* belonged to a New Yorker, naturally — Thomas Clark Durant, builder of the Union Pacific Railroad.

In a well-meaning plagiarism of the New York Yacht Club charter, the Eastern Yacht Club was incorporated in 1871 "for the purpose of encouraging yacht building and naval architecture, and the cultivation of nautical science." And what an encouraging sight it was as the billowing sails of the New Yorkers hove into view from the westward for the first joint regatta of the two clubs off Swampscott on August 11! The Easterners sailed out to meet them behind Commodore Heard's flagship, the schooner *Rebecca,* whereupon the visitors separated with fine precision into two divisions on a signal from Commodore Bennett's *Dauntless* and engaged in a sequence of faultless maneuvers (that is, their professional sailing masters and crews did).

The fleets were on the point of exchanging the traditional salutes when a small sloop slipped tipsily out from under the lee of Nahant, displaying strings of empty bottles in the rigging in place of pennants. She headed, after a fashion, for *Dauntless,* to the rising consternation of those on board, when at the last moment she bore off with shouts and graphic gestures of welcome from her carefree crew. It was Eastern's *Daisy,* whose owner, Captain William C. (Billy) Otis, "having considered the reception as planned somewhat too formal, had decided to inject an element of frivolity and good fellowship to relieve any possible stiffness from the occasion. . . . The joke was taken in good part all around and keenly enjoyed, dispelling at one stroke any risk of too much ceremonial."

That evening the Eastern yachts and bands on board two towboats combined to fill the sky with fireworks and the night with music. In the morning the tugs conveyed a joint party of members to Point Shirley, where they were photographed in attitudes of obvious satisfaction on the porch of Taft's Hotel after one of O. A.'s fish and game dinners featuring "Eaglets from the West," "Owlets from the North" and fifteen less predatory birds. On August 14 hosts and visitors raced through a tangle of spectator boats for cups put up by Eastern and the town of Swampscott; it was the largest regatta of large yachts in American waters to date.

Billy Otis could get away with his saucy salute in home waters. It wouldn't have crossed the mind of a New Yorker even to try. Easterners did not go in heavily for braid and protocol, mindful as many were of one early member who did, firing off a salute so close to a passing yacht that the wad burned a hole in her mainsail, to the annoyance of her owner, who declared with some emphasis that "he had been under fire enough during his service in the Civil War, that he had bought a yacht for pleasure cruising, and damned if he'd stand being bombarded in Massachusetts Bay."

David Sears of Boston and Nahant, one of the first three New England members of the New York Yacht Club, would have bridged the evolution of organized yachting in America by taking his place as the first commodore of the Eastern Yacht Club had it not been for the wreck of his schooner *Actaea* on Chatham Bar in 1868. Her loss left him temporarily without a deck under his feet and therefore ineligible for the honor. Sears's ninety-seven-foot schooner *Caprice* was launched in 1871, however, and in 1873 John Heard resigned and the members accorded Sears their belated recognition of his contributions by electing him their second commodore. But hardly had he been elected when he died. The office was left vacant in memoriam until 1874, when John Murray Forbes, younger brother of the club's Nestor, Captain Robert Bennet Forbes, succeeded to it.

Like Ben and cousin John Perkins Cushing, Commodore Forbes had climbed the family's Chinese ladder and descended, while almost precociously young, with a fortune. Unlike them, from the East and the sea he turned westward and put his money and his energy to work building frontier railroads. One uncle was Colonel Perkins; another was his namesake, the diplomat John Murray Forbes, and John and Black Ben each combined the drive, intelligence and charm of both. The John Murray Forbes of their generation must have seemed omniscient to his members, for his summer retreat from Boston was not the North Shore (though he owned Eagle Head at Manchester until 1869) but the island of Naushon, around Cape Cod in Buzzards Bay, which he bought in 1857 and which remains today the unspoiled preserve of the Forbes family. His flagship was the centerboard schooner *Azalea,* built under his brother's supervision and "all bow and stern," in the opinion of a grandson, until the Commodore cut her in half, as Cushing had *Sylph,* and improved her sailing immensely by adding ten feet to her midriff. (Another early member, attorney Charles P. Curtis, who summered at Swampscott's Fishing Point, acquired the small and slow schooner *Bessie* and turned her into a cupwinner by lowering and lengthening her rig and adding an overhanging stern. One day *Bessie* was in the lead when the family retriever mistook a lobster buoy for a duck and leaped over after it; coming about and retrieving him cost *Bessie* the race.)

John Murray Forbes turned over the stripes in 1878 to another founder, T. Dennie Boardman, who summered above Manchester's Black Cove Beach across from Chubb Island in the converted cow barn that had served the estate when his father bought it from R. B. Forbes in 1865. The Boardman flagship was the schooner *Foam,* and her owner "a bluff and hearty sailor man . . . who preferred a blow to an afternoon breeze, a cruise to the east'ard to tea ashore, and, with a stout keel under him and boon companions aft, he was always ready for any weather — blow fair or blow foul." As for companions forward, *Foam* was a centerboarder, eighty-two feet overall, and in a revealing commentary on contemporary yachting practices, Captain Forbes remarked approvingly that Commodore Boardman rigged her and sailed her for his pleasure and required only three paid hands before the mast out of a crew of seven.

When the Eastern Yacht Club was founded in 1870 the dories belonging to the Nashua campers were about the most pretentious pleasure craft at Marblehead. Appreciation of the harbor's potential as a yachting base was late in awakening and was not wholeheartedly encouraged by 'Headers, as we have seen. The extension of the railroad and the highway up along the shore from Swampscott represented one flank of the summer invasion, and the slow subversion of the Neck by the outside world served as the other. Easterners found the deep harbor a convenient anchorage midway along the North Shore but were divided over its merits as a candidate for their home station. Not until 1880, after nine vagrant years of debate, did the club agree to settle down at Marblehead and build a conservatively gingerbreaded house half along the Neck.

Opening day on June 10, 1881, was to be a blast (and why not, for what is so rare as a day in June?), but it turned into another sort of blast not soon forgotten, a blast of wind and rain from the northeast. Members and guests huddled aboard their pitching yachts in the anchorage, peering at the festivities (such as they were) ashore through the portholes, or got a thorough drenching rowing in. And those disappointed souls from Beverly to the eastward who had fought the long fight to locate the clubhouse closer to home in Manchester Harbor or even the lee of Misery Island, secure from the whims of the northeaster, shook their heads and growled: "We told you so!"

But it was too late. The mantle of destiny had descended on Marblehead Neck.

No sooner had the Eastern Yacht Club settled in its new clubhouse than the porch was taken over by a self-elected auxiliary to the flag officers, comprised largely of elderly bachelors, known as the Piazza Committee. These worthies passed judgment upon all matters of nautical protocol and etiquette arising out of the club's activities on the water and upon the propriety of the behavior of the rest of the members in general, and if nothing happened to be doing in that line, upon such grave questions, "in which money became involved," as Charles H. W. Foster distinctly remembered, "as to the proper way to carve a saddle of mutton."

Question: should the rustle of skirts distract these manly precincts? C. H. W. Foster was the president of Chickering, the Boston piano manufacturer, and summered on Marblehead Neck. At an advanced age he was persuaded to compile *The Eastern Yacht Club Ditty Box: 1870–1900* as a chronicle of the early years. His more than a half-century of membership dated from the opening of the new clubhouse when, he wrote, "man was supreme but, as is usual, the fair sex began to win its way and finally some member under female domination offered a motion that would open the clubhouse to the general use of ladies. Our Piazza Committee was furious, but the motion was carried and what do you suppose happened? Three of the elderly bachelors soon became married! Ah, you sailor men know how it is: 'Tis the old rope that is the easier spliced."

The long and twisted coast of Maine has drawn yachtsmen to its myriad blue bays, pine-scented anchorages and islands uncounted since Robert Carter described so delightfully the cruise of the *Helen* to Mt. Desert Island in 1858. Especially for the North Shore cruising man, down East has been easier to reach than Buzzards Bay and the islands and was even handier before the general adoption of the auxiliary engine and the construction of the Cape Cod Canal not long after that in 1914; besides, Maine is more varied, many would say, and more challenging, more would agree.

Charles A. Longfellow, the poet's eldest son who went along on *Alice*'s transatlantic crossing in 1866, was an early practitioner of the art of the Maine cruise. As a boy he had shot off a thumb with a forbidden gun bought with pennies earned holding horses in Harvard Square; the disability only sharpened the challenge of his first cruise to Bar Harbor with a chum in a sixteen-foot Block Island boat, returning triumphantly with the traditional pine bough hoisted to their masthead. Charley was wounded in the Civil War, traveled everywhere, nearly drowned during a cruise off the coast of Korea, and fancied striding about in an English yachting habit and cap from Cowes, where he sailed several seasons. He died in 1893 after a last summer at Nahant. A noted character around the Eastern Yacht Club and a witty and literate figure, Charles Longfellow was even less successful in getting out from under the shadow of his father than was his younger brother Ernest, the excellent painter who summered at Coolidge Point in Manchester; Ernest admitted once that "anyone who has had the misfortune to be the son of an illustrious parent knows how hard it is to be taken seriously by people," an opinion from which his Beverly summer neighbor, Mr. Justice Holmes, provided living dissent.

Many followed and added infinite variations to the courses charted by the Carters and the Longfellows, and challenges came fast and usually without warning in the 1870s and 1880s when the natives along the thinly settled Maine coast were not prepared to provide amenities for the yachtsmen from up Boston way, and were not especially interested, either. The difficulties involved in foraging when the cook's locker was low cannot be overstated.

One summer Charles H. W. Foster and friends on an Eastern Yacht Club cruise dropped anchor at Bar Harbor when they and the resort were young, inspiring the attractive Philadelphia girls who adorned the colony at the time to get up a quick picnic at Otter Cliffs. All proceeded happily until the sun rose "over the yardarm," when it was discovered that the lunch baskets had been sent by some horrible mix-up to somebody else's spread on another part of Mt. Desert Island. The picnickers had to make do with a few thin crackers and a handful of chocolates, to the absolutely overwhelming chagrin of the girls, who had been tipped "by an experienced chaperone friend that Boston men, though awfully nice fellows and good company, were known as having a most profound regard for their stomachs." All was well that ended well, however. Back at Bar Harbor the Eastern men took their hostesses to supper at Sproul's, "a notable instance of local option in a bone dry state," Foster recalled warmly. "As a result of the mellowing influence of this entertainment, the tribulation of noontime soon faded as such, becoming merely an amusing episode of a summer pastime."

The regard in which Boston cruising men sailing from North Shore harbors held their stomachs after a bout with the bracing

*Thomas Gold Appleton's forty-eight-foot sloop* Alice *lies off Nahant. Nahant Public Library*

*Appleton (in profile) with* Alice's *complement: steward (with spyglass) and three seamen, bearded Captain Arthur H. Clark, H. Stanfield (arms folded) and the owner's nephew, Charles A. Longfellow (cross-legged on floor), son of the poet. Nahant Public Library*

*Charlie Longfellow shoots the sun. From* Eastern Yacht Club Ditty Box

*Before the race at Taft's (note band members). Eastern Yacht Club*

*The start of the first Eastern–New York Yacht Club regatta, off Swampscott,*
*August 14, 1871. Eastern Yacht Club*

*John Heard, founding commodore. Eastern Yacht Club*

*First flagship of the Eastern Yacht Club, Commodore John Heard's schooner Rebecca, 1870. Eastern Yacht Club*

*David Sears, second commodore.*
*Eastern Yacht Club*

*John Murray Forbes, third commo-*
*dore. Eastern Yacht Club*

*Eastern Yacht Club, about 1890. Essex Institute*

breezes off the coast of Maine required, in the days before so many of them had learned to do for themselves, a reliable stove and, to use it, the services of a professional cook, which were not always so easily come by. On one occasion the owner at the last minute had hired, with much misgiving, an old fellow so infirm that he couldn't be allowed on deck while the boat was under way. After a difficult passage the three yachtsmen aboard had anchored and were trying to catch some sleep below when they were awakened by a horrendous splash. Fearful for their cook, all three bounded from their bunks and jumped overboard where they saw bubbles rising ominously to the surface. They were diving, with no luck, when the presumed victim popped his head out of the companionway and inquired, "What's the trouble, gentlemen?" Upon being informed in no uncertain language, he explained: "Why that splash was my ashes."

Almost without exception the schooners and sloops that dominated the Eastern Yacht Club squadron were thirty feet or more of waterline length, most of them much more. Many members also owned boats too small for racing under the club rules. To make a home for these poor relations, Edward Burgess and other North Shore sailors active in Eastern started the Beverly Yacht Club early in 1872. Where his friends were semiserious about the sport, Ned Burgess was intense. From boyhood he had been engrossed in aerodynamics. Bishop Lawrence remembered how his chum "was deeply interested in the study of bugs, moths, and butterflies; drawing sketches, figuring their speed and the curves of their wings. He also studied the models of his boats and improved them each summer." In 1872 Burgess was out of Harvard and turning his bugs and butterflies to account in the graduate study of entomology; his mates in the new club elected "the bugologist," as they called him, their commodore.

Thirty-seven boats started in the first regatta of the Beverly Yacht Club that June; all but twelve were less than twenty feet waterline, and significantly, thirty-two were cat-rigged and every one but three was a centerboarder.

Beverly's espousal of the smaller sailing craft sparked the enthusiasm of South Shore yachtsmen via the curiously roundabout circuitry of Nahant. In 1876 Patrick Grant, Jr., of Nahant (Robert's younger brother) and Dr. John Bryant of Cohasset got up the "Nahasset" Yacht Club among North and South Shore summer residents, many of whom were also members of Eastern. Without benefit of officers or station, Nahasset held a series of union regattas at Nahant and Cohasset that culminated in 1878 off the South Shore with seventy-three starters under twenty-eight feet, the largest yacht race in America to date. The bilateral club disbanded after its 1879 regatta, but its burgee, like the smile of the Cheshire Cat, hovered around and was adopted in 1894 by its lineal descendant, the Cohasset Yacht Club.

If the Beverly Yacht Club pointed the way for baywide yachting, Nahasset had instructed its mentor in the broader implications of the union regatta before it faded out of the picture. In August of 1879 Beverly ran its own first union race — not off the North Shore, nor even in Massachusetts Bay, but clear around Cape Cod in Buzzards Bay, off Monument Beach. The popularity of the catboat in the shoal waters of the South Shore and Buzzards Bay, and the more reliable breezes south of the Cape, and Nahasset's success, no doubt account for the novel experiment. Within two years the majority of the North Shore club's fleet actually hailed from South Shore and Buzzards Bay harbors, and it was running dual regattas every season, north and south of Cape Cod, under different sailing regulations. At the same time the Beverly Yacht Club was marvelously successful championing small-boat sailing in home waters. In 1882 its union regatta off Marblehead broke Nahasset's record of 1878, then broke its own the next year with an armada of 171. Something had to give, and the rest of the camel followed the nose in 1895, when the club left the North Shore altogether and reestablished itself at Wing's Neck in Pocasset. In 1913 the Beverly Yacht Club moved across Buzzards Bay to Marion, where it remains, name unchanged, to the mystification of the uninitiated.

The Beverly Yacht Club's gradual desertion of the small-boat sailors of the North Shore left behind Eastern, which disdained anything under thirty feet on the waterline, and a few scattered local clubs — Lynn (1870), Salem Bay (1879), West Lynn and Gloucester's Cape Ann (1880), Winthrop's Great Head (1881), Rockport's Sandy Bay (1885) and Manchester (1892). (The Nahant and Annisquam dory clubs would not be born of the craze for the Swampscott sailing dory until the mid-1890s.) If the base of yachting was to be broadened, leadership was called for, and that is how Marblehead established itself once and for all as the yachting center of the Northeast: by defending the America's Cup with one hand and promoting the art of small-boat sailing with the other.

Thus it was that in 1885 a group led by C. H. W. Foster and Benjamin W. Crowninshield organized the previously mentioned Corinthian Yacht Club for sailing craft between sixteen and thirty feet waterline and bought part of Jack's Point near the lighthouse on Marblehead Neck, where they erected a clubhouse in 1888. Their dual objective was to advance the design of small boats and racing by amateurs (hence Corinthian, meaning the amateur yachtsman in the tradition of the sailing aristocracy of ancient Corinth). It was about time; the Seawanhaka Corinthian Yacht Club of New York had been dispatching amateurs to the starting line for fourteen years. On the sound theory that good young sailors grow up to be better older ones, the small fry (male only, to be sure) were allowed to be heard from as well as seen with the appearance on the Neck in 1887 of the Pleon, first junior yacht club in America.

Corinthianism was imported to Marblehead, where few Easterners would have dreamed of raising their own sails. Down at Gloucester it was the only way. The old fishing port had long relished its reputation as the saltiest in America, and paid dearly for it, losing twenty-seven of its 350 schooners and 212 of the city's cadre of four thousand fishermen in 1876 alone. The long harbor was the preserve of the big "bankers," but there was ample to spare for a swarm of small craft of every type and purpose, and work enough for some first-rate boat builders such as George Wheeler on Wheeler's Point up in the Annisquam River, and on the waterfront

Samuel Elwell and the partners Isaac H. Higgins and Asa T. Gifford, Cape Codders transplanted from sand to granite.

It was to Higgins and Gifford that Alfred Johnson turned for the decked fishing dory *Centennial,* in which he set sail from Gloucester for England, alone, on June 15, 1876, to celebrate, on a dare, the hundredth anniversary of the independence of his adopted land. The young Danish-born fisherman made his landfall on the Welsh coast after fifty-nine days of buffeting about and sailed into Liverpool on August 21. "Centennial" Johnson's was the first single-handed crossing of the North Atlantic in history and inspired a rash of emulation which a century later is today more contagious than ever.

The first to succumb to the Johnson fever were Thomas Crapo and his wife; they sailed from Cape Cod to Cornwall in a whaleboat in the summer of 1877. Then that September, according to their modestly titled *A Daring Voyage Across the Atlantic Ocean,* brothers William and Asa Andrews, natives of Manchester and Beverly respectively, were perched one day on a Beverly bluff, gazing out over the Atlantic, when one said suddenly to the other, looking down at the boats moored below them: "Let us cross the old ocean in one of these dories." Replied his brother: "Give me your hand. I'll go with you." And they shook on it, with nary a mention of Centennial Johnson. But they followed him to Higgins and Gifford for little *Nautilus,* which the next spring they sailed to Cornwall. In 1880, to show that it worked both ways, Frederick Norman and George Thomas sailed *Little Western,* a wee chip of a Higgins and Gifford cutter, from Gloucester to Cowes, and then, the year after, back to Halifax.

For a mechanic in Chickering's piano works, William Andrews led an astonishing double life. He next had Higgins and Gifford build him a lateen-rigged double-ender twelve feet nine inches long, which he named *Dark Secret,* by way of promoting a current stage show in Boston, and set sail for Ireland (sponsored by the New York *World*) from the Point of Pines on June 18, 1888, while twenty thousand cheered, horns blew, guns saluted and a brass band played

"Yankee Doodle" and "God Save the Queen." The aspirant was plucked from his leaking cockleshell (as the newspapers labeled all these midget vessels) sixty-two days later. Nothing daunted, he succeeded finally in singlehanding to Portugal in 1892 in the canvas-covered folding boat *Sapolio,* promoting a well-known soap. At it again, Captain Andrews and his bride were lost on their honeymoon, trying to reach Spain in a dory.

How far these and later feats of one-upmanship advanced the popularity of yachting is difficult to assess. Such exercises in masochism do not strike most of us as within the realm of pleasure boating; but they did demonstrate (when they succeeded) that strongly built, adequately provisioned and well-sailed small craft of reasonable design could venture forth on the open Atlantic and even cross it in summer weather with seamanship, courage (or bravado born of overweening exhibitionism) and luck, lots of it. And they were attended by enormous publicity.

Three weeks after Alfred Johnson's internationally touted departure in 1876, for example, Gloucester held a twenty-two-boat regatta on the Fourth of July, its first in sixteen years. The next year was skipped, though the harbor was described as "alive" on the Fourth, and then in 1878, while everyone was excitedly following the reported sightings of *Nautilus,* the fever struck Cape Ann full on. The summer people of Annisquam raced thirty-four sailboats on Ipswich Bay in August. A few days later the contagion sent Rockport onto Sandy Bay for its first regatta ever. Then in September the ephemeral Gloucester Yacht Club held one regatta in the harbor and was never heard from again, under that name, until August of 1880 — a few hours after word was received of *Little Western*'s safe arrival in England — when it reappeared as the Cape Ann Yacht Club.

For several years this gathering of natives was content with the practice room of the Gloucester Cornet Club on Main Street, and their lively races attracted much attention on the coast into the 1890s. Small-boat racing out of Gloucester had a unique quality found nowhere else on the North Shore. It was the home-grown, after-hours sport of local workingmen and small businessmen, grown-up wharf rats who just purely loved to sail, like John Bickford, a laborer and fisherman and Civil War Medal of Honor winner, and Aaron Brown, sailmaker and proprietor of a poolroom, and Sam Elwell, boatbuilder, and caulker Frank Gaffney, boat carpenter Joe Cook, and Frank Sanford, guano processor.

Gloucester was a place apart. Let it go its own way. The yachtsmen of the North Shore, some of them with a little grumbling, as we have seen, had already settled on Marblehead for reasons that proved to be good and sound (except when it blew no'theast).

# 13
# Marblehead Defends the Cup

SINCE LOSING THE HUNDRED GUINEAS CUP IN 1851 TO *America* AND the New York Yacht Club, the British Empire had tried four times to win it back; England sent schooners to New York in 1870 and 1871, Canada a schooner in 1876 and a sloop in 1881, all to no avail. Then in 1884 the Irish designer J. Beavor-Webb challenged with a pair of promising ninety-ton cutters off his board — *Genesta,* with a successful season behind her, and *Galatea,* not yet built — proposing that if one were defeated the other be given a crack the next time around. The two were of somewhat different dimensions, of advanced construction and so much longer than its largest candidates that New York set about to build a defender of matching size, entrusting the design of *Priscilla* — with firm orders that she be a conventional centerboard sloop — to A. Cary Smith, who had lined off the club's 1881 cupwinner, *Mischief.*

Smith was an artist, a top racing helmsman and a self-taught naval architect — no rule-o'-thumb whittler like most of the builders who doubled as their own designers in America, but a pencil-pusher who worked some scientific theory into his curves and incurred the scorn of his peers as a "paper boatman." He deplored the extremes to which our British cousins were carrying their cutters, but the opposite mania at home caused Cary Smith such acute anguish for his country that when he was commissioned to embody it in New York's proposed defender, the bald and bearded patriot, who had

the habit of stuttering when in distress, confessed to the young designer Bill Stephens, with the expression of a man about to be
hanged: "Well, my b-b-boy, I've g-g-got to b-b-build a damned steel
s-s-scow."

The problem in America was that builders unschooled in the
dynamics of water and wind seemed to have cast all sense of perspective adrift in an obsessively wrongheaded craving for speed.
Since the Civil War, yards had been turning out centerboard sloops
that each spring were beamier, shallower and more overcanvased.
The ultimate caricature was attained in the New York sandbagger,
whose overwhelming spread of sail was usually but not invariably
counterbalanced by the ballast that brawny crews shifted from rail
to rail, tack to tack, even shifting themselves overboard in light airs,
if need be, to swim for the nearest channel buoy and hope to be
picked up before dark. Capsizes and a drowning now and then were
part of the fun. Schooner yachts, influenced by the swift pilot boats
of the Atlantic ports, betrayed similar if slightly less lethal tendencies.

In the fisheries the race to market for the top price was won (and
in the end, lost) by the broad, shoal-draft clipper schooner, fast and
stunningly beautiful under her clouds of canvas in a smart blow, but
so lacking in the ability to stand up to a sudden squall or heavy gale
that one smashing puff could and frequently did knock her on her
beam ends, heaving ballast, fish and salt tumbling into the lee bilge,
where she would lie, helplessly hove down, until she filled and sank.
When the reckless clippers dominated her fleet in the 1870s,
Gloucester lost 179 vessels and 1,221 fishermen, mainly due to un-
scientific and inexcusably dangerous design that stressed speed and
the shoalness to lie in the city's undredged docks at the expense of
human life.

Across the Atlantic the opposite trend held sway. The deep-
ballasted, virtually uncapsizable hull with none of the initial stability
and little of the speed of the American type was tending toward its
own extreme in the blowy waters around Britain. Yawls and ketches
gained favor over the schooner along the English coast (the yawl

did not begin to catch on in America until the eighties), while the cutter led all, a perfect wedge of a boat that heeled alarmingly and pitched nauseously but refused to ship a drop in the briskest breeze. The deep, narrow hull and more conservative rig had their advocates in America, and from the early 1870s these self-styled "cutter cranks" plumped for the importation of English common sense.

Credit North Shore yachtsmen with a more realistic appreciation of the role of depth and keel in the safety and seaworthiness that were so cavalierly dismissed by the sporty adherents of the sandbag types south of Cape Cod. Yet the cutter craze drew few converts until July 20, 1876, when a sudden squall struck the shallow schooner yacht *Mohawk* where she lay at anchor off Staten Island with sail up and mainsheet, with lubberly unconcern, cleated flat. The 150-foot centerboarder capsized and sank like a stone with five trapped below, including the owner and his wife. The cutter cranks played up the tragedy as a dramatic example of the inherent instability of the American type.

Six years passed with no noticeable evidence that the lesson had been learned. In 1882 Captain Joseph W. Collins of the U.S. Fish and Fisheries Commission, a former Gloucester skipper, mounted a public campaign against the clipper schooners, contrasting the toll they had exacted with the safety record of the English North Sea fishing cutters. By then the case of Uncle Sam's beam versus John Bull's draft, Cary Smith's damned steel scow against the North Shore keel, was a national controversy. Its resolution made Marblehead the yachting capital, for three glorious years, of the world.

The owners of the top boats in the Eastern Yacht Club had raced the New York squadron's finest during its cruises to Marblehead in 1882 and 1883 and were satisfied that nothing their convention-bound brethren might throw into the defense of the America's Cup stood a chance against Beavor-Webb's challengers. Figuring that Boston's day might be dawning, General Charles J. Paine and Vice Commodore J. Malcolm Forbes, son of former commodore John Murray Forbes, formed an Eastern syndicate to build their own candidate for the defense in 1885. Seven of the ten members owned yachts enrolled in the Marblehead fleet; significantly, six wore keels and two were cutters.

General Paine was a lean, balding, hawkeyed, down-to-earth Bostonian with a sweeping mustache, who had commanded a division of black soldiers, and been wounded, in the Civil War. He managed a family fortune in railroads. As a boy he had sailed a catboat in Salem Bay and was an avid yachtsman. He had a summer estate in the country town of Weston, west of Boston, and another on Swallow's Cave Road at Nahant. Paine owned the centerboard schooner *Halcyon,* a slow boat that he had turned into a winner by alterations, whipping many of the New Yorkers; his dual membership in the Marblehead and New York clubs qualified the syndicate's entry.

Of the other members of the Boston group, Malcolm Forbes had the new keel cutter *Lapwing*. His brother, William H. Forbes, sailed the keel sloop *Hesper*. Eastern Commodore Henry S. Hovey the previous year had launched his 109-foot *Fortuna,* which Captain R. F. Coffin, the leading yachting writer of the day, considered the fastest keel schooner in the world. Harry Hovey was the bachelor son of the late George O. Hovey, the Boston dry goods merchant. He wintered on Beacon Street and summered in his father's luxurious cottage on the bank above Gloucester's Freshwater Cove with his sister Marion. The house burned in 1878, and they rebuilt in 1881 in the modish half-timbered style. The commodore was an old friend of Charley Longfellow, who frequently cruised with him. Rear Commodore William F. Weld, of another family in Boston shipping, had already cruised abroad in his handsome new keel schooner *Gitana*. The sixth of the syndicate, William Gray, Jr., was a good amateur sailor who had designed his own keel sloop, *Huron*. Augustus Hemenway of Manchester, Boston merchant scion, owned the keel cutter *Beetle*. The remaining backers were Francis Lee Higginson, J. Montgomery Sears and John L. (Jack) Gardner, the husband of "Mrs. Jack," Boston's flamboyant patroness of the arts, Isabella Stewart Gardner.

For the Eastern Yacht Club to mount such an effort, boldness (New York called it temerity) was in order. The members of the syndicate boldly engaged their good friend and the club's secretary, Edward Burgess, to design their entry, which would be called *Puritan,* and gave Paine, J. M. Forbes and Gray carte blanche to proceed. Burgess was unfettered by preconceptions and unspoiled by success since he was just setting up practice as a professional yacht designer and as yet had nothing much to his credit except the esteem of his friends. He was thirty-six now and camouflaged his ascetic countenance behind sinkbrush whiskers and a string pince-nez that really made him look more like a "bugologist" than a naval architect. His father's business failure in 1879 had forced Ned Burgess to go to work seriously as an instructor in entomology at Harvard, but the summer of 1883, spent observing English yachts at Torquay and the Isle of Wight on the Channel, convinced him to abandon bugs for boats.

On their return to Boston in the fall of 1883, Ned and his younger brother Sidney started the Eastern Yacht Agency on the strength of Ned's thorough avocational acquaintance with design and his drafting skill (he had previously designed and built a couple of boats). No one beat down their doors, and Sid quit the partnership. Ned's first order, showing the influence of his recent overseas observations, was from Dr. W. F. Whitney of the Eastern Yacht Club early in 1884 for the cruising cutter *Rondina* (not quite the club's first, the larger *Enterprise,* with plumb stem and mast aft of the usual sloop position, having been launched for Francis E. Peabody by Dennison J. Lawlor at Boston in 1878).

When caught between extremes, boldness may be the middle course. Burgess's plans for *Puritan* were a compromise between the deep English keel cutter and the shallow American centerboard sloop, even striking a balance between the relative rigs and sail areas. His aim was to combine what he considered the better features of each as to safety, speed and weatherliness in a new design that the Marblehead syndicate banked on to beat both.

Indeed, the approach had already been tried, and had worked

brilliantly, but with no evident effect on the traditionalists. Back in 1871 Nathanael G. Herreshoff designed and his brother John built for a New Bedford owner what is regarded as the initial tentative compromise between the Anglo-American extremes, the centerboard sloop *Shadow,* thirty-three and a half feet waterline, definitely deeper than the "skimming dishes" and equipped with a "railroad" for shifting ballast athwartships — a precocious sign of her creator's inventive genius. Nat was three months Ned Burgess's senior, and the two had been friends since the 1860s, when the Herreshoffs first launched yachts for the Burgesses from their shop at Bristol, Rhode Island. *Shadow* was phenomenally fast, and just before she was sold in 1872 to C. J. Randall, the first of her several Eastern owners (Dr. John Bryant, co-founder of the Nahasset Yacht Club, had her from 1877 to 1896), Herreshoff raced her at Marblehead and won, and she was still almost unbeatable while Burgess was pondering the curves of his aspiring cup defender. Herreshoff had become wholly preoccupied with steamboats and engines soon after *Shadow*'s appearance, however, and was not to resume his interest in sailing craft until 1890.

While drafting the lines of *Puritan* Burgess had the impressive example of *Shadow* before his eyes, and there is some inferential evidence that he was influenced in a general way by the shape of General Paine's *Halcyon.* Kinship with another contemporary flyer, *Black Cloud* of Gloucester, has never been claimed, except that Burgess must have been impressed by the first few racing appearances of this speedy centerboard sloop, because she slid down George Wheeler's ways into the Annisquam River at Gloucester in the late spring of 1884 while *Puritan* was in the conceptual stage and immediately commenced to clean up on every regatta she entered from Hull to Ipswich Bay. *Black Cloud*'s full dimensions are unknown, but she was twenty-two feet waterline and twenty-six overall behind a plumb stem, with a sail plan quite similar to *Puritan*'s, and reportedly she was a wonder on all points of sailing, but especially to windward. Nearing the end of her second season in 1885 the pride of Gloucester had eleven firsts, two seconds and a third in her class in fourteen regattas, and her ecstatic owner, Aaron Brown, the sail-maker–billiard hall proprietor, had refused $1,300 for her from Boston parties. Like *Shadow, Black Cloud* was still copping the silver ten years later.

*Puritan* was launched from the South Boston yard of Lawley and Sons on May 26, 1885. She was ninety-four feet overall, eighty-one waterline, with the plumb stem and counter of the cutter; her twenty-two feet seven inches breadth was the beam of a sloop, while for depth she was more than the one and less than the other, draw-ing eight feet eight inches of keel with forty-eight tons of lead, another eleven feet with the centerboard down. Compromise rig and sail plan. The New York press called *Puritan* a "bean boat" and sneered that she'd be all right for carrying bricks on the Hudson River after her presumed defeat by the New York Yacht Club's *Priscilla* in the coming trials.

With a well-drilled Corinthian crew (all friends of Paine and Burgess) under Captain Aubrey Crocker, a Cohasset professional and veteran of *Shadow*'s helm, the bean boat jolted New York (but not Cary Smith, who had no love for his scow) by beating *Priscilla* in the Goelet Cup Race off Newport in August 1885 (the prize, a silver tankard, was presented to the Eastern Yacht Club by the winner as the perpetual Puritan Cup, the prime trophy thereafter for major yachts in Massachusetts Bay). In the official trials that fol-lowed, *Puritan* finished off *Priscilla* one, two, three.

Meanwhile Sir Richard Sutton's *Genesta* had arrived from En-gland, flying the signal of the Royal Yacht Squadron. On September 14 and 16 *Puritan* outpointed and outfooted the traditional cutter off New York Harbor to retain the America's Cup in two straight races, the second extremely close. In so doing, she catapulted Marblehead to the top of the yachting world, brought down the tyranny of the old shallow centerboarders and the rule of the rule-o'-thumbers, carried off a middle-of-the-road revolution in yacht design and transformed her creator from a relative unknown into the first of the great professional sailboat designers on the western shore of the Atlantic. In boyish celebration (as of all his victories where there was the deck room), Ned Burgess turned a double somersault as his masterpiece crossed the finish line.

Burgess was now beset with orders from eager yachtsmen who wanted to share his secrets. As agreed, Beavor-Webb's *Galatea,* owned by British navy Lieutenant William R. Henn of the Royal Northern Yacht Club, was to have a crack at the Cup in 1886. This time General Paine alone engaged the Beverly designer to improve if he could on *Puritan,* which the syndicate had sold to J. Malcolm Forbes. *Mayflower* was the result, rather larger than her predecessor but along the same lines and also built by Lawley at South Boston. The new Burgess boat was actually defeated by *Puritan* in the early 1886 trials, but a shift of ballast here, and a sail and rig change there, soon brought her up to trim. Under Captain Martin V. B. Stone, General Paine's sailing master in *Halcyon* and one of a horny-handed elite of professional yachting skippers hailing from Swampscott, *Mayflower* sailed to New York in August and drubbed *Puritan,* an altered *Priscilla* under the burgee of the Seawanhaka Corinthian Yacht Club and the new sloop *Atlantic,* built as a contender by members of the Atlantic Yacht Club of New York in an unsatisfactory attempt at incorporating Burgess's major design novelties.

On August 1, 1886, *Galatea* hove into Marblehead Harbor under jury rig from England, with Lieutenant and Mrs. Henn aboard, and was greeted with fireworks, bonfires and salutes, a reception at the Eastern Yacht Club, more fireworks and a serenading by the Salem Cadet Band. The mutual amiability survived *Galatea*'s one-sided defeat off New York on September 7 and 11. Burgess turned his somersaults, and when *Mayflower* returned with her laurels, Marblehead again turned its.

Britannia wasted no time with regrets. The old tonnage rule of yacht measurement, which had placed a premium on depth at the expense of breadth, was repealed after the defeats of *Genesta* and *Galatea,* and the leading English designer, George L. Watson, visited America in the autumn of 1886 to see what ideas he could discreetly borrow. That winter he returned home and drafted the

*Edward Burgess. From* Harper's Weekly, *October 1, 1887*

*Charles J. Paine. From* A Testimonial to Charles J. Paine and Edward Burgess

# HARPER'S WEEKLY.

### JOURNAL OF CIVILIZATION.

Vol. XXIX.—No. 1499.
Copyright, 1885, by Harper & Brothers.

NEW YORK, SATURDAY, SEPTEMBER 12, 1885.

TEN CENTS A COPY.
$4.00 PER YEAR, IN ADVANCE.

*On board* Puritan — *"Getting aft the mainsheet."* Harper's Weekly, *September 12, 1885*

Mayflower, Puritan *and* Priscilla (*the "damned steel scow" from New York*) *cross tacks off Marblehead before* Mayflower*'s defense of the America's Cup.* Harper's Weekly, *July 10, 1886*

Volunteer *runs in from Sandy Hook to win the first day's race. "Keep astern," advises the banner draped from her quarter;* Thistle *can barely be seen at extreme right.* Harper's Weekly, *October 8, 1887*

*Sketches during the* Volunteer-Thistle *series.* Harper's Weekly, *October 1, 1887*

steel cutter *Thistle* for a syndicate of Scots from the Royal Clyde Yacht Club. *Thistle* had more than the usual British beam for a cutter in ratio to depth and exchanged the plumb stem for a clipper bow with cut-away forefoot, a reduction in lateral plane that would have disastrous effects on her ability to claw upwind. But she was faster than anything afloat in her home waters, as she proved, and great things were expected.

As soon as *Thistle*'s dimensions were published (the New York Yacht Club had amended the Deed of Gift of the America's Cup to force the challenger to show something of his hand in advance), General Paine immediately commissioned Burgess to outdesign her. *Volunteer* was rushed through construction and set maiden sail on July 21, 1887. She too was steel and clipper-stemmed, continuing moderately the Burgess trend away from beam toward depth. Yet she was assuredly less cutterish than her Scottish rival, for the challengers still could not bring themselves to espouse the centerboard. In her trials the latest magic from the Burgess board left her parent *Mayflower*, as *Mayflower* had *Puritan*, far, far astern.

*Thistle* crossed with all the hopes of Empire riding on her wake. Her design and construction had been shrouded in secrecy, and she had been a veritable terror amongst the British yachting fleet. The first Cup race was sailed through an armada of spectator boats on September 27 over the thirty-eight miles of the New York Yacht Club inside course. The stunning white *Volunteer* simply walked away from the gallant pretender, passed her in the opposite direction on the homeward run and finished nineteen minutes ahead. The second race on the thirtieth was a formality; the Burgess double somersault set off eleven minutes and fifty-four seconds of whistles and cannon fire before *Thistle* crossed the finish line. There would not be another challenge for six more years.

*Volunteer* sailed in triumph for Marblehead, and while a tugboat towed her the windless last few miles into the harbor on the evening of October 7, the City of Boston held a packed reception for her designer and owner in Faneuil Hall. The briefest of the panegyrics was the best, from the absent Dr. Holmes, who could not resist writing from Beverly Farms, "Proud as I am of their achievement, I own that the General is the only commander I ever heard of who made himself illustrious by running away from all his competitors." Later in the evening the half-encircling shore of Marblehead Harbor blazed with bonfires, and every yacht was illuminated. Into this eerie amphitheater puffed the steamer *Brunette,* towing a serpentine procession of fifty dories strung with Chinese lanterns. As they completed their encirclement of *Volunteer* the harbor exploded with skyrockets, Roman candles and red fire. Then, on a toot from the steamer, every church bell in town pealed furiously and the shores echoed with the blasts of cannon from the squadron. The Lynn Cadet Band burst into a medley of patriotic airs from *Brunette*'s deck, and Town Clerk Felton stepped aboard the third-in-a-row Marblehead defender of the America's Cup with resolutions of congratulation from the selectmen.

It was all slightly ironic. As the designer and yachting writer William P. Stephens wrote, "The majority of American yachtsmen were still unwilling to admit that British ideas were right. After her final victory over *Genesta, Puritan* was proclaimed to be not British, but Boston, — the perfect embodiment of purely American ideas. History was ransacked to prove that depth of hull, outside keel, and outside ballast were all American institutions from the days of *Gimcrack* and *America.* The result of this curious change of course was most beneficial in the immediate demand for a vastly better type of yacht. The effect on British yachting was no less powerful and beneficial. . . . With the tax on breadth and false measurement of depth abolished, British yachting entered on a period of activity and prosperity." The effect on Marblehead, one might add, was to raise it above New York as the Cowes of America — so anointed by the yachting historian Captain Coffin; a mere ten years earlier, as he had observed, the fastest boats on Boston waters were second-handers from New York.

The Cup victories of the Burgess compromise cutters sent out waves of yachting enthusiasm across the United States, and many new clubs were formed. In an effort to rid racing of the forever inexact handicapping nuisance, most adopted the rule of measurement first formulated in 1883 by the Seawanhaka Corinthian Yacht Club making the theoretical designed speed of a boat a factor of waterline length and sail area. The equation was far from ideal, but it was a beginning toward the more sophisticated Universal and International rules and the concept of the one-design classes of boats as alike as fish in a school.

One rasping dissent to the new conformity was tossed in by Captain Robert Bennet Forbes, aged eighty-four. The old sea dog had been responsible for more than his share of design improvements in his time, and he was an admirer of Ned Burgess, but the modern trend was too much. In 1888, the year before his death, he looked back forty years and grumped: "In those days *when comfort was considered of more consequence than racing prizes,* yachts were not lumbered up as they are now, by spinakers with long booms, club-topsails, jib-topsails and balloon sails. As yachts are sailed today I should consider it a great punishment to be obliged to take a sea cruise in one of them. Having saved the Queen's Cup by means of the fine sloops built by General Paine and Mr. Burgess, let us be content with their victories, and go back to the good old days when we were content to win by hard *seaman's* work and good *seaboats,* and not mainly dependant on mere accidents for our victories."

The wisdom of the old man's counsel has oft been borne out since; but in the eighties the chaotic growth of yachting called for rules, rules bred rule-beating, and rule-beating undeniably advanced the art of the designer, if not the comfort of the sailor.

Probably the earliest successful racing class designed to the Seawanhaka Rule was the forty-footer, conceived by Edward Burgess out of the dreams of conquest of the young Adams brothers, Charles Francis the Third, who was twenty-one at the time, and George. The boys summered with other members of their formidable tribe in a compound of close-knit families described by a nephew as a "wooden barracks" at "The Glades" on the west side of Cohasset Harbor, on the South Shore. They were desperate to have a boat that might bring down the fabled Herreshoff *Shadow* of

Marblehead, which had ruled the bay for fifteen years, and went to Burgess in 1887; he drew up for them a keel cutter, thirty-six feet on the waterline, *Papoose* (seven letters with a double *o* for luck), and in her they beat *Shadow* one day off Nahant.

Having accomplished their object, the Adamses sold *Papoose* and in 1888 got Burgess to design *Babboon* along the same lines, but forty feet, the first of four of the class from his board that year for members of the Eastern Yacht Club. Charles Adams the same summer followed brother George's lead in joining Eastern and thus began his famous practice of sailing whatever his current yacht the eighteen miles outside Boston from Cohasset to Marblehead every Saturday morning for the afternoon race, and sailing home that evening — a practice that did much to perfect the helmsmanship with which he ultimately defended the America's Cup and that he continued, summer in and summer out for half a century, even while Secretary of the Navy.

While Ned Burgess was designing his first forty-footer in 1888, his English opposite number, Will Fife, Jr., was creating the forty-foot cutter *Minerva* for Charles H. Tweed, a New York lawyer (not the Boss) who summered at Beverly Farms. *Minerva* was to succeed *Clara,* a Fife cutter of extreme lines that Tweed and an associate had purchased in Britain. *Clara* had cleaned up everything in sight off the North Shore under the professional command of John Barr, the superb Scots sailing master of *Thistle,* who had been induced by Eastern yachtsmen to settle in Marblehead. *Minerva* carried far less sail than her American rivals but had more grip on the water. She was brought across by Charles Barr, John's nephew and eventually the most famous of all the professional yacht skippers in the days when the pros reigned supreme. Under Charlie's touch the Fife cutter showed her wake to every forty-footer from Boston to New York until the whole yachting coast was crying, "Anything to stop *Minerva!*" And so in 1890 the Adams boys commissioned Burgess to design *Gossoon,* more on *Minerva*'s lines than others of the American class, and when they met on the water that year they were well matched.

Edward Burgess was responsible for sixteen of the twenty-one forty-footers which were built before the class gave way to the new forty-six-footers in 1891. He did not live to see the best of his more than two hundred designs, which included several fine fishing schooners, utterly overshadowed by Nat Herreshoff's great forty-six-footer *Gloriana*. For Captain Nat returned brilliantly to sailboat design with *Gloriana*, first of the rule-beaters. With her long overhangs and "spoon bow" that stretched so extraordinarily her measured waterline, and her speed, when heeled, *Gloriana* was as inventive in her construction as she was radical, yet sound, in her lines. Ned Burgess died of typhoid fever on July 12, 1891, having just turned forty-three as *Gloriana* was slipping down the ways at Bristol. "He might have designed the world's handsomest yachts if he had lived to an age of greater maturity, for in my opinion he was a great artist." Thus wrote the Marblehead designer L. Francis Herreshoff of his father's close friend.

The torch passed silently from Edward Burgess to Nathanael Herreshoff that midsummer day of 1891, from the pragmatic bugologist and his faithful North Shore friends, who broke with tradition and brought Yankee sense to yacht design, to the genius who raised it to its glory. Thus dawned the golden age of yachting.

# 14

# Nahant Out-Bostons Boston

WHATEVER NOTIONS ANYONE MAY HAVE NURTURED OF MAKING AN-
other Newport of Nahant went up in smoke with Colonel Perkins's
hotel that September night of 1861, exactly five months after the
Confederate bombardment of Fort Sumter. The fire put a spectacular *coup de grâce* to the last rambling reminder of *la vie gaie*
the left the North Shore's first resort utterly in the clannish (and
clammy, some said) grip of Cold Roast Boston. Nahant had already
achieved the distinction among observers of the social scene of
being more quintessentially Boston than Boston itself. In the Hub,
Henry Cabot Lodge asserted with satisfaction, "everybody knew
everybody else and all about everybody else's family." Since Nahant
had but a twentieth part of the city's everybodys, the interfamiliar-
ity was in inverse ratio.

There was one bad moment after the fire when life seemed to stir
among the ashes, but the distractions of the deepening war took care
of that. There were, too, Fred Tudor's crowd-drawing eccentricities
within the towering fences of Maolis, but death would soon see to
that — his death, and his widow's aversion, as we have seen, for
strong drink. And there was the matter of Bass Point, not yet
troublesome, but it bore watching.

Just to show how unfair, not to say inaccurate, was John Collins
Bossidy's parodic toast to "The home of the bean and the cod/
Where the Lowells talk to the Cabots/And the Cabots talk only to

God," John Ellerton Lodge had returned to Boston in early retirement with a New Orleans cotton fortune at the age of thirty-five when Henry Cabot's daughter, Anna, deigned not merely to talk to him in 1842 but to marry him as well. The bridegroom's curly fringe of chin whiskers and air of poetic contemplation belied his driving nature; not content with one fortune, he was soon pursuing another in shipping. During the gold rush of 1849 one of his vessels paid for herself in freight charges before she sailed on her maiden voyage; by 1853 Lodge had three clippers in the service to 'Frisco.

The Lodges vacationed in the Cabot cottage on Cliff Street. In August 1860 their only son, namesake of his grandfather Cabot, witnessed the "abduction" of his playmate Charley Rice from the school. Late the next summer the Nahant Hotel burned. John Lodge's first reaction was to purchase the thirty acres on East Point and reconstruct the original, smaller hotel; but the war was settling in, and his intended partners pulled out. So he bought up the mortgages and spent the 1862 season resting from overwork and laying plans for his summer mansion on the ruins. On September 11, a year lacking a day after the destruction of the hotel, he died unexpectedly at fifty-five, leaving Anna, their son, and their daughter, Elizabeth.

Cabot was eleven and worshipped his father. Fortunately he had friends and was a Cabot as much as a Lodge, and everybody in his world, after all, knew everybody else. Among his chums was William Lawrence, eighteen days his junior.

The Lawrences occupied a corner of Nahant's genealogical labyrinth that it might be instructive to explore. Young Bill, the Protestant Episcopal bishop-to-be, was a son of Amos A. Lawrence, the textile capitalist. Although the family had old Nahant connections, Amos did not gain a foothold there until 1864, when he forsook his summer place on the Lynn shore of Nahant Bay and bought the Clark's Point estate of that vigorous early yachtsman, Benjamin C. Clark. Bill's mother, Sarah, was a daughter of the dyspeptic merchant William Appleton, who owned the former David Sears cottage on Swallow's Cave Road next to the sailing General Paine, Cup defender. The Appletons and Searses were of course related, and Mrs. Sears was a sister-in-law of Dr. John Collins Warren, who had helped colonize Nahant with his endorsement of its therapeutic properties. Dr. Warren's second wife was the sister of that other Senator from Nahant, Robert C. Winthrop; his son, the third in the medical dynasty, Dr. J. Mason Warren, had married Annie, a daughter of Benjamin W. Crowninshield of Salem, who had a summer cottage on Swallow's Cave Road. As his brother Jacob was Jefferson's Secretary of the Navy, Benjamin was Madison's; brother George had his own private fleet in the form of *Cleopatra's Barge*. The Mason Warren cottage was back of Joe's Beach. A second Crowninshield daughter, Mary, married Dr. Charles Mifflin, and they bought the old Eliot cottage behind Bass Beach, where the President of Harvard spent the summers of his youth; it was later owned by their son George, head of Houghton Mifflin, the publishers. Elizabeth, the third Crowninshield daughter and a great beauty, married the Reverend William Mountford; *their* house overlooked the sea next the Prescotts. The late historian, by the way, was married to a sister of William Amory, who was married to a daughter of David Sears. Dr. Mason Warren's daughter Rosamond married Charles Hammond Gibson (the Gibsons and Hammonds were behind Cedar Point), while his sister married Thomas Dwight and lived on Cliff Street west of the church. The Dwight boys, James and Thomas, studied medicine; later, across the road from his parents, Dr. Tom bought the Charles Amory place from the heirs of Elizabeth Clarke Copley Greene. "Madame Greene," the daughter of John Singleton Copley and wife of Gardiner Greene, the artist's agent in Boston after he had gone to England, lived there many summers.

Thus were intertwined the everybodys of Nahant and Boston, root, branch and twig.

With the Civil War's end, Bill Lawrence and his brother Amory moved sailboats and horses from the old cottage at Lynn to the new one on Clark's Point. Other summer activities stuck in Bill's memory. "As the bowling-alleys and stables of the old hotel were still standing, we boys, Cabot Lodge, Frank Chadwick, Sturgis Bigelow, and Frank Amory, amused ourselves smashing the windows and were chased over fence after fence by Cabot's gardener."

Near East Point and beyond sight of the road was a deep inlet marked by Cupid's Rock. Here, in the properly clothed remembrance of the bishop, "all Nahant boys and men in the garb of nature bathed and dived." Every Sunday after the internal cleansing in the Boston Church, the summer male population headed for Cupid's Rock for a cold dash of the external. One such morning the dignified commission merchant Patrick Grant had stripped himself of all but nature's garb, or so he thought, and was about to plunge into the sea when someone shouted a warning and he stepped back to discover that he was still topped off with his tall beaver hat.

These weekly baptisms continued for years, surviving even the disapproval long afterward of Probate Judge Rollin E. Harmon, who one afternoon observed the rite while on his way to supper with Patrick Grant's son, the jurist-novelist Robert Grant, and complained to the Nahant police. The bathers had to supplement nature until Judge Grant wrote his stiff-necked colleague, "You were within your rights, to be sure, but it is really my bailiwick. I know Nahant better than you do." Judge Harmon retreated, and the garb of Cupid was permitted at Cupid's Rock for a few more years until the prying tourists in their motor cars got too thick along the shore.

In the early 1870s Cabot Lodge and his sister Elizabeth, who had married George Abbot James, divided the East Point estate and built their houses there; Cabot shelved his library in the Greek Revival temple that had been the hotel's billiard hall. East Point was his base for the rest of his life, as indifferent lawyer, as enthusiastic writer and historian, as shrewdest of politicians first elected state representative from Nahant in 1879, then congressman, finally to thirty-one years in the United States Senate, a club only slightly less exclusive than his Cold Roast bastion by the briny blue. The aristocratic squire with his cool eyes and clipped beard, arising every morning to split wood for an hour, riding his horse about town with a nod here and a faint smile there, year after year, though the course of his career shook nations, was the personification of Nahant to itself and to the world.

By insuring that a hotel would not again arise on East Point, the children of John Ellerton Lodge tied the knot in the belt of Boston's Best that girdled the most desirable shoreline of Great Nahant. Little Nahant, being removed from the larger, outer peninsula and having no proper anchorage or private beach it could call its own, never rose above its station as a poor relation; most of it remained the preserve of George W. Simmons of Boston until the death of his son in the 1890s, when a land company was formed to dismember colonial Lynn's windy pasture into house lots.

The Great Swamp and Bear Pond, largely Tudor territory anyway, isolated Bass Point from the main body of Great Nahant in the possession of the Boston colony almost as effectively as Long Beach bypassed Little Nahant. The Phillips family cottages and "Old Castle" held only the western shore, and the remainder of Bass Point — by far the most of it — was not considered worth doing anything with until a Lynn man, Nathan Moore, established a small eatery there, where he treated the overflow from Maolis Gardens to chowder and fried fish. In 1862, the year after the Nahant Hotel burned down, Moore refurbished his place and renamed it the Relay House after the inn outside Baltimore from which the Sixth Massachusetts Regiment marched in the successful assault on the city under General Benjamin F. Butler in 1861.

Within ten years the summer excursion steamers were including Bass Point as a port of call, and the Relay House had been joined by the Bass Point Hotel and the Trimountain House (a play on Boston's Tremont House) at the foot of Bailey's Hill; the Trimountain's best-known proprietor, Sylvester (Vess) Brown, for years hosted an annual reunion of his old schoolmates from Lynn, during which "one might see dignified men playing leapfrog, marbles, and other reminders of days perhaps sixty years agone."

By the 1880s, turned off to a trickle by Mrs. Tudor's teetotalitarianism, the crowds that once surged across Nahant had deserted the Ice King's now-seedy garden of grotesqueries for the brightening lights of Revere Beach and Salem Neck, where an amusement park of promise was arising amongst the ancient willows, and the Bass Point hotelmen were plotting how to add attractions of their own.

Nor was Nahant quite the summer athenaeum it had been when the hotel on East Point was in full though brief swing in the early seventies and it appeared there might be a renaissance. Dr. Oliver Wendell Holmes had reluctantly sold his summer house in the Berkshire town of Pittsfield because it was too far from the city and too expensive to maintain; after fifteen years of visiting around he lit upon Nahant in the summer of 1871, when he stayed with Senator Sumner. He returned for three or four years with Mrs. Holmes, renting the Charles Amory cottage near the Lawrences; to Bill, in his early teens, the Autocrat's talk was "like the running of a mountain brook, fresh and inexhaustible. He dropped in upon the piazza and talked and talked. My father listened, my mother slipped away, and we caught stray sentences. At supper, however, there were always quotations of the bright things the Doctor had said."

*Some* bright things Holmes *wished* he had said. Young Cabot Lodge stood with the great man one afternoon at East Point "when the ocean, lying quiet in the summer haze, was just ruffled by the faintly moving air. As he looked he turned to me and quoted Tennyson's great line from *The Eagle:* 'The wrinkled sea beneath him crawls,' and said, 'How perfect that is. Why did not I think of it first?' "

Dr. Holmes wrote his old friend John Lothrop Motley, then in Europe, a gossipy letter from Nahant on August 26, 1873. As a diplomat first appointed ambassador to Austria by President Lincoln in 1861 on Senator Sumner's urging, the historian had had his ups and downs and was finally down-and-out, having been named envoy to Great Britain by President Grant in 1869 (again on Sumner's initiative), only to be fired after a year by Grant out of pique at the Massachusetts Senator's opposition to his Santo Dominican policy: "I write, you see, from Nahant, where I have been during July and August, staying . . . in the cottage you must remember as Mr. Charles Amory's . . . playing cuckoo in the nest, with my wife, who enjoys Nahant much more than I do — having had more or less of asthma to take off from my pleasures. . . . Many of your old friends are our neighbors. Longfellow is hard by, with Tom Appleton in the same house, and for a fortnight or two Sumner as his guest. . . . I have dined since I have been here at Mr. George Peabody's with Longfellow, Sumner, Appleton, and William Amory; at Cabot Lodge's with nearly the same company; at Mr. [George Abbot] James's with L. and S., and at Longfellow's *en famille,* pretty nearly. Very pleasant dinners. . . . Nahant is a gossipy Little Pedlington kind of a place . . . they are prattling and speculating and worrying about the cost of Mr. J's [James's] new house, which, externally at least, is the *handsomest country house I ever saw,* and is generally allowed to be a great success."

Motley returned to Nahant in 1875 for a last summer, crushed by his wife's death. He was frail and sick; Holmes spent hours with him. Their friend, the haughty Sumner, had died the previous year, embittered by political setbacks. Motley died in England in 1877. Dr. Holmes in his jaunty way had enjoyed the company at Nahant but not its ocean dampness, which aggravated his asthma, and now the company was dwindling. Probably "Th' Haunt" evoked too many old associations. For the season of 1878 he rented a cottage near the depot at Beverly Farms. There, with the warm land at his back, the anatomist of the human frame and spirit was to taper off his own remaining summers.

When the Holmeses stayed in the Charles Amory cottage, Mr. and Mrs. Thomas Dwight and family were across the road. Tom, Jr., had studied anatomy with the doctor at Harvard Medical School and in 1874 was assisting him in the teaching of it. His younger brother, Jim, was graduated from the college that June and would be attending their famous neighbor's lectures himself in the fall; old Holmes was the liveliest professor in the university, but the prospect of the long medical course was sobering nevertheless, and a summer of diversion was not unwarranted, even for a Bostonian.

It so happened that Mrs. William Appleton's son-in-law, J. Arthur

*Barges come and go at the Relay House, Bass Point. Nahant Historical Society*

*Amusement park at east end of Short Beach, about 1870. Nahant Public Library*

*Bass Beach, about 1870, complete with private bathhouses. On the bluff is the Mifflin, formerly Eliot, house, where the president of Harvard summered in his childhood. Lynn Historical Society*

*The Boston-Nahant sidewheel steamer* Ulysses *at Tudor Wharf, 1868. Nahant Public Library*

*East Point from Bass Beach, 1860s. Only the billiard hall stands above the ruins of the Nahant Hotel. Nahant Public Library*

*Cold Roast Boston at the Nahant Club, 1880s. Nahant Public Library*

*Henry Cabot Lodge on his porch at Nahant. From* Town and Country, *May 23, 1903*

*The Lodge mansion on East Point, 1879. Nahant Public Library*

*Richard D. Sears and James Dwight.
From* Harper's Weekly, *September
17, 1887*

Beebe, returned from England that August with the equipment for a new outdoor game that was sweeping all other distractions aside. It was called "sphairistike" by its inventor, an Edwardian-looking cavalry major by the horsey-sounding name of Walter Clopton Wingfield. Beebe's set consisted of spoon-shaped, thirteen-ounce racquets made by Malings of Woolwich, several rubber balls of the sort children played with, a net and rules.

Jim Dwight and Frederick R. Sears, Jr., one of his nearby cousins, measured off a level stretch of lawn on the east side of the Appleton estate on Swallow's Cave Road and strung up the net, taking care to taper the court twenty-six feet on either side back to what the rules called service lines. Racquets in hand, they sallied forth. Their first try was a fiasco. Neither could keep the ball in play. "We voted the whole thing a fraud," in Dwight's words, "and put it away."

Time, however, hung heavy in the somnolence of a Nahant summer, and a month later the cousins again tried "sticky," which was merely Major Wingfield's adaptation to a lawn of the ancient sport of court tennis. Each won a game this time, and they played all afternoon in the rain, in rubber coats and boots. The since-epidemic bug had bitten.

Dwight and Sears at the time had every reason to suppose that they and Arthur Beebe were introducing lawn tennis to America. In reality they were not. Miss Mary Ewing Outerbridge of the Staten Island and Bermuda Outerbridges had played sticky with the British officers of the Bermudian garrison the previous winter and brought a set home to New York in February. That spring, two or three months before Nahant declared the game a delusion, her brother, A. Emilius Outerbridge, laid out a court, indisputably the first in the country, at the Staten Island Cricket and Baseball Club, where he was a crack batsman.

For two summers while he was a Harvard medical student Jim Dwight and his cousins (Bill Appleton and Bob Grant, besides the Sears boys) and friends (Cabot Lodge among them) played obsessively as the informal "Nahant Tennis Club" and in August of 1876 held their first handicapped tournament on the Appleton court with fifteen entries. Fred's younger brother, Richard D. Sears, tried the game for the first time the next summer when he was fifteen, practicing against a barn door with rubber balls that his mother had stitched around with pieces of old flannel shirts — but not 'til Fred was through with them. The Nahanters had their third tournament in 1878, when they used modern tennis scoring and ventured to take on "strangers" in a match at Newport. Bill Lawrence helped canonize the queer fad on his Aunt Emily Appleton's lawn; fifty years afterward at The Country Club in Brookline an old-fashioned racquet was pointed out to him, with the inscription: *Racquet used by Bishop Lawrence in the first lawn tennis game in this country.* Among the first, anyway.

Dick Sears was a natural sort of genius at what a letter writer to the *Harvard Crimson* in 1878 derided as "a seaside pastime . . . well enough for lazy or *weak* men, but men who have rowed or taken part in a nobler sport should blush to be seen playing Lawn Tennis." In 1881, when he was nineteen and a junior at Harvard, Sears won the first United States national singles championship at the Newport Casino, a feat he repeated six years running. He dominated play at the original Longwood Cricket Club. The first site of the club, before it moved to Chestnut Hill, was given by David Sears from the extensive tract he had bought up astride Brookline and Boston, next to the Muddy River; his wife called it "Longwood" out of admiration for Napoleon Bonaparte (a curious hero for a Boston lady), whose last days were lived at Longwood on St. Helena.

With Jim Dwight, Sears captured five of his six consecutive national doubles championships, in the course of which the pair initiated the maneuver of following service to the net: In 1884 they traveled to England, two clean-cut, mustached young Bostonian-Nahanters in white trousers, shirts with rolled-up sleeves, striped blazers, striped belts and striped caps, and Dwight became the first Yank to play on the sacred green of Wimbledon.

Jim in the meanwhile found the spare time to graduate from Harvard Medical School in 1879 and was entering the practice of obstetrics when he was taken ill. Though he recovered completely, he abandoned the active pursuit of medicine, leaving that to brother Tom, who went on to distinguish himself as the successor in the chair of anatomy at Harvard of their revered old Nahant neighbor, Dr. Holmes, who — to make a nice cycle of it — had succeeded their grandfather, Dr. John C. Warren. In 1881 Dr. James Dwight organized the United States National Lawn Tennis Association and was primarily responsible for bringing order out of chaos as the game swept the land; he served a total of twenty-one years as its second president and was gratefully ordained during his lifetime as "The Father of American Tennis."

That summer of 1881, while Dick Sears was in Newport volleying the good name of Nahant from height to height across the slippery grass of the Casino, typhoid fever broke out, to the imminent peril of Cold Roast's good name as the healthiest spa on the coast.

Typhoid was the terror of the summer resort of the 1870s and 1880s, which typically got along without central sewerage and water supply; where hotels were crowded and facilities primitive, housing frequently flimsy, drainage poor, and wells and privies dug indiscriminately on common ground. Bar Harbor was stricken in the summer of 1872; and William Lawrence — having just been elevated to his diaconate — fell one of sixty-three victims of the tap-water at the Profile House while vacationing in the White Mountains in 1875.

In July and August 1881 about seventy-five cases of typhoid erupted at Nahant. Two died. Trying to track down the source of the "Nahant Fever," health officials found that the water in one well used by neighborhood children took on in thirty minutes the flavor of the disinfectant added to a nearby cesspool. The alarmed town rose up and voted for a sewerage system and public water supply, bearing out the worst fears of one old summer resident from Boston, who had very thoroughly been spreading Nahant's dirty linen across the pages of the Boston *Transcript*.

His family, wrote Samuel H. Russell, embraced several households of as many as forty souls and had been summering for fifty-five years at what had always been regarded as one of the healthiest places around Boston. And now there was this epidemic, surely due to an increase in sewage over the past score of years far exceeding the growth in population, which stood at 808 year-round, but was swelled in summer by another 1,600 residents and at least 150,000 transients, who poured in upon the tiny peninsula by land and sea.

The town must be cleaned up, Russell lectured his neighbors (only in the *Transcript* could a correspondent lecture his neighbors in both Boston and Nahant and be sure of his audience), and he exhorted them to follow his example and modernize their cesspools, for "the income of Nahant not derived from personal property invested outside the town is from its summer business. How long will this personal property remain taxable in Nahant, while the owners are liable to five per cent illness in ninety days? The town levy would naturally be increased by the expense of draining and cleaning the town, and the tax on real estate be continually increasing on a declining valuation, while the summer business would be greatly affected by exaggerated reports of the unhealthiness of the town."

Spoken like a true son of State Street. Without mincing any words, and right out in public, Russell was advising his summer neighbors that unless the epidemic in their midst was halted by private measures, Nahant's security as a tax haven was in grave jeopardy.

The practice of the wealthy, most of them from Boston, of evading the general personal property tax in their winter quarters by taking up legal residence in the outlying suburbs, where the rates were incomparably lower, started in Nahant in 1870, and there was not much the Boston assessors could do about it. The dodge was perfectly legal, and because valuations were based on demonstrable holdings, tangible property such as real estate carried the burden while the elusive stock certificate on which the greater wealth was based escaped any detection at all except by the most sophisticated city assessors. Tax collectors in the small suburbs and resorts like Nahant were only too happy to provide havens for the rich commuters and summer residents, assessing them at face value for what they were permitted to see with their own eyes, leaving the hidden intangibles to the owner and his conscience.

The result of Nahant's discovery by the tax-dodgers was that the valuation rose from $2,900,000 in 1869 to $6,000,000 in 1872, while the tax rate dropped from $4.50 to $2.50 per thousand. When the rate commenced to creep back to its former level, one prominent summer resident wangled a sizeable abatement of his $800,000 assessment — and died a few years later leaving millions. Other probate returns likewise opened the eyes of the assessors — too late. In 1908, after the death of Frederick R. Sears, father of the tennis players, the Nahant assessors were directed by the state tax commissioner to go after certain large sums owing in local taxes that had been discovered in probate, and when they were finally collected after a long legal battle they paid most of the cost of the new town hall.

Of course the inequity of these evasions, as they crept into one North Shore resort after another, was as visible to the townspeople as the untaxed intangibles were invisible to the local collectors; as Fred Wilson observed of his native Nahant, "the working man, with only a house and lot, was assessed for a far greater proportion of his total wealth than the wealthier residents, most of whose property was not in plain sight of the assessors."

What if the taxes of the summer resident with no children in the local school did subsidize the education of the natives and enable the town to build town halls and provide services it could not have otherwise? Was it worth it, being the object of that special, super-cooled, Boston brand of noblesse oblige based on family, friends and education, on occupation or the absence of it, and on the possession of an iceberg of wealth of which only the slight eminence above water showed on the tax rolls?

In view of the fact that the sailing men had organized the Eastern Yacht Club back in 1870, one may wonder why the Nahant Club didn't materialize in the old Tudor mansion until 1889. The reason is that there was no need for it; all Nahant beyond the Great Swamp was one water-bound club. But subtle changes were in the works that may have influenced Abbott Lawrence's son-in-law, Francis Peabody, Jr., to lead the move to rent the Tudor field in 1888 and put in several tennis courts and a baseball diamond that led the next year to leasing the whole place as the inner sanctum within the outer.

A newspaper commentator suspected the resort was a trifle *passé* — lowering the bars just an inch. It used to be, he wrote, that "about Nahant there existed an atmosphere that beat the band for exclusiveness and frigid social life. The very name was synonymous then with all that made Beacon Hill the fashionable centre, for to obtain a cottage in that blest region was to attain the right to social recognition anywhere on earth, or at least that was the accepted creed in Boston. . . . New blood and new money were kept at bay for years, and then, when other and more attractive resorts claimed the palm of glory, Nahant had to give in and be more eclectic in its elect."

The Nahant Club drew the circle tighter. To the colony's delight it revived the amenities of the ghostly Nahant Hotel without the vulgar necessity of sharing them with all comers. Once again a bowling alley rang with the clatter of tenpins, and the smoke-filled billiard room resounded elegantly to the *chunk* of polished ivory upon ivory. The old stables came alive with whinny and horse-smell and the shout of groom. The Ice King's parlors served for whist and lavendered letterwriting, his dining room as the setting for the private luncheon party and the candlelit champagne dinner. A generation had come and gone since Nahant had a ballroom, and now, instead of to the quadrille, the Tudor floors bounced to the gay rhythms that were announcing the nineties.

Afternoon tea for the ladies every day, and every Saturday a band concert whose strains "were not restrained," in the grateful words of Fred Wilson, "by the club lot lines, and half the town could enjoy them." And weekly baseball games with the town team when "once or more the club nine had a famous Harvard varsity player, and the Nahant nine would retaliate by finding some crackerjack from another source."

And of course tennis, the ultimate sport of the elite, of the effete, of the Anglophilic easterner, of the blazered Ivy Leaguer, played with strenuous flair before a gallery of parasols and bowlers, upon a velvety turf that only the Nahant Club and the likes of Aunt Emily could afford to have and to maintain, played on and on in the lengthening shadows of the perfect summer afternoon, where it all *really* began.

In the summer of 1893, the year he was appointed a Suffolk County judge of probate, Robert Grant had charge of entertaining the officers of a pair of visiting Russian warships at Nahant. He arranged to have them brought by tugboat from Boston for a very posh reception on the great lawn of the Nahant Club. All the members, who numbered among them some veteran topers, of course hoped their guests would topple like dominoes, and of course the Russians refused nothing, round after round.

When the last cork had popped, Judge Grant surveyed the scene: "The lawn looked somewhat like a battle-field, but with the victors in dignified retreat. The sea dogs had more than held their own." Their chaperone shepherded his Czarist charges aboard the waiting tug. The sea shimmered under the shining moon, while, "gathered in a rug at the stern with their commander in the centre, they indulged in a repertoire of sentimental and patriotic songs worthy of a return from a Sunday-School picnic."

Contrasting with amiable detachment America's two most distinguished resorts back in the middle of the century, George William Curtis had observed that "the repose, the freedom from the fury of fashion, is precisely what endears Nahant to its lovers, and the very opposite is the characteristic of Newport."

Forty years later, on the threshold of the nineties, the two stood in the same relative positions, only more so. "The tendencies to more frivolous and more luxurious habits of life in New York," declared a writer in the Boston *Sunday Herald* early in August 1890, "are at Newport highly accentuated, the season of the latter growing, indeed, more and more to be the climax of the winter gayeties of the metropolis; while Nahant, on the other hand, maintains the pristine dignity and aristocratic quality which have given to Boston her fame among cities.

"Nahant may be said to be even more characteristically Boston than Boston itself," this unnamed correspondent continued. "So generally is this felt with respect to Nahant, that the unappreciative frequently make the charge of its being snobbishly exclusive. To one, however, who sees and feels how dreadful is the trend of our modern American life, this preservation of the old and the true is particularly to be cherished. And it is a pleasure to know that there is a place where people are not in a rush and turmoil over hunts and parades and sumptuous entertainments, but where they live in quiet ease, having indeed entertainment, but not such as puts life to confusion."

The simplicity of summer life at Nahant was attributed by the *Herald*'s reverent observer "in large measure to the very general family relationships and inherited friendships, if one may so speak, among its residents. But, more than that, there are probably more people here, than in any other similar place in America, who may have true claims to aristocracy by reason of cultivation and wealth possessed for generations, back to the first days of the colonies."

Thus Nahant at the close of the nineteenth century.

# 15

Of Autocrats
and Actors

MANCHESTER HAD MANAGED WELL ENOUGH BEING JUST MANCHESTER
until Mr. Fields came along. James T. Fields was the leading book
publisher in Boston and the Daniel among its literary lions, and
he did so well by them, and they by him, that he retired in 1871
when he was only fifty-four and went on the lecture circuit, titil-
lating audiences with anecdotes of his experiences in the den. Two
years later he bought Thunderbolt Hill, as being Olympian enough,
and in 1874 built his summer house on top of it. After a while
Mr. and Mrs. Fields invented "Manchester-by-the-Sea" and started
printing it on their stationery.

The anglicism — dare one call it an affectation? — endures to this
day. Besides steering countless mail, freight and travelers away from
the other five Manchesters of New England, the Fieldses succeeded
in stamping their chosen retreat as an upper-crust watering place
pervaded with a vague air of Englishness and with distinct under-
tones of class. Manchester's tradesmen, desirous of conveying the
assurance that they were fully as discriminating as their clientele,
soon were adding their own "by-the-Seas" to their by-your-leaves.
The publisher's friends reacted irreverently, however. Dr. Holmes
had taken a cottage near the Beverly Farms railroad station and
replied to Fields from "Beverly-by-the-Dépot," and John Greenleaf
Whittier wrote from "Haverhill-by-the-Hollyhocks." At Cape Ann
someone muttered, "Gloucester-by-the-Smell." But Manchester-by-

the-Sea stuck — only in certain quarters, to be sure — in spite of the jibes, showing that Mr. Fields knew how to pick a catchy title.

Fields was a child of four in Portsmouth, New Hampshire, when his father, an improvident shipmaster, died. Want stunted the boy's formal education but not his curiosity. He read everything he could lay his hands on and got a job clerking in Boston in William D. Ticknor's Old Corner Book Store at Washington and School streets. The rest is literary history. He rose to partnership and then to ownership of their publishing firm on the strength of his almost infallible judgment of America's tastes in reading in a day when America read. In the process Fields influenced those habits profoundly, as book publisher and as editor of the *Atlantic,* for his authors were Holmes and other members of Boston's Society for Mutual Admiration, tolerated outsiders like Mark Twain and Bret Harte, and the English Victorians whom he introduced to his countrymen. Most of his den loved their great, hearty tamer in his Scottish tweeds, with his shaggy beard and roaring laugh, "guardian and maintainer of us all," as Emerson called him. When Fields retired in 1871, Dr. Holmes expressed mock doubt that without his friend's praise and encouragement he would ever "write anything more worth mentioning."

In arriving at the North Shore, Fields and his beautiful and brilliant second wife, Annie, followed the trail broken by Richard Henry Dana, first to the Pigeon Cove House at Rockport, where they vacationed during the Civil War, then to Manchester, where they rented a cottage in 1865 and every summer until they bought Thunderbolt Hill in 1873.

The tireless travel writer Bayard Taylor looked in on them in August of 1875, the couple's first full season in their "quaint, old-fashioned residence," and was bowled over by the view of the coast and the ocean from the veranda. "We have but to turn our heads and we see the inlet, the village, the bluff, and swelling waves of forest, melting into distant grays and purples under a sky which (just now at least) is more English than American. [Was this the inspiration for "by-the-Sea"?] There is a perpetual breeze, with strength enough on its wings to refresh and not exhaust. The foliage is opulent and varied in color, the fields and meadows are exquisitely green, and there is a mixture of savage nature and laborious culture throughout the landscape which continually surprises us with the effects of contrasts."

In Boston James and Annie, seventeen years younger than he and very much of a literary and sociable figure in her own right, resided at 37 Charles Street, the foot of Beacon Hill, where a procession of international celebrities occupied their guest room. Dr. and Mrs. Holmes for some years lived a few doors off at number 21, and there was much passing back and forth. No great coincidence, then, that three years after Fields moved to "Manchester-by-the-Sea" for his first summer on Thunderbolt Hill, Holmes popped up at Beverly Farms, not much above two miles up the shore; on September 22, 1878, the doctor wrote James Russell Lowell, their cohort in the Saturday Club, who had been made Minister to Spain by President Hayes as reward for his political support: "We are at a small wayside house, where we make ourselves comfortable, my wife, my daughter, and myself, with books, walks, drives, and as much laziness as we can bring ourselves to, which is quite too little, for none of us has a real genius for the *far niente*. [*Dolce far niente,* sweet doing nothing, an expression then in vogue.] All round us are the most beautiful and expensive residences, some close to the sea beaches, some on heights farther back in the midst of the woods, some perched on the edge of precipices; one has a net spread out which she calls a baby-catcher, over the abyss, on the verge of which her piazza hangs shuddering. We go to most of these fine places once during the season. We see the fine equipages roll by (the constable does *not* take off his hat), and we carry as contented faces as most of them do."

A sometime neighbor of the Holmeses by-the-Dépot was the Beverly-born poetess Lucy Larcom, a large, good-humored, humorless maiden lady who had relinquished teaching for the wider didactic opportunities of publication. She padded out a sparse living with sentimental homilies and effusions on nature such as (from

*Wild Roses of Cape Ann*): "I never knew the world in white/So beautiful could be/As I have seen it here to-day/Beside the wintry sea" — verses, as one gentle biographer put it, "of the kind that pass with the generation to which they belong." Holmes wrote her after thumbing through a presentation copy of *Wild Roses* in 1880, "My wife and daughter were sitting opposite to me, and I had to shade my eyes with my hand that they should not see the tears shining in them." Whittier wrote Holmes that *Wild Roses* gave Larcom "a right to stand with the rest of us."

Time would have its toll — "as if an autumn wind were tearing away the last leaves all around me," the doctor lamented to Lowell. Richard Henry Dana, who led off the summer march to Manchester, died long beyond his time in 1879 at ninety-one. Fields died in 1881; his widow and the Maine storyteller Sarah Orne Jewett became almost inseparable companions, traveling abroad, wintering at the Charles Street salon carried on by Annie, summering on Thunderbolt Hill. In 1882 Emerson and Longfellow died, and Dr. Holmes retired from guiding generations of Harvard medical students through the twists and tunnels of the mortal coil. About this time he pulled out of his cottage by-the-Dépot and rented one recently built by the Marshall family on Hale Street within sound of the surf on West Beach.

In the spring of 1884 roistering, rotund old Tom Appleton died, and the blows redoubled. That summer Holmes lost his younger son, Edward, then his wife, Amelia, in 1888; and the next year, his eightieth, his daughter, Amelia Sargent. Stoically, the old man surrendered himself to the care of his surviving son, then a justice of the Massachusetts Supreme Court, and his daughter-in-law Fanny.

In his last years Oliver Wendell Holmes was without rival the most famous figure on the North Shore, and because his birthday fell on the twenty-ninth of August, when he was invariably in their midst, everyone made much of it, to his great satisfaction.

Flowers and fruit from far and wide were heaped within the cottage. The postman groaned under the weight of letters and telegrams. Adulatory poems were addressed to the celebrant, and loving cups were inscribed. The newspapers sent reporters, the summer people called, the neighbors came by, and each year the schoolchil-dren of Beverly Farms — scrubbed and dressed in their holiday best — were admitted en masse by Judge Holmes and Fanny to recite their greetings and then ushered out, each with a souvenir of the occasion. His nephew and biographer, the Boston historian John T. Morse, Jr., summered nearby at Pride's Crossing and observed how these fetes took more out of the old gentleman every year, "but his courteous soul would not permit him to say 'not at home' to any one who showed to him the kindness of calling. Then, for days after-wards, he struggled to make due acknowledgment for all the tokens sent to him, sometimes trying to write briefly, and always insisting upon at least signing whatever had been written by his secretary after his own tired eyes had given out."

The Autocrat of the Breakfast Table had to be centerstage himself too much to play with any consistency the passive role of theater-goer. Soon after his retirement, though, Dr. Holmes was drawn under the marquee of the incomparably elegant Boston Theatre, which filled the block between Washington and Mason streets and seated 3,140, by the twin billing of the great English players, Ellen Terry and Henry Irving. The Goldsmith of Boston made his way backstage, "and while I was talking with them a very heavy piece of scenery came crashing down, and filled the whole place with dust. It was but a short distance from where we were standing, and I could not help thinking how near our several life-dramas came to a simul-taneous *exeunt omnes.*"

Well-nigh all the brightest stars of their day transited the prosce-nium of the Boston Theatre, and when one chanced to be pulled slightly out of orbit one summer by the attraction of Manchester's heavenly shore by-the-sea, others followed, in the clustering manner of stellar bodies, until every summer a galaxy of them was heaving into view across the coast, pausing for the season, and passing on over the autumnal horizon, as reported in the New York *Dramatic News:* "Hidden snugly among the pine woods and granite rocks of the Eastern shore of Massachusetts is a romantic spot beloved by many members of the profession, a quiet retreat to where they can hide and dream away the summer months in *dolce far niente*. It is currently reported that this Lotus-land was discovered by the eminent tragedian, Joseph Proctor, who with his characteristic unselfishness introduced other actors to the scene, until regularly, every off season, there came a full company to the Old Neck, transforming what had been an unprofitable tract of stony property, into valuable estates, and, in ten years doing for the spot what its regular inhabitants would not have accomplished in a century."

Joseph Proctor was a lofty presence in the romantic theatre. He specialized in Shakespearean heavies and had mouthed, snarled, growled, threatened, roared, wept and expired his way all over America and Britain since emerging from the country town of Marlboro at seventeen to debut in Boston, ever after his home base. Some measure of his polemic ability was his frequent appearance as the tattered and wild-eyed "Jibbenainosay" in *Nick of the Woods,* a ridiculously melodramatic role which he was able to lift to the verge, at least, of tragedy. Like many another actor, Proctor wed an actress, and after she died, married another, Elizabeth Wakeman, who sometimes played supporting roles with him onstage as well as off.

In 1864 the Jibbenainosay was forty-eight and a sure box-office draw when he bought the snug, colonial Sally Samples House on Sea Street, at the tip of a finger of Manchester Harbor, for a summer place.

Why Manchester? In 1856, two years after the Boston Theatre was built, Joseph Proctor made his first appearance there, filling in on the off-nights of the opera with a repertoire of tragic roles. The theatre went broke in the financial panic of 1857. One of its reorganizers the next year was the Boston real estate man Benjamin W. Thayer. In 1864 Thayer acquired part control, and he and Proctor acquired their summer cottages at Manchester a quarter of a mile apart. Thayer's Old Neck Road neighbor on his other side, almost to Eagle Head, was Samuel H. Bullard, who had built the previous year; he too was an incorporator of the Boston Theatre. The plot was thickening.

*Enter* Junius Brutus Booth.

On April 14, 1865, five days after Robert E. Lee handed his sword and his beaten army to Ulysses S. Grant, John Wilkes Booth — considered by some critics the most brilliant, and certainly the most erratic, of America's most erratically brilliant family of actors — shot Abraham Lincoln in the President's box at Ford's Theatre in Washington. John and his older brothers, Edwin and Junius, had last acted together in *Julius Caesar* at the Winter Garden in New York the previous November. Ned and June had argued violently with Johnnie over his fervor for the Southern cause and his raging hatred of the President, whom at that moment — if they had only known — he was plotting to abduct.

Edwin Booth was playing at the Boston Theatre when he heard the news of John's latest aberration. Junius, the eldest and the spitting image of their late glowering, heavyset actor-father of the same name, was playing in Cincinnati. A mob stormed his hotel. He was smuggled out and sheltered by friends, made his way to Philadelphia, and on April 26 was arrested by federal agents who suspected him (by erroneous interpretation, as they later learned, of a letter he had written his deranged brother) of complicity. Aboard the train to Washington and prison, Junius told his guard: "I wish John had been killed before the assassination, for the sake of his family." That peacetime summer was the worst in a lifetime of nightmares for the Booths, bad scenes such as an evening years before when a crazed, drunken actor had rushed at James Wallack, a rival, and Thomas Handasyd Perkins, Jr., with a knife as they emerged from a Boston theatre. Shortarm Tom was wounded but knocked Wallack's would-be assassin to the ground. He turned out to be Junius Brutus Booth, Sr., the *pater familias*.

James and Annie Fields spent the bittersweet summer of 1865 by the sea discovering Manchester. Three years earlier they too had had a brief experience of the Booths. Next to literature the publisher was most addicted to the theatre and had accepted with delight the invitation of Mrs. Julia Ward Howe to her after-the-show reception for Edwin, a rising Shakespearean tragedian, and his wife, Mary Devlin, whom he had met when they were playing at the Boston Theatre in 1857. Beacon Hill was there at Mrs. Howe's, and Mary observed in her fiercely protective way how curious and condescending everyone seemed to be, and none more so than Mr. Fields — or so she imagined. But Fields was notoriously shy on first meeting, and a day or so later he called on the Booths. Edwin made up an excuse not to see him. "And the cad," Mary fumed to a friend in vehement *nonsequitur,* "returned with a request to see them at their home tonight: a regret is already written. How I hate such hypocrisy! They don't care for us."

Edwin fled into anguished seclusion after the assassination, but 1866 found him back in Boston with his sister Asia's actor-husband, John S. Clarke, leasing the Boston Theatre from Benjamin Thayer and his partner, Orlando Tompkins. Never the passionate soul that his brother was, but a competent actor and the steadiest head in the family, Junius was forty-five and had been several months out of jail; he joined Ned and Clarke in Boston as acting and stage manager. One of the female leads in the company was Agnes Perry, daughter of a British army officer and a pretty, robust and versatile actress from San Francisco. She was three years widowed after two sublimely happy years of marriage to a handsome young actor, Harry Perry.

Junius fell for Agnes. Within a year his brother and brother-in-law turned over the lease and management of the Boston Theatre to him. He married the girl and was feeling flush enough besides to buy a piece of land above Old Neck Beach in Manchester from Ben Thayer, co-owner of the theatre; in 1869 they built a cottage on it.

The new Mrs. Booth was twenty-five years younger than her husband and younger by three than his oldest daughter by his first wife. The elder Junius had set the example by running out on his family in England when he came to the United States to seek his fortune behind the footlights and could not marry the mother of his numerous American children until his first wife back in England finally gave him a divorce in 1851. The accompanying scandal so shook up the younger Junius that a month after it broke in public he ditched his own first wife, Clementine De Bar, an actress eleven years older than he, and their daughter Blanche, and sailed for California with a Boston actress named Harriet Mace. There they lived, on and off

*Dr. Oliver Wendell Holmes poses in his favorite rock seat at Beverly Farms on September 9, 1894, a few days after his eighty-fifth birthday and a month before his death. Boston Medical Library in the Francis A. Countway Library of Medicine*

*The Holmes cottage, Beverly Farms. The Autocrat's outdoor throne nestles in the ledge at left. Essex Institute*

*James T. Fields, Nathaniel Hawthorne, and the author's close friend and publishing partner of Fields, William D. Ticknor. Essex Institute*

*The actress sisters, Mrs. Bowers and Mrs. Conway. From History of the Boston Theatre*

*Manchester's Theatre Lane appears more a skyway in portion of a panorama from the Congregational church steeple, about 1876. Joseph Proctor's house is behind trees at left; Fred Conway's massive place dominates Ocean Hill; that of his sister-in-law, Mrs. Bowers, is lower and immediately to its right; then the Fieldses' "Thunderbolt Hill" squarely on the ledge; finally, at far right, the Booths' cottage just before they added on the Masconomo. Procter Brothers, Howard collection*

*John Wilkes Booth as Mark Anthony, Edwin Booth as Brutus and Junius Brutus Booth, Jr., as Cassius in* Julius Caesar *at the Winter Garden, New York, November 25, 1864. Harvard Theatre Collection*

*Agnes Perry.* History of the Boston Theatre

*A summer day on Day's Creek, Manchester, early 1880s. The Masconomo House looms at the end of Beach Street. Estate of Alfred C. Needham*

the stage, in what proper people called sin (though Clementine divorced him in 1855), until Hattie's death during the Civil War, when Junius returned east with their daughter Marion, and events propelled the family into a vortex of tragedy such as none had ever mimed before an audience.

*Enter* John Gibbs Gilbert.

Old men were the forte of this polished Bostonian, one of the top comic artists of his day, which was a long one, for he played 1,150 lifetime roles, rolling the customers in the aisles of Wallack's Theatre in New York from the day it opened in 1862 until it closed in 1888, the year before his own final curtain dropped when he was seventy-nine. Gilbert uttered the first words spoken publicly on the stage of the Boston Theatre, the dedicatory poem at the opening on September 11, 1854, then turned around and walked back on as Sir Anthony Absolute, one of his virtuoso roles, with his actress wife, Maria, in Sheridan's *The Rivals*. The couple reappeared periodically until Maria's death in 1866. Rather reserved and solemn offstage, Gilbert remarried and in 1868 bought a summer cottage on Old Neck Road between Bullard and Thayer, whose fine hand may be suspected in the deal.

*Enter* Mr. and Mrs. Frederick B. Conway.

Conway was English, and though a familiar figure on tour in America was one of the few on the circuit who had never appeared at the Boston Theatre when he and his better-known second wife, an actress, bought land on Ocean Hill above Sea Street in 1868, next to Joseph Proctor. A year later they moved into their summer mansion, which "rises up prominently from a kind of central eminence, forms a striking picture in the landscape, and seen either from the bay, or distant hills, it awakens admiration and reflects much honor on the genius of the builder." (The new house of Conway's neighbor Booth seemed to the same observer less imposing, though striking enough — "the stars and stripes are floating over it and a cordial welcome is extended by himself and his accomplished lady to visitors.")

Fred Conway was a competent actor, who in later life did not exert himself much beyond sentimental Irish roles and the like. In 1852 he married the daughter of a Methodist minister, Sarah Crocker; she and her sister Elizabeth had escaped from their Connecticut cloister and taken up with the naughty world of the professional theatre. The Conways toured the circuits together until 1864, when, like many other actors hungering for a larger bite of the box office, they leased the Park Theatre in Brooklyn and put their own name on the marquee. As many actors did not, however, they made a success of it, playing to the popular madness for melodrama and romance, appearing on most of the bills together and debuting their daughters, Lillian and Minnie.

In Conway, who was a large man, what struck one critic as pomposity impressed another as burlesque. One summer day in 1870, as a newspaper correspondent reported with great relish, Mr. Conway was at Manchester "in a dory with his son and servant off some distance from the shore, when suddenly the boat was upset and over they went into the 'vasty deep.' The boat came up, but Mr. C., immense in weight, was floundering about — as I had the story — like a whale harpooned and hampered, 'swilled with wild and wasteful ocean.' He 'blew' at last — the actor was the father here — and out of the engulfing brine the gurgling cry came up from the cave of Aeolus: 'Save the boys, the boys; I'll shift it for myself!' The boat took up the boys — the father would have swamped it in an instant — and he had the presence of mind to see it. So resting his right hand on the bow, he was towed, still floundering through the water like a captured whale, or huge leviathan, in safety to the shore, and amid the acclamations of the audience the curtain fell. Mr. C. is, by the by, very much of a gentleman, and highly respected by the citizens of Manchester."

Two years after Fred's death, in the evening of December 5, 1876, fire broke out backstage during a crowded performance in Conway's Theatre, and 297 people suffocated or were trampled or burned to death trying to get out.

*Enter* Mrs. D. P. Bowers.

Elizabeth Crocker, that other daring daughter of the Reverend

Mr. Crocker, married David P. Bowers, a Philadelphia actor, in 1847 when she was seventeen; he died in ten years, but not before she was well launched on the stage as a popular actress with pretty eyes and, so said a critic, "a voice of fascinating sweetness, a refined manner and a cultivated mind." In 1866 she played Romeo to her sister's Juliet at the Winter Garden; three more years, and they switched roles at the Boston Theatre. Having surely paid many an off-season visit on her quite as handsome sister and her "leviathan" of a brother-in-law (her second husband, a chemist, died in 1867), Mrs. Bowers bought a cottage a few rods down Old Neck Road from the Conways in 1873 and so completed the already famous actors' summer colony of Manchester known by then as "Theatre Lane."

Junius Brutus Booth, in the meantime, had become involved in North Shore summer property speculation, joining with Thayer and Tompkins and the English actor E. A. Sothern, among others, as already noted, in forming a land company to purchase Marblehead Neck for $250,000 in January 1872. Edwin had built the lavish Booth's Theatre in New York in 1868 (Mrs. Bowers played Lady Macbeth to his Macbeth there) but ran into such financial problems that at last, early in 1873, Junius agreed to give up the management of the Boston Theatre (the company staged a farewell benefit for Agnes on May 10) and to take on his brother's opulent white elephant in order to free the Prince of Players for the road, where the real money was. Then all were engulfed in the panic, and in January 1874 Edwin Booth was forced into bankruptcy.

Junius must not have made out so badly while all about him were excursions and alarums, because in the spring of 1877 (the Marblehead Great Neck Land Company even then was on the brink of foreclosure) he embarked in his own spectacular fashion on the summer hotel business in Manchester. And since he proposed to tack an enormous dog on the tail of the cottage he and Agnes had occupied for eight years in the heart of the summer colony, the reaction of their neighbors was mixed. (As one observer said, all such ventures had hitherto been held at bay by Manchester "with a view to keeping the society somewhat select.")

Edwin had settled in Boston on Beacon Hill and wrote a friend
that "June is building a hotel at Manchester — sits still — smokes
and bewails his hard lot. Aggy *jobs* and looks as though her hair dye
had affected her health." In other words, Agnes was doing acting
stints to help with the mortgage. Their inspiration in this hotel-
building (a form of showmanship, at that) may be inferred from
the observation in the New York *Dramatic News* that summer
that the Manchester colony had entertained "almost every actress
and actor of note, many of whom would have been delighted to purchase summer residences in this earthly paradise, but, as usual, no
sooner was it known to the world, than every foot of land was
bought up, and Manchester has become a select seashore resort for
a number of wealthy persons and a few artists and literary
men. . . ."

The Masconomo House, invoking the name of the last sagamore
of the Agawams, which Black Ben Forbes had applied to his estate a
score of years before, opened for the season of 1878. Some tongue-
tied wag said that one guest who tried to pronounce it "died the
following day of complications resulting from lockjaw." Presiding
over twelve acres of lawn that rolled sedately down to Old Neck
Beach, the Booths' greatest production extended 240 feet from their
cottage and contained 106 rooms. At four corners of an octagonal
hall in the center were four mammoth fireplaces "that glow merrily
with their great log fires on cold and stormy days." Above the roof
the chimneys bounded an eight-sided observatory. The North Shore
guidebook first published by Hill and Nevins in 1879 called the
Masconomo "a good facsimile of some of those charming hostelries
to be seen around the shores of the Swiss lakes among the Alps, the
best hotels in Europe."

June's and Aggy's bowling alleys and billiard tables were joined
by tennis courts, then by bathhouses above the high water mark of
Old Neck Beach, whose sands beguiled the ear with a strange music,
described by one who walked there: "As you step briskly over it, a
distinct and somewhat clear, shrill note is heard, which seems to be
upon the key of C of the treble scale. By scraping or shuffling the

foot over the sand, the tone may be prolonged; and it is loudest, I have noticed, when the sand is dryest." The early summer people who found the geographical nomenclature of the settlers too brusque for their romantic sensibilities changed Old Neck Beach to Musical Beach, which evolved, with the appearance of the Masconomo on the scene, into Singing Beach. Various explanations have been advanced for the music of the sands — "some wise," in the words of a local historian, "and some otherwise."

Overnight the Masconomo was a hit. Of course it was, for how could it have flopped in such a setting, with such a management, such a company and such guest stars?

Junius Brutus Booth died in 1883 after only five flush seasons of his final extravaganza and was elaborately interred in Manchester. Mrs. Bowers's second husband had joined her first by then, and later that year she took her third, her occasional leading man of long but lesser standing, James C. McCollum. In 1885 Aggy Booth married her third, John B. Schoeffel, owner of the Tremont Theatre in Boston.

Under the Schoeffels the Masconomo House kept right on flourishing. They knew how to put on a show, all right. One summer night in 1886 it was *A Midsummer Night's Dream,* outdoors under the stars as it should be. Special trains steamed into the Manchester depot from Boston, and by early afternoon the audience was streaming onto the grounds. That evening, before an enthralled throng on the great lawn that rolled down to the musical beach and the twinkling sea, Shakespeare cast his spell under the glare and glow of the novel electric lights, Chinese lanterns and a score of locomotive headlamps, all to the swelling sounds of a full orchestra and chorus above the murmur of the surf.

By the dawn of the nineties those romantic, bombastic, melodramatic, comic, and tragic players on Manchester's charming Theatre Lane were in the wings or in their graves.

*Exeunt omnes.*

# 16

# The Gold Coast

THE MAIN BODY OF THE INVADING LAND-GRABBERS FROM THE CITY WHO
had captured the Beverly shore before the Civil War did not reach
more distant Manchester until after the restoration of peace, when
they struck on the crest of the brief postwar boom. Poet, publisher
and player publicized the pleasant potential of the resort, but with
land values on the verge of explosion, it was the perspicacious and
the powerful who populated it.

Down from Boston came Greely Curtis in 1868 to buy the headland just east of Dana's Beach. He called the mansion he built
"Sharksmouth," because the outline of his shore looked like one on
the map. Curtis was married to Tom Appleton's sister Hattie
(Longfellow to another sister, Fannie). He had been an undistin-
guished general in the war. Driving by, Bayard Taylor was impressed with his "castle by the sea, built of gray stone, and of a very
original design, an Italian *loggia* being combined with Norman-
Gothic features. . . . Around it the roughness of the native pine
forest has been softened in the most admirable manner, turf borders
melting naturally into huckleberry thickets, and geraniums growing
amicably in the midst of ferns."

Close on the spurs of General Curtis trod John Henry Towne, a
wealthy Philadelphia industrial engineer; in 1869 Towne bought
Eagle Head, formerly Old Neck, at the tip end of the actors' colony,
"Theatre Lane," from John Murray Forbes, built a summer man-

sion above the surf and put together an estate of seventy-five acres before dying in Paris six years later. Both Towne and Forbes had wrestled with the prewar problems of railroad financing and construction. During the war Forbes had much influence on its naval conduct, and Towne made the engines for several Union vessels, including the ironclad *Monitor*. At about the time he acquired Eagle Head he set up his son Henry in partnership with Linus Yale in the manufacture of Yale's patented locks. After the elder Towne's death the University of Pennsylvania created the Towne Scientific School for engineering studies as a mark of his benefactions.

John Henry Towne's daughter, Mrs. Alice Towne Lincoln, started a campaign among Manchester and Beverly summer residents in 1879 to raise the money to acquire a strip of land on either side of the country road through the thick "Essex Woods" from Manchester to Essex. Between purchases and gifts most of this road came under public protection, and with Essex and Western avenues was adopted as the third leg of the "Big Heater," a popular pleasure drive connecting Manchester, Essex and the Blynman Canal at Gloucester, resembling on the map a triangular horse-drawn snowplow, a "heater" — or, as some held, a flatiron.

The fast-pedaling author of the bicyclist's guidebook *In and Around Cape Ann*, John S. Webber, Jr., was exploring Theatre Lane one summer day a few years after Towne's death and found himself wheeling toward Eagle Head, where "we soon enter the private grounds of Mrs. J. H. Towne of Philadelphia and continue over the well kept avenue to the turn-off, where a politely worded sign-board tells us that 'Strangers are requested to turn here,'" which he did. Mrs. Towne died in 1892, and in three years Eagle Head was sold to James McMillan, the rich and powerful senator from Michigan, for upwards of $200,000, they said.

It applied almost as well, at least in the case of Manchester, that, as the psalmist sang, *the meek shall inherit the earth.* And meek, on first appearance, was Cyrus Augustus Bartol, the third of the strangers to invest heavily in the Manchester coast after the Civil War.

Diminutive and delicate, elfish even, whimsical, learned and literary, Dr. Bartol was the Unitarian pastor of the old West Church on Cambridge Street in Boston. Up until around 1870 his flock had supposed him to be preoccupied with the transcendentalist abstractions of the Emersonians, of whom he was a leading spirit. Under this impression, someone — probably a parishioner — remonstrated with him for sinking his spare dollars into shoreline down at Manchester when he should be stashing them in a sound Boston bank where they belonged, like the prudent but impractical man everyone knew him to be.

"Ah, my friend," the shepherd is said to have responded, with a knowing shake of his snow-white locks, "you and a lot of other folks seem to forget that the Lord Almighty has stopped making sea coast."

*His* Maker, however, had not forgotten His servant. Quite possibly getting his tips from on high, Dr. Bartol took his baptismal plunge in 1870 at the age of fifty-four when he bought for a modest sum the long stretch of magnificent shore in West Manchester called the Glass Head Pasture. The seller was Lewis N. Tappan, a native who was considered an especially astute real estate man.

On the choicest elevation of Glass Head Dr. Bartol built his mansion, and on a nearby bump the natives proudly called The Mountain, his observatory and study. When the spirit took hold of him he would ascend to the summit of his Sinai by a spiral staircase and through a trapdoor in the floor, which he was wont to shut after him and sit upon in his easy chair so as not to be disturbed as he contemplated his earthly domain and how a man of God should be so mysteriously blessed with the best of both worlds. When, in another twenty-five years, Dr. Bartol did move on to the next, his daughter sold Glass Head to Gordon Abbott, president of the Old Colony Trust Company in Boston, reportedly for $135,000.

While he was overseeing the construction of his manse in 1871, Dr. Bartol looked out across the water and sighed for what he saw (it was not his nature to *covet*) — the seventy-five acres of the Great Pasture, that is, most of Smith's Point, which provides Manchester its harbor. The tract was, in the words of a New York journalist, "dotted with juniper and barberry, gay with wild roses and golden-rod, an immense green pasture of hill and dell lying open to the ocean, whose cliffs are its utmost bounds."

The minister of the West Church "with childlike simplicity saw the best in every man," wrote a biographer, "and the world was to him a temple of the living God in which it was good to dwell." And so Dr. Bartol gladly paid the $600 an acre that Williston Smith was asking for the family's seventy-five on Smith's Point and laid out a road; before long he was sharing his new corner of the temple with converts eager for niches at from ten to twelve thousand apiece. For good measure he picked up House Island, half a mile offshore. In 1872 he recrossed the harbor and gave David Leach $1,225 for Norton's Point, inside Tuck's Point (which he bought too) on the western shore, rocky and barren of all but a gnarled cedar standing near the tide. As the opportunity presented, he added to these holdings.

This was the bread that Cyrus Augustus Bartol cast upon the bay. Years later, when it had come back to him ten- and a hundredfold, he surveyed the results for which he was chiefly responsible and pronounced in benedictory tones that "Manchester has become in our day a splendid watering place, known as such throughout the United States; so she finds gold eagles stitched into her dress" — and into the clerical cloth. An unlikely colossus, Dr. Bartol — and yet, there he stood astride the entrance to Manchester Harbor in 1872, one foot firmly fixed on Glass Head, the other on Smith's Point.

Chiseled more from the classical stone were Augustus Hemenway and Thomas Jefferson Coolidge, two titans of Boston finance, who the same year descended on the prime remaining seacoast unbought by the pastor. Hemenway picked up Pickworth Point, the smaller jut of pasture-crowned ledge east of Smith's Point, but he had short use of the house he built above Bellyache Cove, for he died four years later.

Coolidge, on the other hand and at the other end of town, lopped off the old Goldsmith Farm that occupied the whole of the kettle-shaped peninsula east of kettle-like Kettle Cove and behind Kettle

Island, which does not resemble a kettle at all but was named after a family of Kettles. Old man Gifford Goldsmith was an original; he grew tobacco and claimed the sun circled the earth, figuring from the length of the shadow of his cane that it was only 3,000 miles away.

In the mansion he built on "Coolidge Point," the textile-banking-railroad capitalist spent most of his remaining forty-eight summers until his death in 1920 at eighty-nine. T. J. was old Boston through and through. After Harvard, he set his cap for money and a daughter of William Appleton and got both. He was as honest, they said, as he was shrewd, which makes a hard bargainer. In later life, after he had his pile, Coolidge served Harvard and country as overseer and minister to France. His gift to Manchester of its public library (he would not have his name over the door) was in hopeful, if partial, retreat from the political creed of his youth, a creed that would have grieved his Great-grandfather Jefferson: "I believed myself to belong to a superior class, and that the principle that the ignorant and poor should have the same right to make laws and govern as the educated and refined was an absurdity." The Coolidge purchase in the lee of Kettle Island, as the Louisiana Purchase had been for his farsighted ancestor, proved to be one of his characteristically sagacious deals and has remained essentially intact in his family ever since.

The doldrums in the wake of the financial storms of 1873 took some of the wind out of luxury land sales, and it was four years before Cyrus Bartol's initial subdivision of Smith's Point produced any summer cottages. The first of these, built while the Booths were adding the 240-foot ell to their place farther back on the road in 1877, were J. Warren Merrill's on the hill above Lobster Cove, jokingly dubbed "The Extinguisher House" by his neighbors in reference to his tower, and E. E. Rice's on the harbor shore above Long Beach.

Dr. Bartol's third buyer, as clever an actor as any on Theatre Lane, was "Professor" Orson Squire Fowler, who in 1878 built on the Point of Rocks at the north end of Long Beach. Fowler was then

*Smith's Point from Gales Rocks, 1880s. Mrs. William S. Fraser*

*Cyrus Augustus Bartol.*
*Essex Institute*

*Dr. Bartol's cottage and observatory at Glass Head, West Manchester. From a private collection*

*Group on the porch of the Haven cottage above West Beach at Beverly Farms around 1870 includes, right to left, Salmon P. Chase, Chief Justice of the United States Supreme Court and Lincoln's Secretary of the Treasury during the Civil War; Franklin Haven, president of the Merchants Bank of Boston, an early summer settler; the Reverend Mr. Lothrop; Mrs. Haven; Mrs. Rantoul at window (probably Harriet, a neighbor); Nettie Chase; Mary Haven; Nellie Haven, at window. This was the Havens' third cottage, the previous two having burned. Beverly Historical Society*

*The Beverly Farms Coach on Summer Street, Manchester, around 1890. Manchester Historical Society*

*Manchester Harbor in a glassy calm, looking out, 1880s. Essex Institute*

*The mysteries of photography had given way to good amateurs, and formal poses to holiday antics, when H. W. Belknap, curator of the Essex Institute, snapped this picture in West Manchester on Decoration Day, 1888. Belknap Album, Essex Institute*

*Greely Curtis's "Sharksmouth," built in 1868 above the east end of Dana's Beach —*
*forerunner of splendor to come. Manchester Historical Society*

*Belknap's family and friends in West Manchester on the Fourth of July, 1888.*
*Belknap Album, Essex Institute*

*Chowder House at Tuck's Point, Manchester, 1880s, showing "Fort House" on Norton's Point, designed by Arthur Little, at right. Manchester Historical Society*

*Coolidge Point from the Magnolia steamer landing, June 1890. The mansion of T. Jefferson Coolidge is at the extreme left. Manchester Public Library*

sixty-nine and at the peak of his fame and fortune as a practitioner of phrenology and what he termed "physiology," by means of which, he claimed to believe, every problem known to man could be solved. No professor (though an Amherst College graduate), "Doctor" Fowler lectured everywhere to audiences only too willing to believe, and published a prodigious mélange of pseudoscientific mishmash such as two volumes which went to forty editions, extending *Important Directions and Suggestions to Lovers and the Married,* and advice on *Amativeness: or, Evils and Remedies of Excessive and Perverted Sexuality.* He was married three times, and after he was seventy he fathered three children, so it may be unjust to state, as one unsympathetic biographer has, that only Orson Fowler's conceit saved him from deliberate charlatanism. At all events he was acceptable enough to Dr. Bartol and Manchester.

The professor had published *A Home for All; or, the Gravel Wall, and Octagon Mode of Building* in 1849. The book started a fad in eight-sided houses and earned for its author a footnote in the annals of architecture by advancing the octagonal as cheaper than the conventional, easier to heat and illuminate, space-saving and step-saving. The fad died out with the Civil War, and his Manchester cottage (since torn down) looked more logical than phrenological.

As late as 1879 Hill and Nevins could get away with suggesting in their guidebook to the North Shore that since few of the estates between Pride's Crossing (where the venerable station agent was an unreluctant spout of information) and Beverly Farms could be seen from the train, the tourist should get off at the first depot, proceed on foot or otherwise and resume his ride at the next. "These 'mansions by the sea,'" they advised, "are surrounded by extensive natural forests, meadows, fields, lawns, and flower gardens interspersed with ponds, streams, carriage roads, bridle paths and footpaths. . . . These private grounds . . . and the roads through them are mostly open to the public in summer, and a drive or walk through them should not be omitted. But in doing so the visitor should bear in mind that the least recompense he can make for so much pleasure is to conduct himself decorously and not stray from the beaten paths picking flowers, trampling the lawns, or breaking the limbs of tree and shrubbery. He ought at least to be as considerate as his English cousins who, year after year, travel through the broad acres of the 'Lord' without ever stepping to one side or the other, thankful that his more favored fellow being shares with him thus much."

Unhappily for the Lords of the Shore, base ingratitude toward the more favored fellow was growing into the curse of the eighties in America. The Western farmers were rising up against the Eastern "interests," the Knights of Labor were breaking their lances upon the walls of capitalism, and, worst of all, the Democrats were running things.

As for the North Shore, those conveyers of the masses from the ovens of the city to the seaside, the horsecars, had already been insinuated into Swampscott and Marblehead like so many quadrupeds of Troy, raising the threat of conquest by a fifth column on tracks so feared by Ben Ware and other anxious shore-owners in their hapless attempt of 1885 to carve out a new town from the contiguous villages of each.

In March of 1885, even as the cries of "B-Ware!" were being raised in the streets of Marblehead and Swampscott, the Naumkeag Street Railway proposed to extend its horsecars from Beverly Center to Pride's Crossing and Beverly Farms. "A mere entering wedge!" expostulated Thornton K. Lothrop, retired lawyer and summer resident. If the cars came, he warned, "a great many of Beverly's citizens would avail themselves of a fine ride and visit the beaches and drives," and the value of shore property would go all to hell. Let us control our own destiny, said he, by getting incorporated as a separate town.

Lothrop persuaded his Pride's neighbor, John T. Morse, Jr. (Dr. Holmes's nephew), that disaster impended. The two were among some ten out of the seventy summer residents of the Farms and Pride's Crossing who paid their general property taxes in Beverly, which entitled them to vote locally. The natives were willing enough to go along with the promised prospect of lower taxes, and many of them, having bartered their birthrights to the Lords, were now by way of being their lieges in any event. A petition was got up; a bill for the incorporation of Beverly Farms was filed in the General Court, and in due course it was rejected in March of 1886 (not for the first time; back in 1717 the Farms, on account of some now-forgotten gripe with Beverly, had tried without avail to unite with Manchester).

John I. Baker, chairman of the Beverly selectmen, veteran local politician and business leader, a patriarch long of beard and sharp of wit, cut the ground out from under the Boston lawyers. Regard the summer people, he declaimed to a committee of the legislature (where he had served as state representative for eighteen years), driving their fancy turnouts over town roads and running town water from their taps (as a matter of fact, summer taxes made possible the public water supply, the library, the extension of roads, and better schools, police and fire service) — look at them, and now they propose to pull out and throw the whole tax burden on the rest of us!

Furthermore, argued Selectman Baker (and here is where he cut the ice with his old cohorts in the legislature), these fellows are nothing but Boston tax-dodgers, whose real aim is to set up their own private summer colony as a tax haven, and unless the legislature stops them short, the epidemic of evasion for the benefit of the rich and privileged that started at Nahant will infect the entire North Shore!

Not for nothing did they call John Baker "King of Beverly." As long as King Baker reigned, the Lords of the Shore would wrest no Magna Carta from *his* realm.

In retaliation against the defeated summer secessionists, the Beverly assessors raised valuations wholesale along the shore, uncovering in the process nearly two million dollars concealed in paper assets, including $900,000 of Lothrop's. Their draconian sweep naturally caused the residents of the Farms and Pride's Crossing, summer and year-round — "the first-rate, native, old-fashioned

Yankee population" to whom John Morse appealed — to rise up almost to a soul in righteous wrath.

A Farms committee (with Lothrop and Morse keeping a low profile this time) went to work on the legislature in an extraordinary lobbying campaign financed with a slush fund of $18,000 raised by a Boston-based committee of summer people. Charges and countercharges flew thick as snowflakes during the winter of 1886, and the Beverly separation issue threatened to blow the dome off the State House. The Beverly Farms–Beacon Street axis put the pressure on the state government, which the Republicans had always presumed to be their private preserve, and John Baker countered with his damnedest.

But King Baker had long since split with the Republicans over the temperance issue; he had run twice as the Prohibitionist candidate for governor. And the most the forces of union could raise for lobbying and sundry purposes was $3,500; that did not go very far when you were up against division lobbyists who buttonholed House members to "bet" them $200 that they would vote against division. That spring of 1887 a thoroughly cozened legislature bestowed its tentative blessing on this second, ferociously fierce, campaign to keep the horsecars off Hale Street.

There was a most terrible stink. Traffic in votes was charged. Committees of both branches held hearings, condemned corruption but released no evidence, if they found it. The votes held firm, and the division bill was finally passed over the objections of no less a figure than U.S. Senator George Frisbie Hoar, the Republican leader of the state, and sent to Governor Oliver Ames.

The governor's blood was as blue as any that coursed through the veins of the separationists, and he was in their camp, but it was all too much; his friends had gone too far; the reputation of the party (and the outcome of the next election) was at stake. He vetoed the bill to incorporate Beverly Farms, declaring that to sign it would be "to excuse and encourage a monstrously bad and corrupt practice" that had endangered the legislature's reputation of two hundred years for honesty and probity.

Governor Ames's veto was sustained. The Beverly assessors relented and passed around some downward revaluations in the right places. And of course the charges of tax-dodging, and the well-publicized slush fund and the scandalous lobbying were an awful embarrassment to the summer residents of the Gold Coast, who were mightily relieved to be out at last of an adventure upon which they had embarked, as John Morse sighed, "with scant foresight."

Beverly was never quite the same after its civil war. The cynical and roughshod tactics of the rich men from Boston failed to split the town on any map, but they succeeded in drawing class lines where before few on either side were disposed to bear witness to their existence. "Nobody can bring back the beautiful fields, stretching from the woods to the sea, where cows and oxen grazed," grieved Mary Larcom Dow years later. The old schoolmistress could not conceal her bitterness over the transformation of the Farms — "nobody can bring back the roadsides bordered with wild roses. . . ."

At Manchester, which was not involved except by empathy, the lines were also drawn, as indeed they were being drawn across the land. On his estate near Lobster Cove, in 1880, Russell Sturgis built Emmanuel Church, a half-timbered Protestant Episcopal chapel, for his summer neighbors. The Reverend D. F. Lamson, who had been called up from Hartford as pastor of King Baker's Baptist church and later was commissioned to write Manchester's history, described this more or less friendly rival as "a churchly little building, with lych-gate, mantling ivy and 'storied windows richly dight,'" which during the summer season "receives within its walls more wealth and fashion and culture than are often found in churches of much larger size and greater pretensions. It is viewed, however, rather as an exotic by some of the permanent residents." Of his own parish Mr. Lamson said only that "it has never been a strong one in numbers or in wealth."

Looking about him as his adopted town entered the final decade of the century, Lamson came to the conclusion that as a noted resort Manchester "has lost much of its individuality, greatly to the regret of its older inhabitants who remember it as a place which had life in itself. . . . From the first Richard H. Dana . . . to the latest representative of the new aristocracy, from senator, ex-governor and minister plenipotentiary to champion golf player and imported flunkey, from 'tally-ho' to donkey cart, from Russian wolf-hound to my lady's lap-dog — an influence more or less perceptible, but often indefinable, has been exerted upon the town by its summer population. It has furnished a new social problem.

"[This] will be considered by some the period of the town's prosperity and glory, and by some the period of its decline and decay. It must be left to some future historian fully to tell the story, and to strike the balance between the advantages and disadvantages of a modern summer resort."

# 17

# The Shingled Shore

EVERY KIND OF "COTTAGE" WAS TO BE ENCOUNTERED ALONG THE NORTH Shore in the 1870s, from the rude tent on the beach to Major Henry Lee Higginson's "Sunset Hill" at West Manchester, described wonderingly by one guidebook as "a sort of Schönberg castle." Somewhere in between, for the plain people, was the "piano box," commonly rented for a few weeks. (Why not stay home and move into the attic, grumbled a disenchanted vacationer, for there one can "enjoy open stud construction and one layer of boards between the occupant and the almighty sun, and never have to pay for the temporary change of address.")

If there was a denominator of design common to the open stud box and the gingerbreaded atrocity in America's age of architectural know-nothingism, it was the "stick style" of construction, which sawed and hammered the most plentiful building material in the land to conform to a practical compromise between mid-Victorian hearts and flowers and the requirements of domestic routine. The Stick Style was all planes and awkward angles of boards, battens and braces, dull at best, and like boredom everywhere, subject to mindless and unpredictable explosions of vogue as in the case of the otherwise unexceptionable late-Stick house of the Eastern Yacht Club on Marblehead Neck, whose piazza columns and fence posts were of barked tree trunks bristling with the naked stumps of their former branches like sloppily put together hat racks for wearers of all statures.

Nosing around Cape Ann for *Harper's* in 1875, the restless writer-painter Samuel Greene Wheeler Benjamin liked the sea, the natives and the scenery and scoffed at the cottage architecture, which was typical of most of the North Shore. "The weather-worn and quaint gambrel-roofed farm-houses are turned for the nonce into villas. They are garnished with new porches, lace curtains, and croquet grounds; and cottages presenting a cross between an Italian villa and a Chinese joss-house are perched on the hill-tops and planted among the buildings of the early settlers, not always with perfect success as regards effect. There is hardly anything that will so test the sense of propriety and artistic taste as the location and construction of a country-seat, whether simple or pretentious. . . . The ideal country residence is yet to be designed; but one thing in its construction, and the last thing usually thought of, should be fitness. A building that would look well by the Thames or in Venice is not suited to Cape Ann."

As much had been dreamed of thirty years earlier by Alonzo Lewis in his vision of "a style in which the cottages shall appear to grow out of the rocks and to be born of the woods."

If money could purchase propriety, taste and fitness of design, the segment of the shore from Swampscott to Manchester that wealth was turning into the Gold Coast was as natural a laboratory for architectural innovation as Newport, say, and within the shadow of Boston besides . . . given a fresh hand at the drafting board and an owner not too Brahmin-bound.

There was no noteworthy evidence that such a combination had yet clicked when Bayard Taylor came down on the train in the summer of 1875; only signs that the rocks and woods were being manicured. Beyond Beverly Farms, Taylor wrote, "the scenery becomes wild and rugged, and the signs of wealth and luxurious leisure increase. The bald headlands are crowned with mansard-roofed villas, the former briery slopes are civilized into grass and shrubbery, and there are more pony carriages than farm wagons on the country roads. . . . All this picturesque, irregular coast is dotted with charming summer castles and cottages." The attention of an

English traveler was arrested by the "Swiss-looking cottages of wood." The Eastern Railroad advised its riders that Beverly Farms "is not yet overrun by a promiscuous swarm of visitors [though it was doing its best], as the land is almost entirely held by a few wealthy proprietors, who are constantly adding to the beauty of the shore by reclaiming swamps, laying out lawns, and building most inviting-looking houses."

On the contrary, the most inviting-looking houses ever to grace the New England coast, cottages that would herald the first renaissance of American domestic architecture, had not yet been built; but they were about to be, and they would grow out of the rocks of the North Shore and be born of its woods. There *was* a fresh hand at the drafting board, and it belonged to that true master of the third dimension, Henry Hobson Richardson of Boston.

Richardson was supervising the construction of his massive Trinity Church in Copley Square when he designed a large cottage for Watts Sherman in Newport that was like nothing seen before in America. Spacious and pleasant, with stately gables and fluted chimneys, aproned roofs, wide bay windows, masonry below and half-timbered above, and an open, interconnected interior layout emanating from a central living hall, Richardson's "Shavian manorial" creation was his admiring application to the New England coast of the innovative Queen Anne style revived and embroidered by the progressive English architect Richard Norman Shaw; where Shaw used the plentiful tiles of his homeland to plasticize his exterior planes, Richardson substituted common wooden shingles.

The Watts Sherman house of 1874 was an eye-opener for the more imaginative American architects, who were quick to appreciate that their doyen had broken the brittle bounds of the Stick Style with his emancipation of living space, his feel for native wood and fieldstone, his sense of site. Before the decade was out, Watts Sherman adaptations (Richardson was impossible to copy successfully) had sprung from other boards into the suburban and seaside setting, showing ever more shingle, fewer distracting derivative doodads, and the pleasing effects of this new spatial liberation. With the design of the C. J. Morrill cottage at Bar Harbor by William Ralph Emerson of Boston in 1879, the first to be sheathed in shingle from sill to eave, the enchanting, all-too-fleeting "Shingle Style" had arrived.

Nostalgic, picturesque, irresistibly inviting in the maturity it attained on the North Shore in the 1880s, the Shingle Style was uniquely a seaside phenomenon. Here was a house of cool dreams above the ocean, at ease with ledge and lawn, every window thrown open to a vista of beguilement, every ceiling ashimmer in watery reflections, a languid sprawl of space wrapped in an undulation of shingle roasted in the sun and seasoned to a silver gray by the salt of the winter spray.

During the early eighties Emerson and two or three other architects planted an experimental crop of shingled cottages where the soil of the North Shore was richest and still to be had for a price, at Manchester, Beverly and Swampscott. The architectural historian Vincent J. Scully, Jr., singled out ten as leading examples of the genre in his definitive study, *The Shingle Style and the Stick Style*.

First to sprout were two by Emerson, a distant, Illinois-born cousin of the Concord Sage, who grew up in Boston and was five years older than Richardson, though still in his late forties. Both cottages illustrated how rapidly and successfully Emerson "Americanized" Richardson's original hybrid. The better of the pair was built for General Charles Greely Loring at Pride's Crossing as if it had been summoned forth from the sheer ledge on which it crouched. The owner, a man of superb taste, was the son and namesake of Squire Loring, Beverly's original summer settler. When he got out of Harvard his health was delicate and his means independent; instead of entering business or a profession he toured Europe, dabbling in Egyptian archeology, and on his return assayed to farm the family summer estate in gentlemanly fashion. A life of pleasant underachievement was not for a Loring, however. He joined General Ambrose Everett Burnside's staff in 1861 and overcompensated for his retiring nature so thoroughly that he emerged from the Civil War a major general himself. Loring returned to Egypt, schooled

*Sticks and gingerbread were the style in summer housing at Pigeon Cove, Rockport, 1870s. Procter Brothers, Howard Collection*

The "River House" on Norton's Point, Manchester, designed by Arthur Little and built by Dr. Bartol — a palace of shingle. Manchester Historical Society

himself in archeology and the arts, and when the Boston Museum of Fine Arts opened its new building in Copley Square in 1876 his culture and generalship were combined in the curatorship. For twenty-five years the modest, goateed General Loring stamped the Museum's early development as its executive until shortly before his death in 1902.

Emerson's companion design of 1881, for Alexander Cochrane at Pride's Crossing, was more spreading and somewhat more refined with its flat surfaces, scalloped shingling above a touch of brickwork, and palladian and eyebrow windows.

The third of these first shingles to break North Shore ground in 1881 was "Shingleside," a bastardized and overblown colonial saltbox of ungainly proportion with indented porches and an awkward pepper grinder of a bay built on Swampscott's Little's Point by James L. Little to the design of his son, Arthur, who was twenty-eight and had studied at Massachusetts Institute of Technology and in Paris. Arthur Little's first commission had been a successful Colonial Revival house, "Cliffs," which he designed in 1879 for George Dudley Howe, who bought his commanding lot on Smith's Point from Dr. Bartol in 1878. Although "Cliffs" proved to be an influential design, Little characteristically abandoned it and turned to shingle with enthusiasm. After "Shingleside" he designed "Grasshead" nearby for his father the next year; it was longer, lower and more satisfactory in shape, marred only by the same broken-branched tree trunks for piazza posts that discouraged leaners at the Eastern Yacht Club.

Cyrus Bartol had done so well as a speculator in land that in 1883 he built three speculative cottages in shingle to Arthur Little's plans on Norton's Point in Manchester and two others on Smith's Point, probably by Little also, since he is known to have designed one that year at Lobster Cove. The former were the "River," "Barn" and "Fort" (on the site of an 1812 earthworks) houses, with a common stable that practically flowed in shingle over the meadow.

His Norton's Point collection shows how rapidly Arthur Little was mastering the new milieu, adapting his design by sections to the rugged terrain above the water, breaking up the space horizontally and vertically, sculpting the shell with vistas, towers, turrets, swelling bays, nooks, walkways and peekaboo windows, and then shingling it all together. As much can be said of Arthur Little's Lobster Cove creation and of one of his last efforts in shingle, the happily contoured cottage he conceived for J. Henry Sleeper on Marblehead Neck above the harbor in 1888.

Augustus Hemenway's death in 1876 had left his widow Mary, who had always been regal, rich as well, and she was not chary of spending her mite. She developed into a determined and effective philanthropist, giving $100,000 to help save the Old South Church in Boston from destruction, introducing cooking instruction and physical education to America by way of the Boston public schools, and covering considerable eleemosynary ground in between. In 1883 Mrs. Hemenway commissioned William Ralph Emerson to design a shingle-above-stone cottage for her daughter, Mrs. W. E. C. Eustis, on her Pickworth Point estate at Manchester. It was an angular yet pleasing arrangement of contrasting building materials. Someone interested Mary Hemenway in financing archeological expeditions in the Southwest, and in the summer of 1886 Manchester was treated to a visitation by three Zuni Indians from New Mexico whom the grande dame had invited to Pickworth Point after hearing that their tribe believed it had arrived in the desert over "a great salt water." Down at the edge of Mrs. Hemenway's lawn the Zunis offered prayers to the Great Spirit over the sea.

(And not only the Zunis. The descendants of the Indians for whom the entire coast was once their exclusive resort were occasionally allowed back on the white man's reservation. Thomas Grattan had not been at Nahant a week in 1839 when several families of Penobscots paddled ashore in their bark canoes and pitched their tepees near the hotel — using old sails instead of skins; the men spread their fishing nets to dry, while the women and children set silently to work weaving baskets. Consul Grattan was dismayed at the plight of the once-proud Americans and commented that no one could regard them with indifference except "the accustomed

Yankees, the descendants of the spoilers, who speculate on turning the labours of the semi-savage wanderers to account." Later, Penobscots at one time or another tented as crowd-attracting curiosities in Maolis Gardens and near the hotels on Phillips Point in Swampscott, at Magnolia and elsewhere. One summer when Buffalo Bill's troupe encamped at Stage Fort Park in Gloucester the Indians found some ancient mounds and astonished the "natives" with a ritual dance in full regalia.)

Of the other Manchester cottages of the early eighties praised by Professor Scully, one was a spacious place designed by Arthur Hooper Dodd of Boston for William Pratt and built for $11,000, which was above average, although Beverly mansions were costing as much as $75,000. (Over a span of ten years one Manchester contractor put up thirty-two summer houses for a total of $225,000 and twenty-one stables for $75,000.) Scully's other choice was G. Nixon Black's "Kragsyde," an arresting pile-up of airy rooms and porches wrapped in shingle and clamped down on the cliff above Lobster Cove in 1884. "Kragsyde" was designed by Robert S. Peabody and John G. Stearns of Boston; the name was a transparent plagiarism of "Cragside," an English country home conceived by Richard Shaw, whose Queen Anne revival inspired Richardson and was greatly admired by Peabody. Scully regarded Black's mansion as the partners' domestic masterpiece, with its gigantic drive-through wooden arch à la Richardson supporting a boudoir-library, its free-flowing surfaces and variety of textures.

A generation of shingle grew out of the rocks and was born of the woods of the North Shore, but no more. McKim, Mead and White of New York (McKim and White were graduates of Richardson's office) raised the style to its highest plane in the late 1880s and then moved on to other forms. Emerson was a romantic aesthete, an artist in space and texture for whom the Shingle Style was the ultimate medium. Little swung along with the times and wound up designing vast Georgian piles for the filthy-rich Edwardians who were buying their way into Pride's Crossing. "By far the finest things in the late 'eighties," Lewis Mumford wrote of the shingles in *Sticks & Stones*. "This new note, however, was scarcely sounded before it died out; and in the twenty years that followed the conflict between industrialism and romanticism was swallowed up and finally forgotten in the rise of a new mode."

Were they too virginal to perpetuate themselves, too captivating to be recaptured, too possessively the expression of a coterie of architects and clients who collaborated, for a moment in time, in the incarnation of a fancy as fleeting as the dance of ocean sunlight on their ceilings?

It is tempting to associate the shingled shore with the easy noblesse of those early arrivals from Boston, the Lorings and the Paines and their friends and their children, who felt, and were, much too secure to succumb to the anxious exclusiveness that gripped each successive newcomer. Size and show were the new clients pounding at the door. The age of pretension swaggered in with the nineties, and our first try at wrapping our houses lightly and loosely around the angularities of our lives was over.

# 18

## From Magnolia to Eastern Point

ONLY ALONG HER FLANKS, OPEN TO THE OCEAN AND HENCE UNCLAIMED by the fisheries, was Gloucester exposed to the nips of the land-hungry pack that ranged the North Shore in the wake of the Civil War. The nearest straggler for the picking-off was the snoring hamlet of Kettle Cove, which lay partly along the shore of Gloucester a mile and a half west of the harbor, part within the easterly limits of Manchester.

This coastal anomaly consisted of the twin points of Coolidge in Manchester and Magnolia in Gloucester, of nearly equal size and separated by a fine crescent of beach inside Kettle Cove (sometimes confused, to add to the confusion, with the smaller inlet to the west of Coolidge Point), so named not for a kettle, as already indicated, but for a family of them which settled there in colonial times.

Kettle Cove was so far from both town centers that it was of no particular interest to either; consequently the natives were left by both, for 220 years or so, to their own vices and devices — small farming, slight shore fishing and less lobstering, and the heroic consumption of rum on every excusable occasion.

Magnolia Point took its name from the exotic flowering shrub, common to the South but found in Massachusetts in its wild state only in the swampy ravines that furrow the depths of the primeval forest behind the West Gloucester and Manchester shore. This stretch from Freshwater Cove to Kettle Cove is all bold red ledge, during winter storms a continuous explosion of white water, in summer offering safe harbor only for a few small craft in the two coves. The railroad was a mile from Kettle Cove, and even the shore road through Manchester to Gloucester passed it by, so that the first summer boarders (the family of Mr. Day, a Boston ship chandler, in 1861) had the warm sands of Crescent Beach and the sleepy upland of the Point satisfyingly to themselves.

Like its twin across the cove, which had been owned originally by the Goldsmiths, Magnolia Point was the family farm of the Knowltons until Daniel W. Fuller came along in 1867 and made them an offer. Fuller was a Swampscott man who had witnessed the transformation of his home town into a prosperous resort and fore-saw similar possibilities farther along the North Shore, where the owners of the land were still unsullied by the sins of speculation.

The Knowltons sold most of Magnolia Point to Daniel Fuller. East-west across its shoulder he laid out Hesperus Avenue in honor of the imaginary ship that Longfellow wrecked on the very real rock of Norman's Woe a mile alongshore toward Gloucester; with in-creased traffic this new road took over the ancient cart path, Master Moore's Lane (after a famous teacher of navigation to local sea captains, whose house still stands at the head of it), above the ledges that tied in with Western Avenue behind Freshwater Cove, and the old name went out of use.

North-south from Lobster Lane (later extended around the Point at the water's edge as Shore Road) Fuller cut through a road to Hesperus Avenue and named it after himself. The tenting craze was in full pitch, and he encouraged campers; to some he sold lots, and to others he sold or rented cottages that he built himself. In 1873 this enterprising developer opened a café for the benefit of his expanding colony at the corner of Hesperus and Fuller, in charge of Mrs. Maria H. Bray, a West Gloucester housewife who knew something of botany besides; she called the place "Ptilota" after a seaweed she found down on the beach.

Magnolia, as the divided village of Kettle Cove was renamed,

developed rapidly during the 1870s into a hotel resort second only on
the North Shore to Daniel Fuller's native Swampscott. Up behind
the cove Allen Knowlton opened the small Crescent Beach Hotel in
1873 and did so well that he enlarged it year by year and soon had
150 guests. Success gave him grander ideas. In 1877 he dusted off
and elaborated on a project his father, James Knowlton, had vainly
pushed in 1847 when he attempted to get Manchester to annex
Magnolia Point from Gloucester. Allen petitioned the legislature to
carve a new town of Magnolia out of Gloucester and Manchester,
but the son fared no better than the sire.

Behind the east end of Crescent Beach Allen's brother-in-law,
Barnard Stanwood, fixed over the Knowlton homestead into
Willow Cottage and hired Mrs. Bray away from "Ptilota" to run it
in 1876. This time mine hostess was restrained from venting her
passion for botanizing; Willow it remained, and her hospitality and
its location on the crest of a billow of meadow that rolled down to
the ocean soon brought waves of vacationing celebrities to the comfortable summer boardinghouse set so invitingly in the shade of its
giant trees at the end of a driveway fenced with the bleached bones
of a stranded whale.

Halfway out on the point, on Hesperus Avenue, Daniel Fuller
built the Hesperus House in 1877, so popular that after only two
seasons he matched it with a wing seventy feet to the west and
joined the two with a covered walkway that bulged eclectically at
the middle into a pseudo-Chinese pagoda entered through a porte
cochere, which was the latest thing to arrive under, especially by
private conveyance, with coachman up. The Hesperus was Magnolia's first definitely fashionable hotel, and long after the grandness of
the resort had left it behind retained the loyalty of quiet Bostonians
of breeding, perhaps due in some measure to its practice of feeding
children with nurses at separate hours.

The winter after he doubled the Hesperus House the founder of
Magnolia traveled to the young state of Colorado to visit Lewis N.
Tappan, the Manchester real estate man who in his younger days
had followed the pointing finger of Horace Greeley and pioneered

the territory. Tappan owned an interest in underground real estate
at Leadville, where the friends descended into the Virginius silver
mine. Daniel Fuller was being hoisted back up in the ore bucket
when it let go as he neared the surface and dropped him 140 feet
back down the Deer Lodge shaft to his death. A few hours later
Tappan also died, in shock.

By the 1880s the rocketing popularity of Magnolia kept six summer hotels filled, including The Oceanside, which opened as a
homey boardinghouse with a sweeping view of the sea and betrayed
as yet no hint of its future glitter as the North Shore's preeminent
*pied-à-terre.* Excursion steamers touched at the Kettle Cove wharf
when their owners and masters felt so moved, and solvency allowed,
which was irregularly, and the Eastern Railroad built a depot barely
over in Manchester to serve East Manchester, but Magnolia primarily, bringing the point to within a twenty-minute trot by hotel
barge.

Thus officially addressed by the railroad, and stamped by
Baedeker as "a pleasant little watering-place," the resort soon had its
own postal substation, to keep Magnolia in touch with the world,
and then a library, built by the wealthy summer people in 1889 to
keep the world in touch with Magnolia.

Previously the books which the little library housed had been
shelved in a small church on Magnolia Avenue and ministered to
from the proceeds of an annual fair run by the summer folks. *Magnolia Leaves,* the summer monthly founded by the energetic Mrs.
Bray, observed that by making it available to the natives (who really
had no use for it), its sponsors invested the library with the necessary
flavor of charity. "Idle women, however, must have something to do
to pass away the time. Fancy work for a fair is at once pretty, and
supposed to be charitable. I, for one, have never seen the charity in
young women of wealth devoting their time to embroidery to be
sold at fairs. They are really taking the bread and butter out of the
mouths of those poor girls who have to live by their needle. It would
be charity to buy the fancy work from the needy working girls, and
then give it to the fair to be sold. This does not enter the heads of the

fair workers, who enjoy the fun of selling their useless knick-knacks at exorbitant prices."

Fashion frequently follows fame, and the descent upon Magnolia in 1877 of a figure both famous and fashionable doubled the effect on the resort. Bearded, bald and burning with the fires of a spectral palette, William Morris Hunt had captured Boston on his return from Europe a score of years earlier with an exciting portfolio of paintings such as America was not used to, with his enthusiasm of the proselyte for Millet and the novel techniques of the Barbizon School. He married a granddaughter of Colonel Thomas Handasyd Perkins, and when he felt so disposed, charmed the city's innermost circles. But Boston pleased him not, and less so than ever after he lost his studio and much of his work in the Great Fire of 1872.

Hunt roamed to remote places like Newport, his native Vermont, the sun-splashed Azores and North Easton, where Henry Hobson Richardson was creating architectural monuments to the Ames shovel family (his brother, Richard Morris Hunt, was a monument-maker in his own right). North Easton's inland heat in the summer of 1877 drove him to sea-cooled Magnolia on the invitation of another architect friend, William Ralph Emerson, who had a small cottage above Crescent Beach for the season. The two searched lucklessly for a fish house or shed whose owner would let them cut a studio skylight through the roof until "a cultivated lady from Gloucester" assured Barnard Stanwood, who had an old barn across the road from Willow Cottage, where Hunt was staying, that he was a great artist and that his choice of Magnolia for painting would be "the making of the place."

Hunt bought Stanwood's barn and adjacent carpentry shop that July. Emerson oversaw its conversion into a studio that looked like a stranded ship; they christened it "The Hulk." The barn was doubled in length for horse stalls, painter's van, buggy and dogcart. In a nod to the nautical they hung davits and swung ropes here and there, and in admonition to the creative screwed a vertical sundial to an outside wall with the spoilsport legend NOW IS THE TIME.

The artist probably had some late-season use of The Hulk in 1877 but was dissatisfied with the loft as a studio and made what he called a "barracks" of it for himself and visitors, doing his painting in the carpentry shop. Every morning Hunt set forth in his interesting van with a student and driver. Once upon the scene, as one of them told it, he "would leap from the van, take a camp-stool and a block of charcoal paper, and, with a stick of soft charcoal seize the salient points of the subject to be rendered. The assistant would . . . 'lay in' the first painting — reproducing the effect of the charcoal-sketch, while Hunt would watch intently for the right moment . . . when he would seize palette and brushes, and perhaps complete the picture in one sitting." To ward off kibitzers he is said to have worn sandwich boards advising I CAN'T TALK and I CAN'T HEAR.

For the 1878 season Emerson and Hunt perched a one-man gazebo on a pole thirty feet above the ground, reached from The Hulk by a catwalk with a drawbridge by which the artist could isolate himself. From this unique nest he surveyed Magnolia Point, the sea and Eastern Point beyond with eagle eye, and sketched, and meditated Bartolian style, in lofty loneliness. But for most of that summer he was kept in Boston drafting the murals for the Albany State House and broke away to Magnolia for only a few weekends. Almost prostrate with overwork, Hunt fled the next summer to the Isles of Shoals off the New Hampshire coast. On September 8, 1879, his body was found in a tidal pool. He was fifty-five. Whether he had died by suicide or accident was never satisfactorily resolved.

Five months after the artist's death an auction of his unsold works in Boston revealed that the painting van had not ranged far from The Hulk during his brief encounter with a shore that inspired the culminating production of his life. Of twenty-one canvases and charcoal drawings, all but two or three were set in Magnolia. The best was *Gloucester Harbor,* shimmering through a windless midsummer haze, a large oil now in the Museum of Fine Arts, Boston, which sold for $3,000. He dashed off this masterpiece in an afternoon and sized it up with satisfaction: "I believe that I have painted a picture with *light* in it!"

Its distinctive light was what attracted William Morris Hunt to Gloucester, and it shines through the works of his predecessors there: the native Fitz Hugh Lane, who produced calm, glowing, suspended animations of the harbor and its shores (though he could paint a coaster wallowing through a sloppy swell to make a stomach somersault), and Winslow Homer. Lane died a dozen years before Hunt's arrival; no painter since has matched his achievements with atmospheric light, and he stands with Homer as the greatest of American marine artists.

Homer painted Gloucester as early as 1871, six years after Fitz Hugh Lane's death. His first stay of any duration was in the summer of 1873, when he undertook to tackle watercolors seriously. He returned in 1880, the summer following Hunt's mysterious demise, literally getting inside his subject by the device of boarding with the lighthouse keeper on Ten Pound Island in the middle of Gloucester Harbor. The artist was rowed back to the mainland in a few weeks with fifty or more watercolors of haunting beauty that attest to his absolute mastery of the medium and to the harbor's theatrical effect on the painters to come for whom Lane, Hunt and Homer raised the curtain — or lifted the veil.

*Gloucester Harbor* — that tidal amphitheater of ever-shifting scenery, of glorious light and friendly dark, of restless rise and fall and to and fro. . .

The year that Winslow Homer withdrew behind his harbor moat for a summer of watercoloring, a popular female author from Andover built a cottage in Wonson's Field at the north end of Niles Beach on Eastern Point. Elizabeth Stuart Phelps was her name, and she called her place "The Old Maid's Paradise." From her window Miss Phelps was seduced by the sunset breaking through the scudding clouds of a storm's tail end: "All Gloucester harbor tossed against it. The bows of the anchored fleet rose and sank angrily. The head-lights came out one by one, and flared, surging up and down. Ten Pound Light flashed out for the night; but her blinder was on, towards us. The little city, glorified now, forgiven of her fish, and her dust, and her bounding roads, loved and dreamed over, and sung in heart and pen, melted all through her pretty outlines against the massive colors of the west."

Forgiven of her fish under the spell of Gloucester Harbor tossing in the tempest, perhaps, but by the light of day Miss Phelps had regained her chronic irritation at the imperturbability of the place in the face of visitors. "Her summer guests may come and go, may pay or not, may criticize or adore, but her fish bite on forever. The result of my own observation has been that Gloucester, in her heart of hearts, regards her large summer population with a certain contempt." Of course, the more the lady criticized the more she adored, and like all unrequited lovers, the worse she was rebuffed. But oh, that dust and those bounding roads!

Gloucester's notorious indifference to her summer guests was fairly exemplified by the easygoing attitude of the natives, who never went anywhere since they were already there, concerning the matter of public transportation. The train ride down from Boston took an hour by the clock; by the dial of time travel it was a hundred years, because the local public conveyance until almost 1890 was the stagecoach.

The extension of the rails to Gloucester in 1847 drove the Salem stage off the old colonial shore road, but the coach still clattered from the depot across the cape until 1861, when the first train steamed on to Rockport. The stage line from the Gloucester station to Annisquam and Lanesville was not finally forced to give way until the trolley cars scared the horses off the road.

Excursionists by sea fared no better, and rather worse if the bay was bumpy. From that August day of 1817 when the paddle steamer *Massachusetts* barely beat His Snakeship into Gloucester Harbor, thirty years drifted by before Menemon Sanford started sporadic summer service to Boston in his sidewheeler *Yacht*. In 1859 the Boston and Gloucester Steamboat Company was organized and put *Mystic* in regular year-round service. A succession of steamers during and after the Civil War carried fish from the company's wharf on Duncan's Point for the Boston market and general cargo on the return from Central Wharf.

Some effort to accommodate the summer excursion trade was

*William Morris Hunt.*
*Essex Institute*

*"The Hulk," William Morris Hunt's summer studio at Magnolia, showing his elevated gazebo and, at right, behind the trees, "Willow Cottage." Watercolor by Ernest Bruno de Gersdorff, 1878. Cape Ann Historical Association*

*Croquet at the Foster Cottage, Magnolia, in the 1870s. Procter Brothers, Howard collection*

*A picnic on the granite summit of Mt. Ann, West Gloucester, late 1880s. Belknap Album, Essex Institute*

*Camping in style at Magnolia, 1870s. Procter Brothers, Howard collection*

*Archery was an acceptable sport for ladies summering in Magnolia at the Perkins House, nucleus of the grand Oceanside Hotel. Procter Brothers, Howard collection*

*Elizabeth Stuart Phelps and her "Old Maid's Paradise," East Gloucester. From* Chapters from a Life

*Eddie Parsons's famous omnibus in East Gloucester Square, about 1870. Dorothy Buhler*

*View of Niles Beach, looking south on Eastern Point about 1890, reveals a barren moor and the solitary summer cottage of John J. Stanwood. Photo by George Bacon Wood, author's collection*

*Arched à la Richardson, the Gate Lodge guards Eastern Point above Niles Beach and behind John Perkins Cushing's stone wall. Procter Brothers, Howard Collection*

made during the late 1860s, pausing long enough in Gloucester for passengers to take a swim at Pavilion Beach, down a fish dinner at the Pavilion or the Atlantic House and have a quick look around the waterfront before the reboarding whistle. Eleven more steamers, mostly sidewheelers — five of them operated by a rival company in the early 1870s — plied the thirty-two miles along the North Shore, sometimes touching in summer at Magnolia or Salem, until the Boston & Gloucester settled down with the sturdy little 108-foot screw steamer *George A. Chaffee* in 1876; "The Bed Bug" (so-called from her size and shape) remained in service for nineteen years.

The real heroine of the run, and the most famous of her long day in Massachusetts Bay, was the line's first custom-built steamship, the 142-foot *City of Gloucester,* with the profile of a warehouse, topped off by two masts and a single stack, yet as squat as a tugboat, slow, powerful and unbelievably ugly. The *City*'s trial trip from Gloucester on July 28, 1883, was planned as a gala to Nantasket, where she was to come to anchor while the large and happy party of local men and their ladies on board indulged in a catered collation to the strains of the Gloucester Cornet Band. But the day broke stormy, and outside Eastern Point the waves capered uncooperatively. "The hilarity did not continue with all on board," wrote the reporter for the *Cape Ann Advertiser.* "A spirit of uneasiness was manifest. Some of the ladies and gents whose smiles and laughter added much to the pleasure of the occasion began to look pale. They did not appear so lively as before. They had an all-gone expression, a don't-care-whether-school-keeps-or-not look. Vainly they tried to overcome it and to make themselves believe that nothing was the matter with them — a praiseworthy effort, but it proved a failure, and the seasick victims paid tribute to Father Neptune and felt all the better after the account was settled." And very much better after the captain mercifully put about at Halfway Rock and returned to harbor, where the collation was brought out in the calm lee of Eastern Point.

That was the first and very nearly the last time the *City of Gloucester* reneged on a trip in her forty-two years on the run, and it wasn't her fault. Only the dirtiest weather daunted the dirty old girl, and if she didn't move, nothing moved. She endeared herself to generations of year-round and summer folk such as Gloucester native Theodore S. Ireland, who remembered the boyhood thrill of the 3:30 A.M. departure for Boston.

"At the wharf," Ireland wrote, "bright stars, creak of lines on the bollards as the engine was idled, then the churning of water as we slid away from the dock, and later the sun coming up out of the ocean. A mug-up from the galley with coffee and donuts. . . . I doubt if any ship had a whistle like the *City*. It was single tone and I believe high C. Just after daylight on a thick foggy morning it was really something to hear the *City* leave the harbor, blowing every 20–30 seconds."

Most guests booked for the few summer hostelries on Cape Ann arrived by train and were met at the depot by the hotel barge. Those bound for camp or cottage on the cape's more distant shores had to wait with luggage, patient spouse and bawling children for the stagecoach that four times daily lurched over the dusty road skirting the Annisquam and Mill rivers to Squam and beyond to the Back of the Cape on Ipswich Bay. Vacationers off for the handful of small hotels and boardinghouses of East Gloucester and Rocky Neck were rewarded with the delight of a four-cent ride across the busy harbor on the midget steam ferry. Or they could make one of the hourly trips around behind the pungent wharves in the lumbering horse-drawn omnibus, of which the *Advertiser* reported one June that "when a very fat lady got in last week a passenger grumbled 'Omnibuses were not made for elephants.' To which she retorted with a twinkle 'Sir, omnibuses are like Noah's Ark, intended for all kinds of beasts.' A burst of applause from the other passengers, and soon somebody got out, but it wasn't the fat lady."

Miss Phelps was not fat, nor did she come upon East Gloucester by omnibus. She was the well-formed daughter of Professor Austin Phelps of the Theological Seminary at Andover. Like countless other girls, Elizabeth had lost the boy she loved in the Civil War. From her grief emerged *The Gates Ajar,* in which she laid bare her own spiritual torture and recovery. The novel appeared in 1868 when she was twenty-four and brought her fame and fortune, selling 78,000 copies. Not long after, she jounced in her buggy on an exploratory trip over that abhorrent dirt road, past the snowy acres of split salt cod curing in the sun above the wharves where the schooners nudged and creaked, paused on the crest of Patch's Hill, "and drew the breath of unexpected and undreamed-of delight. We had discovered Eastern Point . . . the fairest face of all the New England coast."

After boarding with the Wonsons for a few trial seasons, the authoress in 1880 built "The Old Maid's Paradise." She never could conceal her distaste for anything remotely connected with fishing — the smells, the clatter and the coarse talk, the gurry, dirt and inconvenience — and the heart of Gloucester, its waterfront, was a purgatory to be endured along the road to the heaven of Eastern Point.

No, Elizabeth could not forgive Gloucester her fish, and she could not forgive her her fishermen. When one was killed during an affray in an East Gloucester saloon she raised a cry against the rum sellers and drunkards of the port. She harangued temperance meetings, and "I used often to be asked to drive down the North Shore and tell the summer people what we were doing for the fishermen. These parlor talks always resulted in something less evasive than pleasant words. Generous and hearty to a surprising degree were the contributions to our always clamorous needs from people to whose tastes and experience our work was quite foreign."

Down on the wharves, though, they wondered whether this meddlesome female and a cabal of other influential North Shore summer swells were not more concerned with getting the poor fisherman home from a night on the town than from one on the grounds.

Over the years a lengthening litany of vessels, most of them Gloucester schooners returning from fishing, had piled up on the rocks of Brace Cove at night or in storm or fog, mistaking this small of Eastern Point's back for its head, beyond which lay safe harbor. In 1880 several veteran mariners suggested that because the light and bell at the end of the point frequently were neither seen nor heard under adverse conditions, a loud whistling buoy, activated by the tossing of the waves, should be moored a mile off shore to guide vessels away from the lure of Brace Cove and into Gloucester Harbor.

This prudent advice raised a tempest of hysteria. One alarmed opponent wrote the *Advertiser* that when a whistler was moored off Newport an ailing summer visitor "died raving for want of sleep" and reminded landholding readers that Beverly property owners had recently blocked attempts to locate one of the dreadful things off their shore; he (or she) warned that the bellowing buoy would most certainly drive summer visitors away and result in the abandonment of improvements and depreciation of land values from Eastern Point clear around to Magnolia.

And so nothing was done. Two years later, after several more wrecks, the wise heads of Gloucester again brought up the whistler and this time brought down on themselves a regular hurricane of letters and petitions from the shore owners, real estate agents and summer visitors. The Lighthouse Board ahemmed and ordered a heavier hammer for the fog bell at the Eastern Point lighthouse. Another year passed. A returning mackerel schooner drove ashore in the night, mistaking a lamp shining through a red window curtain for the ruby beam of the lighthouse.

At last Washington acted, and late in 1883 "Mother Ann's Cow" was moored, over the groans of the summer people, half a mile south of the Eastern Point light, where it has remained to this day — except during the vacation seasons from 1885 through 1888, when Miss Phelps, a chronic insomniac with friends in high places, had it removed.

Luckily for the lowly fishermen, the old maid just then finally found the paradise she pined for in the person of the Reverend Herbert Dickinson Ward, seventeen years younger than she. The knot was tied by the father of the bride in October of 1888; soon after, the Boston *Record* reported that "since her marriage Mrs.

Ward is much better, and the officer who had to remove the buoy has put it back with the assurance that next summer he will have no orders to disturb it."

How much of this hue and cry against Mother Ann's Cow, this scare talk about sleepless nights and ruined land, can be laid to what might rightly strike the reader as the preposterously irrelevant imminence of the twenty-first birthday of my grandmother in 1882?

Well, my Great-great-grandfather Thomas Niles had died in 1872 at the age of seventy-five. He had seen the worth of his Eastern Point Farm increase tenfold since 1844, and with fifteen children between the ages of sixteen and forty-seven to divide it amongst, he counted on his investment to continue upward under the rising pressure on shore property. Therefore in his will Farmer Niles had forbidden his executors to divide the four hundred acres until his youngest granddaughter, Sarah McClennen Rogers, reached her majority. Meanwhile two of his sons managed the farm. My grandmother was twenty-one in 1882. The executors immediately published a subdivision plan; no satisfactory buyers approached, and since the taxes then were only about $720, they bided their time.

A quarter of a century after they had first rattled north from Boston into Lynn, the horsecars finally breached Gloucester's unconcern about such conveniences in 1886, and it appeared that inevitably (as it was, in three more years) proper public transportation would be extended from the Eastern Railroad depot around the harbor through East Gloucester Square and probably as far as Rocky Neck, which was but a short trot from the Niles gate. In 1887 the Niles executors sold the entire farm to a syndicate of American and Canadian capitalists, lawyers and entrepreneurs, the Eastern Point Associates, for $100,000.

The key to the deal may have been the syndicate's clerk, A. Spalding Weld of the real estate firm of Atwood and Weld, the only member who did not subsequently build. Weld lived in the Jamaica Plain section of Boston, where also resided his friends, Charles F. Farrington, a businessman, and David S. Greenough, an importer. David and his brother John, a New York railroad financier, had

first come to Gloucester as boys in 1855, when they stayed at the
Pavilion with their family; they would row across the harbor to
Eastern Point and "spy out the land," taking care to keep clear of
Mr. Niles, and they vowed that someday they would build their
summer homes on its Black Bess Point. This they did in 1888. The
three Canadians were from Toronto: Henry J. Scott was a retired
merchant and Member of Parliament; J. Hamilton Kane was a
banker; Walter Barwick was an attorney who had been vacationing
at the small Seaside Hotel on Niles Beach for several years. The
Greenoughs must have had a strong hand in engineering the deal
through their friends Weld and his partner, L. P. Atwood, who
bought one of the first cottages to be built . . . as did Barwick in
bringing in the Canadian money.

During the fall and winter of 1888 eleven pleasant Shingle Style
cottages, incorporating the ready supply of native fieldstone and
schoonerloads of lumber from Maine, were strung out along the outer
harbor shore and up the dirt road that led to the abandoned Civil
War earthworks on the point's highest elevation, which they called
Fort Hill Avenue. Barwick, Kane and Benjamin S. Calef, a Boston
insurance man, had Arthur Hooper Dodd design their houses
grouped around the old water-filled quarry on the nubbin of ledge
below the lighthouse at a cost of $7,000 each. On the end of this
Quarry Point across the small cove from the lighthouse, John V.
Lewis, Cincinnati Standard Oil magnate, built the grandest (many
years later the house of the Eastern Point Yacht Club), a spacious
$12,000 cottage designed by Appleton and Stephenson of Boston,
who that same winter did the Gate Lodge at the north end of Niles
Beach, where Farmer Niles had dropped the bars on Farmer Patch;
here the Associates' porter was stationed to screen all who entered
their private sanctum through the lodge's stone arch designed in the
manner of H. H. Richardson. John J. Stanwood, Gloucester fish
dealer and land speculator, built on the rise behind Niles Beach, and
Captain Albert Lewis, owner of Lewis Wharf in Boston, raised his
cottage next to Farrington on Fort Hill Avenue.

These first dozen houses, designed and located to set the tone, were pictured in a promotional brochure. But the Eastern Point Associates had more in mind than an "exclusive" colony of 250 cottages. The center of it all was to be the classiest summer hotel on the North Shore, presiding over Gloucester Harbor from behind the embrasures of the old fort. Guests and summer residents were to have direct service to Boston and Gloucester on the *City of Gloucester* and *George A. Chaffee,* which would touch at the end of a 300-foot pier the syndicate built into the harbor from the foot of Fort Hill Avenue. While they worked on the financing they bought the diminutive Seaside Hotel opposite Niles Beach on their new dirt boulevard to the lighthouse, as a stopgap, refurbished it as The Beachcroft and hired Mrs. Maria Bray away from Magnolia as their hostess. And then with splendid flourish they brought a boatload of prime prospects down from Boston on the *City* for a catered *déjeuner à la fourchette* under a striped tent, followed by a tour of their magnificent resort-to-be *à la barouche*, and otherwise tried to prime the pump of its development.

But the well was dry, to the ultimate relief of their heirs and assigns. Not a shingle of the syndicate's fortress hotel materialized. The steamship stop at the expensive pier was abandoned from lack of patronage. Although a few lots were sold, not one beyond the first dozen was built on for five years, and in 1892 the Eastern Point Associates declared themselves bankrupt and were reorganized on less ambitious lines.

"The scheme was doomed to failure from the beginning," reflected a later summer resident. "There were no water mains, no gas mains, no electric wires, no telephones. Purchasers for such land could not be found." The clouds of dust and lurking potholes that beset the wayfarer on the road through East Gloucester after the watering carts had fallen victim to local politics, predicted the *Cape Ann Advertiser,* "will down more summer visitors than the cars and steamboat will bring to town."

And the fish bit on forever.

# 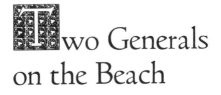wo Generals on the Beach

DESERVED THOUGH LESS THAN TRIUMPHANT WERE THE SUMMER "VACA-tions" of a brace of Union generals of the Civil War, far from the sounds of shell and shot on the lonely sands of Ipswich Bay. One was a famous commander, relieved of his command at his own request by President Lincoln. The other, more infamous than otherwise in the eyes of his enemies on both sides (who were as legion as his friends), pitched his tent not four miles away after his outright sacking by the hard-pressed Commander-in-Chief.

The plain bad luck of General John Charles Frémont, rendered worse by his poor judgment and the brilliant tactics in the spring of 1862 of his adversary in western Virginia, General Thomas Jonathan (Stonewall) Jackson, had confirmed the President in his doubts about the conqueror of California, whom he had commissioned with some misgivings in the first place, in deference to the radical antislavery wing of the Republican Party. In June he placed Frémont and his corps in General John Pope's Army of Virginia. Frémont disliked Pope for what he regarded as his insubordination when their roles were reversed earlier in Missouri and asked to be relieved. Lincoln promptly obliged and gave his corps to General Franz Sigel. It was the onset of the long anticlimax of John Frémont's remarkable career; he went home to New York with his staff, on full pay.

Early that August the Gloucester *Telegraph* revealed under "Personals" that General Frémont was passing a few days with a friend in West Gloucester. A week later it was noted that he had ridden over to the Methodist Camp Meeting at Asbury Grove in Hamilton with a Major Haskell and given a talk on the war. His companion was in fact his aide, Major Leonidas Haskell of West Gloucester, and clearly the unnamed friend who had induced the general to get away from it all.

It was not Frémont's first visit to the North Shore. Some years before the conflict, when he was living in California, he had taken a cottage near Nipper Stage at Nahant. How the western explorer penetrated Cold Roast Boston is obscure, unless it was through his neighbor on East Point, John Ellerton Lodge, who may have met up with him in the course of pursuing his Pacific shipping interests, and probably did politically; Lodge was an ardent abolitionist and mounted the stump for the only time in his life when he exhorted the longshoremen assembled below his office on Commercial Wharf in the candidate's behalf when Frémont ran unsuccessfully for the presidency against James Buchanan in 1856. The westerner was rarely at Nahant, although his beautiful and brainy wife, Jessie, daughter of Senator Thomas Hart Benton of Missouri, was there with their daughter for several seasons.

A speaker at a recruitment rally in Gloucester told how he ferreted out the Frémonts and the general's skeleton staff in their camp on the sand near Two Penny Loaf, a hill of ledge that marks the west end of Coffin's Beach: "I went to see Frémont; he was out fishing, but I saw Jessie. God bless the day when my eyes beheld *Jessie*. (Tremendous applause). If the stones could be ever animated they would turn to soldiers in her presence! (Loud cheers for Jessie)."

Another who went out to see the general, with more luck, was Fitz Hugh Lane. The Gloucester artist was widely known by then and sketched with pencil the tents pitched neatly on the beach (two of them evidently tepee-fashion), while a pot cooked contentedly over an open fire from a tripod of saplings. He worked this up into an oil painting for the general's lady. Perhaps Lane's presence is accounted for by the fact that his mother, a West Gloucester Haskell, was related to the general's aide.

After nearly a month on Coffin's Beach, John Charles Frémont broke camp on August 27 and returned to New York.

The tides washed over General Frémont's footsteps in the sand that wartime summer of 1862, and no remembrance of his presence remains but as sketched by Fitz Hugh Lane and so casually noted in the newspaper. Not so the Union commander who followed him into rustication twelve months afterward: Benjamin Franklin Butler came, saw and carved his name in solid granite.

Both men were appointed major generals by President Lincoln to cement the support of the radicals of both parties, although Frémont, the Democrat, was too extreme even for the Republican Butler, who called him "a candidate for dictator" after he issued the unauthorized proclamation abolishing slavery in his Missouri command that eventuated in his falling out with the President. Butler burst upon the world from the mill town of Lowell, where as a young lawyer of poor-boy background, ill looks and ferocity of wit and ambition he took up the cause of the workingman, clawed rapidly up the political ladder and had accumulated a fortune as a mill owner himself, among his various interests, by the age of forty-three when the war broke out and he marched off to Baltimore as a volunteer brigadier general at the head of the first contingent of Massachusetts militia.

Unschooled in any field of war but the drill, Butler parlayed his already powerful political leverage with the President and to his credit took New Orleans with the support of Admiral Farragut's gunboats. Thereby was bred the discredit in which the South held and hated "Beast Butler." Tough and efficient, he restored and maintained order in the subdued port by such measures as hanging a local gambler for desecrating the flag and decreeing that ladies of New Orleans who persisted in taunting his soldiers would be treated by the army as women of the streets. In New Orleans, too, were sown the seeds of the reputation (perhaps not wholly deserved) for corruption and venality, which, along with a certain uncontrollable vindictiveness, was the principal flaw in a character shot through with paradox. His brother, Andrew Jackson Butler, profiteered extravagantly, and the general was rumored, apparently without any evidence, to have purloined the silver spoons from the house he occupied, a canard that has dogged him into posterity. It seems to have been his summary dealings with foreign legations, however, that provoked diplomatic pressure on Lincoln to relieve him in December of 1862.

Home in Lowell and still without a command in the summer of 1863, General Butler came upon the expanse of rocky pasture that tumbles down to Hodgkins and Diamond coves on Ipswich Bay between Annisquam and the next stage stop at Lanesville. The location struck his fancy. He bought forty-seven acres of it, pitched his tent with his two sons and their tutor, and they all went fishing. In November the President put him in command of the Department of Virginia and North Carolina, with two corps, a tour of duty that terminated ingloriously when the Confederates bottled him up at Bermuda Hundred, aborting his support of General Grant's campaign against Richmond. In January of 1865 Lincoln relieved Butler for the second time. The war ended. The President was assassinated and succeeded by Andrew Johnson, and for the second summer General Butler and his boys "spent a very delightful season in sailing and fishing and the full enjoyment of a free life," as he described it, at "Bay View," which he had decided to call his estate.

Vehemently opposed to President Johnson's conciliatory Southern policy, Butler reentered politics with a run for Congress in the summer of 1866. Not wishing to take on the incumbent in his home district of Lowell, he claimed residence in Gloucester and campaigned at the invitation of the retiring John B. Alley for his seat from the Essex district, "feeling a little curiosity to know whether I could be elected in a district where I was only a carpet-bagger," and won, "while I lived in a tent on the beach."

In Washington Congressman Butler led the almost successful vendetta to impeach President Johnson and was a feared spokesman for the harsh interpretation of Reconstruction. "Make the best of it you can," wrote one reporter, "it is a terrible face, this of Butler's; it looks like a pirate's — the strong, unscrupulous, cruel face, the low wide head, the crossed eyes, the hatchety Roman nose, the thin lips, make a combination powerful and pitiless. Yet we know this man has room in him for large magnanimities, for gentle charities, for good-will and tenderness." A Scottish writer heard "The Beast" address a black audience in Richmond (Butler's hotel was hung with pictures of him, horned and hooved; he ignored them).

"A short, stout man," he wrote, "with large head, a round body, and short spindle legs . . . speaking in a somewhat harsh but very fluent and articulate voice. It was easy, even at a glance, to see how this man had the power to make himself an object of such deadly hate to a whole people. There was power in the big bald head, in the massive brow, in the vulture nose, in the combatively bullying face, in the heavy eyelids, and in the keen, scrutinizing gaze. . . . His speech . . . was delivered with an audacity of manner that made one reluctant to admire even what deserved admiration."

Ben Butler provided an amusing example of his stump technique in his autobiography, *Butler's Book,* when he parodied the attempt of Richard Henry Dana, Jr., of before-the-mast fame, to explain his aristocratic and unbending nature before a crowd of Lynn workers during his campaign to unseat the congressman in 1868, and his own response. Both of course were North Shore summer "carpet-baggers." The incumbent had sneered at Dana's white gloves and distant demeanor, to which he claimed his opponent replied:

"I do wear white gloves for the purposes of society. . . . When I was a young man, and was a sailor before the mast on the coast of California [and] washing [hides] and stamping out the filth, I assure you, fellow-citizens, I was as dirty as any of you. But how does my opponent live? If you will come down to my cottage at Manchester-by-the-Sea and visit me, I will take you in my one-horse wagon and drive you around the town and show you our beaches, which are a very pleasant sight, my friends; but as we are riding along over our seashore roads we will hear a noise behind us and

*General John C. Frémont. Essex Institute*

*General Frémont's encampment on Coffin's Beach, West Gloucester, sketched in pencil in August 1862 by Fitz Hugh Lane. Cape Ann Historical Association*

*A less formidable camp on the Presson Farm in West Gloucester, about 1870. Procter Brothers, Howard collection*

*General Benjamin F. Butler in 1890.
From an engraving of the portrait by
Darius Cobb that Butler chose as the
frontispiece for his autobiography,*
Butler's Book (*Boston, 1891*)

*Previously unpublished photograph of the yacht* America, *about 1880, taken when
Butler owned the grand old schooner. Mrs. Jerome S. Bruner*

turning around see a carriage with two or four horses driven at full speed and with perhaps out-riders on horseback, and it will come dashing by us covering us with dust, and in that carriage will be my opponent."

To these clever paraphrases Congressman Butler quoted himself as responding:

"As to the averment that it is necessary to be dirty in order to get to be your equal, I assure you I shall not have to get into a manure pit to be fit to associate with you, but simply be a respectable, well-clad, decent American citizen who knows that one man who behaves well and does his duty to his country and his family is as good as another. As to horses, fellow-citizens, when I came down here into this district from Lowell, where I used to live, I brought my horses with me, and I thought I had a good span; but when I got among you I found that my constituents had better horses, and I proposed to get as good a pair as I could, and I have got a good pair, and if you will come down and ride with me I assure you we won't take anybody's dust."

"Mr. Dana was beaten out of sight," Butler hardly needed to add.

For eighteen years after the Civil War, fighting for the rights of blacks, the rights of labor, the rights of women and the rights of Butler; as lawyer, as congressman, as governor of Massachusetts, finally as presidential candidate; as Democrat, Republican or Greenbacker according to the winds of political change, the general was on center stage or maneuvering in the wings, always in the swirl of controversy and tumult that he thrived on and promoted by his very presence, or the threat of it.

The demand for granite in the construction of public buildings, monuments, bridges and roads, and the bottomless supply beneath the private soil of the coast around Bay View, met in the fertile mind of the congressman from Gloucester, with the result that in 1869 he effected the formation of the Cape Ann Granite Company with Jonas H. French, a Boston lawyer who had served on his staff during the Civil War.

The satrap's military background paralleled the master's (French had been commander of Boston's ceremonial and political Ancient and Honorable Artillery Company), and his chief had elevated him to a colonelcy and made him provost marshal of New Orleans. The old comrades gathered in close to two hundred acres of rock-rich real estate above Hodgkins Cove and soon were quarrying it, Colonel French at the active controls. At Bay View, with wholesale views of Ipswich Bay, they erected neighboring cottages and stables of their stone (French, with good reason, called his "Rock Lawn"). The company thrust a granite pier into the cove for stone schooners and sloops to load from, ran its own railroad down from the pits and within ten years was hiring as many as six hundred workers, many of whom lived in its tenements and bought from its store. Public edifices uncounted and streets without end rose and were paved with their granite, including one private mansion in Washington, Congressman Butler's, built on the southern boundary of the Capitol grounds at a cost of some $125,000 and sold quite profitably to the government when he put public service behind him.

The merest whisper that Ben Butler had been retained as counsel was frequently sufficient to bring the other side to terms out of court. His fees ran into the tens of thousands, yet no adversary was unworthy of his blade, so loved he to get the better of the bargain. One summer day, it is told, he was accosted by the Annisquam butcher:

"General, if a dog should jump into my cart and run away with a piece of meat, could I collect damages from the owner?"

"Certainly."

"Are you positive?"

"Of course I am!"

"Well, General, it was your dog."

"How much was the meat?"

"Five dollars."

Cape Ann's most famous summer resident dug out a piece of paper, scribbled on it and handed it to the butcher, who was thinking he had the old fox by the tail.

"There, you owe me a dollar."

It was a bill for six dollars for legal advice.

The fast deal that brought Ben Butler his greatest joy brought him the glory-covered old first-time captor of the America's Cup. He was already keen on sailing, had a mosquito fleet of small boats moored below his house in Diamond Cove in the charge of Cap'n Jabez Marchant, Jr., when opportunity, which never had to knock more than once, rapped on his door in 1873. Butler had won the claim of Gazaway Bugg Lamar, a Georgia banker turned blockade runner, for compensation for cotton condemned during the war. His grateful client apparently contended or offered to contend that he owned another property seized but never properly condemned, the famous schooner *America,* which had been found by the Union Navy sunk, presumably while she was serving as a Confederate blockade runner; the navy salvaged her and placed her in service on the blockade and, after the war, as a school ship. Now she lay in some disrepair at the Annapolis Navy Yard. Navy Secretary George M. Robeson, a Butler crony subsequently investigated by Congress on charges of extravagance and corruption, posted her for auction over the hot objections of naval officers who had learned their ropes on her as midshipmen. Rumors that Lamar might press his claim to *America* evidently scared rival bidders away, and she was quietly if not secretively knocked off for $5,000 to a straw for Butler and Jonas French, who was not a sailor and thereafter had little to do with her. Jabez Marchant and a crew of Gloucester fishermen set sail from Annapolis with the prize on July 2, 1873, and dropped anchor at Bay View after an eventful passage of storms and squalls during which they almost lost their precious antique in a series of knockdowns. Gloucestermen always were notorious sail-carriers.

For the remaining twenty years of his life *America* was General Butler's pride, his joy, his source of relaxation from the cares of politics and legal practice, especially after the death in 1876 of Sarah, the actress wife he worshipped, when he all but abandoned Bay View to his daughter and her family. Her owner maintained the rakish yet old-fashioned schooner to the nines under a smartly uniformed crew, dressed ship at the slightest excuse, was ever on the lookout for a race and cruised with his sons and friends as far off as

Labrador and Havana. Under sail as in politics, he was gifted with a stout pair of sea legs and reveled in tempestuous weather. On advance notice from the Coast Survey of an approaching storm he would hurry to sea out of pure zest for the battle, ordering his sailing master to "hold her to it." Small wonder the Butlerian advice to the prospective guest aboard that a yachtsman must "be able to eat and drink unlimitedly, not be seasick more than one-half of the time and keep goodnatured under difficulties."

Having gained admission to the Boston Yacht Club, where he had friends, the year he "acquired" *America,* General Butler displayed his disdain for Eastern, where he didn't, by sailing her up and down the starting line of the annual EYC regatta off Marblehead the following July, raising cries of rage and frustration from the cockpits of the jockeying entries whose bows he crossed. Among his targets that day was Edward Burgess, who did not, nevertheless, disdain the maverick owner's invitation later to modernize somewhat the most famous yacht in the world. Butler's professed contempt for Boston and North Shore blue bloods and Harvards was heartily reciprocated (mixed with not a little trepidation), and it is a curious fact that after that initial caper on the Eastern starting line his entire career afloat appears to have belied his reputation ashore.

William U. Swan, the yachting writer who was instrumental in returning *America* to the navy in 1921, observed of Butler's sportsmanship that "at times he was reluctantly permitted to enter regattas held by clubs whose members turned their backs on him socially when ashore. At other times he was barred altogether. Neither circumstance affected his good natured enthusiasm for yachting, and eventually, it may be added, he broke down many social barriers in yachting circles. . . . But for all his disregard of accepted yachting usages and customs General Butler took his numerous defeats like a true sportsman, seldom offering excuses; and no matter how badly he was beaten, he was ever ready for another race. Often he was laughed at when the old yacht came trailing in at the finish, but he brought a touch of color and human interest to the sport, such as no other American had offered up to that time."

Benjamin Butler's old sidekick and summer neighbor on Cape

Ann, Jonas French, with his good, solid, imperial-whiskered, broad-browed look of Sunday school superintendency, was arrested in 1891 on charges of embezzling from the Maverick National Bank of Boston, of which he was a quarter-owner. He and another director and the cashier were alleged to have loaned themselves fifty times the legal limit — $800,000 in the colonel's case alone. French's Cape Ann Granite Company (of which Butler was still a director) went into receivership against French's liabilities, estimated at $900,000. The pair played for big stakes, but though many echoed (not loudly) General Robert Schenck's characterization of "old Ben as a cross-eyed cuttle-fish swimming about in waters of his own muddying," no one was ever able to pin anything on him through the murk.

Benjamin Franklin Butler died in 1893 in his seventy-fifth year, still going strong. He left Bay View and *America* to his only daughter, Blanche, and her husband, General Adelbert Ames, whom she had married in 1870. Ames was a West Point graduate, winner of the Congressional Medal of Honor for bravery in the First Battle of Bull Run. In Virginia he served under his future father-in-law, the citizen major general who at every opportunity had made a point of scorning Pointers since he was politically passed over for admission as a boy. Ames rose to general, commanded a military department in the South after the war and was appointed to the Senate from Mississippi in 1871 at a time when Congressman Butler enjoyed great influence with President Grant. In 1874 he was elected governor of the former slave state. At the head of a corrupt carpet-bag government and caught up in the forces that were tearing Reconstruction apart, Governor Ames was impeached by the white-liners when they regained control of the Mississippi legislature. Butler got a smart ex-Confederate lawyer to defend his son-in-law, and the charges were withdrawn in exchange for his resignation. Adelbert and Blanche returned north for good, continuing to summer at Bay View with their children, and the "Ames Estate," where General Butler ran for Congress from a tent on the beach, has remained in his family ever since.

Paul Butler, the general's surviving son, was more interested in canoeing than yachting and in 1897 turned *America* over to Butler Ames, his nephew, who the next year joined the New York Yacht Club and reenrolled its greatest boat after a separation of nearly fifty years. She raced for the last time in 1901 and was laid up in Boston until 1917, when C. H. W. Foster, historian of the Eastern Yacht Club, bought the old schooner to save her from being sold in the Cape Verde trade. Four years later Foster, William Swan and other Bostonians returned her to the navy. Back at Annapolis she rotted in the dock for lack of funds. At last in 1941 limited restoration was undertaken. Then World War II broke out. Work was suspended. On Palm Sunday of 1942 her shed collapsed under the mass of snow dumped by a freak blizzard, and *America* was crushed to pieces.

As for the Jonas French sequel: William Henry O'Connell, an immigrant Irish millworker's son who grew up in Ben Butler's bailiwick of Lowell, no sooner was back in Boston from Rome with the red cap of a Prince of the Church in 1911 when he bought Rock Lawn for his summer archdiocesan seat. The new cardinal was determined to elevate Irish Catholicism to a position of respectability in the historically dominant councils of Yankee Protestantism. His Eminence Romanesqued the grounds with hundreds of trees and shrubs, lawn seats and statuary, installed a tennis court and had cherubs and seraphs painted on his kitchen ceiling. But after a while he forsook Bay View for a cottage in the more fashionable Devereux section of Marblehead.

# 'Round the Cape

AS THE EASTERN POINT ASSOCIATES LEARNED TO THEIR COST, CAPE ANN was no ripe plum for the picking. If their summer nirvana lay well nigh unattainable at the end of a trail obscured by dust and mined with potholes, all of West Gloucester beyond walking distance of the depot, Coffin's Beach and the four marshy, meandering miles of the Annisquam River estuary had surrendered to scarcely any roads at all and were ambushed at every turn on a hot and windless August day by squadrons of greenhead flies with the jaws of crocodiles, armies of bloodthirsty mosquitoes and legions of insects called midges, each too tiny to be seen yet equipped with the teeth of a greenhead.

And as for Cape Ann proper, all roads to Gloucester and Rockport had to squeeze across the Blynman Canal that had connected Squam River and the fishing port since colonial days. This feat was accomplished, when it chanced to be shut, over the drawbridge that was installed over the "Cut" in 1868 as a sort of cork in the bottleneck, a function it has served ever since. Once into Gloucester by the means of choice or necessity, the summer visitor discovered that the stagecoach was the sole public conveyance to the shore almost until the advent of the electric trolley cars.

Add to these natural obstacles the sublime indifference, if not the studied contempt, of the native population, and grand ventures for its colonization, like lost ships in the night, had a way of foundering on the Cape Ann shore.

The mile and a half of Coffin's Beach, as an example, was simply a sandbar cast up between Two Penny Loaf and Farm Point by a few millennia of storms sweeping across Ipswich Bay. On his deathbed the old Revolutionary hero Peter Coffin gathered his sons and cautioned them to husband the stand of timber that held the vagabond sand from drifting over his fields. But the trees went to the mill anyway, and the farm went to hell, and Frémont made camp on the outermost dune of a seashore desert.

Superb as it was and is, the beach was miles from the main road, much too far from anywhere to serve the pleasure of any but Gloucester folk fowling, wading and digging for hen clams. In the 1870s and 1880s the solitary year-rounder on the several hundred acres of the deserted Coffin farm was Solomon T. Trumbull, a quarryman who sold off a few lots for summer camps. Where the cart track dignified as Atlantic Street disappeared amongst the dunes he put up a rough-and-tumble roller skating rink that doubled as a dance hall and clam chowder canteen.

In about 1888 Edward C. Hawks, a Buffalo lawyer, came upon this wasteland by the sea, so clean and beautiful in its very barrenness, and bought Trumbull's land and several smaller abandoned farms and integrated the titles. Far out on the Loaf in 1890 he built a pair of "castles" of granite barged to the beach from a local quarry and dragged up to the site on sandsleds by oxen. With a faint smile, one imagines, he called this outpost "Hawksworth Hall." Later he was joined by his brother, James D. Hawks of Detroit, an engineer then runging it up the ladder to the presidency of the Detroit and Mackinac Railroad; James built his own castle, "The Bungalow," at the other end of the beach on Farm Point.

Did Edward Hawks grow lonely in the solitude of his splendid spit of sand, or merely land-poor? In the 1890s he cut Two Penny Loaf into 106 slices around the core of Hawksworth Hall and chopped the beach into another fifty, all with results as barren as his real estate. No one wanted to build a summer house on sand, exposed to storm and sea, isolated and without conveniences of any sort. Local speculators carved the land below Farm Point into yet another hundred lots; they named the small pond there Sleepy

Hollow Lake, and their dream resort Willoughby Park. Sleepy it all remained, and hollow the hopes, and they tiptoed away, most of their land unsold.

James Hawks survived his brother and summered at Coffin's Beach for thirty years. At one time he owned about a thousand acres, of which he restored a hundred to cultivation, and he planted ten thousand Austrian pines on the dunes in atonement for the prodigality of the Coffin boys. In 1924 his widow donated Wingaersheek Beach, the stretch southeast of Farm Point across the river from Annisquam, to the city of Gloucester, and not until the break-up of the Hawks estate did summer cottages finally sprout on the sands where John Charles Frémont sought solace after his beating at the heavy hand of Stonewall Jackson.

The variety of transport that George H. Procter had to make use of in order to commute summers to Merchant's Island six days a week from his *Cape Ann Advertiser* in downtown Gloucester suggests why more of the Annisquam River cottagers were not from out of town until the first motor car crossed the Cut.

Pearce's Island it was originally, about midway along the Squam River, owned and farmed by Captain Elias Day and James Thurston until 1864, when the farmhouse burned and they sold out to Simeon Merchant, a Gloucesterman recently returned from the California gold rush. Twice a day the tide swirled back and forth around the island; behind it and Rust and Ram islands, clear back to the West Parish woods and the Coffin farm, Jones Creek filled and drained through two miles of marsh where the farmers cut and stacked the salt hay, which they poled across to Gloucester in their gundalows in the fall of the year.

Uncle Sim resumed the farming, and after the war his produce, meat and sundry supplies attracted Gloucester people to tent on his island. In 1869 he built several small summer cottages for rent. The Procters were among his first tenants.

To get to town from Merchant's Island the editor had to row his dory three hundred yards across Squam River to Brown's landing (or be ferried by his children to the flats if the tide was out) and hike through the fields a half a mile to catch the Gloucester-bound stagecoach from Annisquam. Returning, if he had not been able to leave the dory, Father would hail the island across the quiet of the water and soon hear the thump of oars in tholepins and much juvenile excitement as the family boat approached.

One day a large party of Gloucester friends was shuttled over for a day of boating, swimming from the low-tide sandbar in the bend of the river, chowdering and dancing; as they were about to recross, a downpour intervened that lasted all evening. But the picnic tent was dry and ample; spare bedding was rounded up among the hosts, and the river rang with song and laughter 'til past midnight.

Merchant's Island was made for memories. Lobsters then abounded around the scattered rocks in Jones Creek, and the flats were gorged with clams. Uncle Sim initiated the boys in the art of bobbin' for eels, made up "bobbins" for them (lines and hooks squirming with garden worms) and dispatched them in the dory with instructions to anchor by the light of the moon over a certain spot in the creek off the long stone wharf. In an hour one night they hooked fifty of the critters; Uncle Sim skinned the lot, and the island had an eel fry next day. And the annual mackerel run, when the tinkers schooled into the river from the bay: one afternoon two of the boys hooked, split and salted an entire barrelful, hove it aboard their dory, rowed to Squam the next morning and sold their catch to a dealer for $3.50. And the gunning, when in the 1870s Lloyd Lewis, father of my Uncle Phil Lewis, came down from Lynn as a young fellow with a pal to camp on the island and shoot game birds in the marshes for the city market; the day's bag was taken into Gloucester and handed to the Eastern Railroad station agent, tagged for delivery to the chef of the famed United States Hotel in Boston.

At the end of his six-day week Editor Procter would buy the Sunday groceries, board the last Annisquam coach, trudge through Brown's field with his basket to the landing, shove off in the waiting dory, or shout for it, and slide across the tide to his island retreat. "What a sense of freedom it was," he rejoiced, "to have twenty-four

*Annisquam, across Lobster Cove from High Town, or Blueberry Hill, early 1880s.*
*The great boulder on the heights is Squam Rock, once known as Young's Great*

*Rock; to its left is solitary "Crown Cottage," built by D. A. Bulkley about 1880, one of the earliest summer houses in the community. In the distance are Ipswich Bay and Coffin's Beach. Procter Brothers, Howard collection*

*The vacationers at the Ocean View House present a scene of gaiety in contrast to the stern visage of their host, Eben B. Phillips. William D. Hoyt and* History of Essex County

*The Ocean View House presides over the ledges of Pigeon Cove and its bathhouse, at right, about 1870. Procter Brothers, Howard collection*

*Fishing at Pigeon Cove in the early 1870s is for gentlemen, in full attire.*
*The favored spot is Singer's Bluff, also known as Angling Point. Beyond is the*

*breakwater built by the granite quarry works of Rockport.*
*Procter Brothers, Howard collection*

*The Pigeon Cove House and (opposite) a reflective group of guests on the porch, about 1870. Procter Brothers, Howard collection*

*Summer scene on the Annisquam River, from the long-forgotten vantage of "Maiden's Retreat Bluff," Merchant's (Pearce's) Island, about 1874. William D. Hoyt*

*After the death of George H. Rogers in 1870, porches were added to his house and it was renamed the Bass Rocks Inn. Procter Brothers, Howard collection*

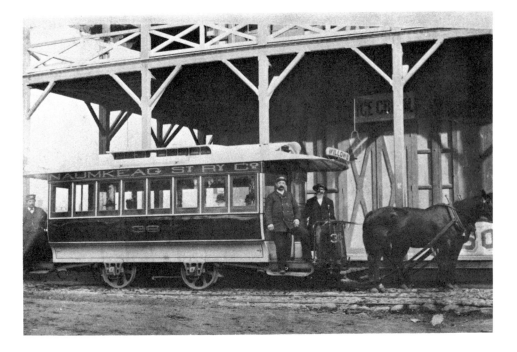

*The amusement park at Salem Willows was brand new and the horsecars had just started the run out to Salem Neck when number 36 was photographed in 1877. The Pavilion (below) fourteen years later. Essex Institute*

hours of real exemption from business cares, to breathe the pure air of heaven, to sail or row or bathe in the life-giving waters which flowed over the clean sandy beaches, or to sit on the piazza and watch the others enjoy the day in an orderly manner."

There was never anything fancy about summer life on the Annisquam River. The cottages that cropped up on the shores of Merchant's and Rust islands and Wheeler's Point — later at Wolf and Ferry hills, Riverview and Thurston's Point — were solid middle-class, inexpensive, unplastered, with piazzas that gave sweeping views up and down the river to Annisquam and its blinking lighthouse, the line of Coffin's snowy dunes, Ipswich Bay beyond. Before the invention of the naphtha and gasoline engines, ownership of anything so grand as a yacht was, with rare exceptions, out of the question. The twisty channel was narrow, and beset with rocks and shifting sandbars, the finest kind of nursery for young sailors in small boats; but the passage south and through the tide race at the Cut to Gloucester Harbor was hazardous, even when taken at the flood, and has long been forbidden to sailboat except under power. So, the practical "way out" for the river-bound who hankered for a taste of open-water sailing was to work wind and tide in the long haul out to Ipswich Bay, and hope to regain his mooring by nightfall.

That was the slant of George W. Smith, who in the 1850s put "Shiloh Lodge," the first summer cottage in the Annisquam River, on Rust Island. A score of years later George Procter accompanied the affable Boston ironmonger aboard his *Ida Belle* for a day's fishing in the bay with a party of cronies, "although many of them gray-bearded, as lively and happy as young school boys." With Captain Eben Brown at the tiller of the sloop, they had a smart sail out the river and into the bay, where the skipper found his landmarks that told him that he was on top of a favorite fishing hump, brought to and anchored. All tossed coins into the kitty for the first fish caught and threw over their lines. "Having secured a good fare, and partaken of the substantial luncheon provided, the home run up river was made for Shiloh Lodge, and later on one of Mr. Smith's famous fish dinners, with toothsome accompaniments, furnished a meal which was redolent of pleasant memories."

So much for summer life on Squam River in the well-ordered seventies and eighties.

East of the sand-swirled mouth of the river on Ipswich Bay the village of Annisquam jealously guarded its peninsular privacy, part of Gloucester but a world removed from the hustle and clatter of the port four miles away. In early colonial times Squam's narrow Lobster Cove was as busy with fishing and shipbuilding as the Harbor, but the maritime activity naturally gravitated to the larger, leaving the village's bay fishermen, clammers, lobstermen, sometime smugglers and farmers to their twisting lanes and weathered cottages, almost surrounded by the sea, which suited them just fine.

For several summers during the Civil War "a party of ladies and gentlemen," so described in the Gloucester *Telegraph,* pitched their tents on a rise of pasture near the old Village Church at the head of Lobster Cove. August of 1865 saw "quite an accession to their numbers, and they have three tents and quite a spacious camp ground. They have also a fine little yacht and a fancy row-boat moored in the cove, below the bridge, and a span of horses stabled in the vicinity." Next summer the contagion of canvas had spread to Wigwam Point on Ipswich Bay and Squam Point on the cove.

Pioneer Annisquam cottagers, the "Cambridge Settlement," came from Cambridge to Babson's Point above the village, leaving their mark on Cambridge Beach and Cambridge Avenue. In the 1870s Isaac Adams, the wealthy inventor of a nickel plating process, set his summer mansion on "Adams Hill," where beds of shells told of Indian clambakes, and walled up nearby springs to make a goldfish pond. On the bank of the Squam River at the end of Cambridge Avenue Pennsylvania steel magnate Luther S. Bent placed his "bungalow" and decreed that gardens bloom among the rocks; after his demise his son, Quincy, vice president of the Bethlehem Steel Company, tore the place down and in 1921 substituted a $250,000 Italianate villa.

Another early summer Squammer (though a little off-Squam on the south shore of Lobster Cove) was the Harvard marine zoologist Alpheus Hyatt, disciple of Louis Agassiz and curator of the Boston Society of Natural History. In 1878 Professor Hyatt bought the 1664 Norwood house, where he set up the first oceanography laboratory in the United States. The location did not quite suit him, however, and after two or three years he and his associates founded the marine biological laboratory at Woods Hole in Buzzards Bay. When not aboard his research schooner *Arethusa,* the professor sailed a boxlike catboat with name lettered in Chinese characters; the neighbors called it "Hyatt's Old Tea Chest." One of his two sculptress daughters, Mrs. Anna Vaughn Hyatt Huntington, created the triumphant equestrian statue of Joan of Arc in New York's Riverside Park; her near-duplicate of it prances through Gloucester's Legion Square, immortalizing a local firehorse.

The summer colonies of Norwood Heights and Rockholm rose out of the windy pasture above the Ipswich Bay shore around the turn of the century; but the village, with its intimate lanes, compact old houses and air of snug security against the sea, never surrendered to the twentieth century. "Squam is kinda pretty," allowed one old lady, "when you get used to it."

Just about the time that Ben Butler and Jonas French, the Goliaths of the granite industry, were buying up Bay View, the Fish Oil King from Swampscott, Eben B. Phillips, was mapping the North Shore's first extensive summer subdivision across the top of Cape Ann on Andrews Point in Rockport. Back in 1855, when they were talking of extending the railroad from Gloucester to Rockport, Phillips had shrewdly bought a large section of pasture and woodland north of Pigeon Cove, to which he added acreage east of the Babson Farm in partnership with George Babson, finally gathering in about all of Andrews and Halibut points.

The Oil King made his money selling his own brand of salt fish ("Phillips Beach Dunfish") and cod-liver oil and was a heavy investor in Boston and North Shore real estate. A hard worker and a strenuous player. In his time he had gone fishing, farming (he claimed to have dug a hundred bushels of potatoes single-handed one day), gunning (and once bagged nineteen pigeons out of a flock of twenty), rowing (for miles in subzero temperature) and yachting (as a familiar figure, bearded, bald and broad of beam at the helm of his schooner *Moll Pitcher* and her successor in the 1870s, *Fearless,* said by some to be the fastest by the wind of her day). Taciturn yet restless and keen of mind, a devotee of the poetry of Alexander Pope, Phillips was by the admission of an admiring biographer "a very peculiar person."

The Oil King bided his time and around 1870 launched into a well-publicized summer development of Andrews Point as "Ocean View," which he subdivided into some 225 building lots crisscrossed with roads linked to a mile-long peripheral boulevard that someone, perhaps he, named Phillips Avenue. In 1871 he opened a small summer hotel, the Ocean View House, at the south entrance to his project, sold a few lots and built a few cottages along the shore; he was planning a large hotel at the very tip of Andrews Point when he died in 1879, "so fully impressed with the idea that constant employment was one of the greatest duties in life that he kept in active operation up to his last sickness."

Pigeon Cove and the rest of Rockport owe no mean debt for their calm and sober atmosphere to two hundred determined women armed with hatchets, who marched on Dock Square on the eighth of July, 1856, at the instigation of one Hannah Jumper and noisily chopped their way through fourteen illegal rum shops; thereby they established, possibly forever, the moral tone that almost ever since has sustained the voters of Rockport in their resolve to remain publicly dry.

Eight days after this smashing victory over the demon, Ralph Waldo Emerson arrived at the Pigeon Cove House for a week of contemplation that must not have been sundered by a single discord of revelry from across the water of Sandy Bay, judging by his *Journal* entry of July 23: " 'Tis a noble friendly power, and seemed to say to me, 'Why so late and slow to come to me? Am I not here always thy proper summer home? Is not my voice thy needful music; my breath, thy healthful climate in the heat; my touch, thy cure? . . .' "

Be such sentiments as they may, Robert Carter and his shipmates in the cruising sloop *Helen* spent an un-Emersonian evening over claret two summers later, locked in behind Pigeon Cove's quarry pier with the fogbound fishing fleet. They had rowed her there through the thick all the way from Rockport, where they had re-solved not to remain another minute, for the stench of rotten fish in that tight little harbor had rendered it "so unpleasant on deck that, immediately after supper, we had lighted our cigars and closed the cabin doors, to smother with the fumes of tobacco the fishy odors from the shore." Anchored there in Pigeon Cove, as the drinks were about to give out they mixed and poured a final round with the toast "Confusion to the fog and success to the last of the cocktails" — only to discover in the midst of a general spluttering that in the dark of the cabin someone had reached for the jug of lamp fluid.

Such antics in the bosom of the friendly, fogged-in fishing fleet were barred from shore, where Pigeon Cove, in the words of the Reverend Henry C. Leonard, a summer habitué, "though not de-parting from simple, unfashionable ways, donned a habit somewhat new, and became widely known as a watering place. Gentlemen, whether with or without families, came to Pigeon Cove, not to waste their substance and wear their life out in excesses and follies, but for rest and quiet and healthful pastimes."

After the Civil War the Pigeon Cove House changed hands and in 1871 was moved to another site and replaced by a large new House. Down on the shore below, bathers of both sexes waded and paddled in the Bath (there was a Gentlemen's Bath at Hoop Pole Cove), a natural basin in the ledge, behind ropes tied to bolts driven into the smooth rock.

"Here they come tripping down with bathing-dresses on arm and bathing-hats on head," wrote one female guest fascinated by the ritual. "A few moments suffice for change of dress, and then they come forth from the bathing-houses a merry company. Some bathe from a sense of duty, others for pleasure and excitement. You can tell the different motives of the bathers at a glance. The former go into the water as they would into a dentist's chair. They nerve themselves up to it. They stoop down, take off the hat, which they fill with water and pour over head and shoulders, then catching the rope they venture three or four plunges, and the thing is done, the duty is performed: they come out, and go dripping back to the bathing-house, 'a damp, moist body.' "

The absentee landowner Eben Phillips developed Ocean View as an out-and-out speculation, gambling on the extension of the railroad to Rockport. Ten years earlier, at the other end of Cape Ann, Thomas Niles had been similarly motivated by the prospect of train service to Gloucester in buying the Eastern Point Farm. George H. Rogers must have been seized with the same idea when a few months after plans were announced to push the rails on to Cape Ann in 1845 he started quietly buying up the ancient colonial "cow rights" to the pastures north of the Niles and Patch farms, on the ocean side of East Gloucester overlooking some of the boldest coast on the North Shore; its most prominent feature is the precipitous promontory of Bass Rocks, at the south end of Little Good Harbor Beach, where the fighting striper lurks in the foaming surf.

George Rogers was a merchant of Gloucester, genial and generous, humorous and outspoken, and possessed of an insatiable appetite for real estate. He commenced his career as an apothecary, but rolling pills was not for him. With a small stake he got in on the ground floor of Gloucester's profitable trade with Surinam. When that showed signs of flagging during the darkening years before the Civil War, he pushed his surplus into real estate with such verve that they called him "The Great Conveyancer" and moved buildings over land and water so offhandedly as to merit the subnomen "The Great Remover."

Rogers paid fifty dollars for the first of his cow rights in the Bass Rocks section and by 1862 owned all fourteen, for which he was out of pocket $1,359.98. His investment was described at the time as "completely wild, abounding in swamps, rocks and berry bushes, presenting as rough a piece of territory as could be found on the Cape." He spent $120,000 clearing forty acres for tillage and mowing and four miles of roads, kept forty head of cattle, sold milk and vegetables over town, planted three hundred fruit trees and put in "a large grapery, peach house, greenhouse and conservatory." On the heights above Bass Rocks he laid the foundation for his summer house, which he bought in Boston and brought up on one of his vessels. Across the road Rogers assembled from parts of demolished Boston mansions a combined boarding house and sanitarium, Whiting House. In the same way one of The Great Remover's two massive barns had served the Methodists of Gloucester as their church, "The Old Sloop," before he hauled it from Prospect Street to his estate.

Apparently overextended, The Great Conveyancer in 1868 offered fifty summer building lots for sale. But there were few buyers, and when George Rogers died broke at sixty-eight in 1870 his 250-acre investment went on the block against $85,000 in debts. Henry Souther, a Boston brewer, headed a syndicate that took it over for $46,000 and had the controlling hand in the casual development of Bass Rocks over the next two decades until his death in 1892. Like Daniel Fuller, Henry was a Forty-niner — indeed, president of the Society of California Pioneers. His cousin John Souther was a South Boston locomotive manufacturer and inventor, who built the prototype steam shovels that loaded the gravel that filled in the Back Bay; John's almost equal claim on posterity was staked through the awesome person of his granddaughter, Miss Marguerite Souther, who for fifty-five years drilled young Bostonians (the writer among them) in the proprieties of ballroom dancing at Eliot Hall in Jamaica Plain.

Henry Souther's friends thought Bass Rocks a poor business venture, but he saw it as an investment for his grandchildren and let the farm continue to dominate. The Rogers home was converted into the Bass Rocks Inn. Whiting House became the Bass Rocks Hotel until the match of an incendiary took care of that. The Pebbly Beach

House was built on the shore, also burned suspiciously in 1884, and was replaced after ten years by the Moorland Hotel.

Among the more interesting of the few cottages of the era is the ungainly, cupolaed landmark of Judge Edgar J. Sherman of Lawrence, a former state attorney general, who was a trustee of the development after Souther's death. The house is literally bolted to the highest ledge of Bass Rocks, and with reason. John Webber paused there on his bicycle circuit of Cape Ann in 1885 and looked down from the veranda, where "seventy odd feet beneath us the 'sad sea waves' dash with terrific force against the huge jagged rocks, sending a thick blanket of snow-white foam afar out over the restless surface of the little cove. To see Bass Rocks in its glory one must visit the place during a storm; then the waters roll up in mountainous waves, and breaking against the rocky shore send thousands of tons of water completely over the dwelling on the cliff above."

And what befell these grand strategies to honeycomb the Cape Ann shore with summer colonies? Willoughby Park and the dreams of David Hawks to make the desert bloom never got off the paper; the myriad cells of Ocean View were integrated into substantially larger estates by 1900; likewise a similar attempt of the Southers at Bass Rocks. Reality sundered the web of lot lines with which the Associates sought to entangle Eastern Point, as it did the almost as ambitious plan of another partially interlocking syndicate to slice Rockport's Emerson Point into two hundred summer parcels that same year of 1889. The Rockport group bought up five hundred acres behind Loblolly Cove and on Emerson Point, which they renamed Lands End after its opposite across the sea. They laid out streets with quaint Cornish handles such as Wessex Road, Tregony Bow and Penrhyn Lane, and actually built a three-wing, three-story hotel above the cove, the Turk's Head Inn.

But like the rest, the Lands End Association had to pull in its horns. Cottages refused to spring from checkerboards. Land prices were too high, locations too remote, ledge too prevalent, services too primitive for the buyer of average means. The wealthy scooped up the lots by the handful, and before the end of the century most of the prime shore frontage on Cape Ann, from Magnolia along Gloucester Harbor through the Annisquam River and all the way back around by the sea to Eastern Point, had fallen to the summer people, by design or by default.

# The Great Invasion
# of Salem Willows
# and Other Picnic Parties

*It's not very far from old Salem*
*And from Lynn it's a half an hour's ride.*
*You don't mind the trolley because you can jolly*
*The nice little girls by your side.*
*On moonlight nights, Gee! it is dandy,*
*And on Sundays it's simply divine.*
*You can have all your "Coneys,"*
*To me they're all phoneys,*
*But Salem Willows for mine — it's mine.*

WHEN LOU COLLINS AND GEORGE HARDY WROTE THE MUSIC AND LYRICS of the "Salem Willows for Mine Waltz" in 1919 they struck just the note of good clean fun (laundered of the effects of the bloody noses and skinned knuckles suffered during the infrequent forays of the bully boys from Boston) that had marked the Willows as the healthy prototype of the all-American small-city amusement park for forty years.

Everyone knew, of course, that a couple of generations of jolly fellows and their nice little girls had been sneaking their flings along Boston's "phoney Coney," with its miles of sand and sensation, not to mention sin, yet the dig is not entirely disingenuous. By 1919 the Age of Innocence was on the skids, and so was the amusement park, no thanks to world war and the Tin Lizzie; but the merry-go-round and the midway and the trolley party, and all they evoked of that grandest of small-time, small-town larcenies, the stolen kiss, lingered on in the afterglow of the national self-image. Naughty Revere Beach was the creature of the big bad city, dismissed by the American Baedeker as "a popular holiday resort of Boston's lower classes"; furthermore, although it was the creation of the Narrow Gauge Railroad, the big beach was never under the control of the busy Little Wiggler and rapidly outgrew the feeble efforts of the town of Revere to check its excesses and remedy its deficiencies.

By contrast, old Salem's mini-resort had to do without the attractions of the beach; its Neck offered naught but rocks and mud flats. But the Willows was as handy as it was dandy, only twenty minutes from town, and it lay firmly within the grasp of the municipal authorities and of the horsecar company that operated and filled with customers what was among the very first of the hundreds of amusement parks organized by the street railways of the United States.

Salem sticks its Neck a mile into the bay between Beverly and Marblehead. Out at the end of it is rocky Juniper Point; off toward Marblehead hangs Winter Island from a causeway, offering some shelter to Salem Harbor and the focus of activity in the days of its commercial glory, Derby Wharf. Surrounded by tidal flats, the Neck and Winter Island have long been unapproachable by vessels of deep draft.

This was not always so. Dr. Bentley, Salem's ever-curious diarist, took his morning constitutional out to the Neck for years and knew it intimately; he had it in 1812 from an elderly acquaintance, who had it from his grandfather in 1760, that when the colony was founded, the Neck and Winter Island were forested to the water's edge. The settlers stripped off the timber to build defensive blockhouses and to clear ground for the drying of fish; there was deep water up to shore then, and Winter Island for a long time was Salem's fishing and commercial base. But they reckoned not on the northeast storms, unimpeded any longer by the forest, which ripped across the lowlands, eroded the soil and shoaled the coves in their lee until finally Winter Island had to be abandoned for the deeper water farther in the harbor.

Once it had been rendered more or less useless as a maritime facility, Salem didn't know quite what to do with its Neck. As it was a mile out of town in the bay and "cleansed" by the breezes off the water, the Neck pasture was regarded as a likely location for the pesthouse, which was duly erected halfway along the northwest shore of what came to be called Hospital Point; thence were ostracized the victims of smallpox and other contagious diseases, to die in isolation. No such privacy was accorded three convicted murderers who were hanged by and on the Neck (a fourth was executed on Winter Island in 1821), the first in 1772 when twelve thousand spectators in holiday mood ignored the January cold and streamed in from the countryside, munched their box lunches, heard the Reverend Mr. Diman preach a highly satisfactory sermon on the wages of sin and watched Bryan Sheehan collect his.

In the main, though, Salem Neck was the scene of more joy and jollity than such grim proceedings would suggest. The blockhouses of the settlers had given way to permanent earthworks with successive wars and scares of war — Fort Pickering out on Winter Island, Fort Juniper on Juniper Point (where the Neck Farm was) and Fort Lee midway on the Neck. Fallen into disuse after the Revolution, the old, grassed-over redoubts were magnets for the boys of Salem and for boys at heart such as Dr. Bentley, who on the thirtieth of May, 1792, "went down to the Neck Farm & dined on fish, & after dinner left the concourse of boys, men, & negroes, & went upon Juniper Head, where I took a soft lodging upon a stone, & relieved myself by an hour's nap under the Junipers. I confess still a pleasure in seeing the busy pleasures of children, & cannot think there is so great difference in the great world & little one as I have been taught to imagine."

On more serious business, the boys found Juniper Point and Winter Island good vantages from which to watch for returning East Indiamen — and a Spanish silver dollar for the winner of the

race in to Derby Wharf with the good news. The lads had a competitor in the pastor of the East Church, so sharp of eye that his
parishioner, Captain George Crowninshield, built Dr. Bentley a
watchtower on the Neck, the higher to raise his spyglass to the
horizon while pausing in his daily walk. Along the way, the pesthouse was an all too visible reminder of Salem's sick poor, and in
1801 a conscience-stricken board of health had forty willows planted
nearby "in such direction as they may think will be most conducive
to the comfort and convenience of the sick." The hospital burned in
1846, but the trees held their ground, grew stately and o'erspreading,
and around 1858 the Willows was embraced by the Salem park
system.

After its abandonment by the maritime interest, Winter Island was
considered fit for no other very great enterprise and was adopted as a
training ground by the militia. "The Artillery & Infantry with the
Targets went this day upon Winter Island," wrote Dr. Bentley on
September 21, 1808, "but from the wind or some other cause nothing
was done to discover expert firing . . . not a man was upon the
ground who even knew what the art of Gunnery was."

By the 1850s the Massachusetts Volunteers were closer to the
mark. Their annual displays of preparedness for come-what-may
attracted vast throngs that funneled by vehicle and afoot across the
Neck and through the Willows to Winter Island. The progress of
the day would be marked by immense clouds of midsummer dust as
the patriotic citizenry with gala spirit followed the drills and the
parades, fraternized with the volunteers, settled down with their
lunch baskets and attuned their ears to the strains of band after
band. The champion, of course, was the Salem Brass Band, under
the baton of a recent émigré from Dublin, the handsome young
cornetist Patrick Sarsfield Gilmore, later the leader of his own
famous band and originator of the "monster band concert," massing
hundreds of musicians and choruses in the thousands. The Salem
players, however, were content during evening concerts to arrange
themselves on the grass and read their music, like coal miners, by
the flickering light of miniature oil lamps affixed to their caps.

The volunteers and their bands marched off to war, and straggled back, but the surrender of Salem Neck to its destiny did not begin until the year 1873. This came about, as related in an earlier chapter, when the land company that had gobbled up most of Marblehead Neck advised the summer colony of Lowell people who had been leasing their camps there since 1866 to buy or get out. Most chose the latter course and, having a manifest partiality for necks, snooped out some available land on Juniper Point in 1873 and transplanted themselves there.

That was the start of it. Two years later Daniel B. Gardner of Salem purchased the Neck Farm, which Dr. Bentley had made the frequent destination of his constitutionals seventy-five years earlier, and divided the forty-two acres into summer cottage lots. History had come full cycle in a sense. One of Dr. Bentley's East Church parishioners, Captain Edward Allen, acquired the rock-strewn tract in 1803 and that May moved out from his town house for the summer — "the first time," his pastor observed, "the Neck has been the residence of any family but for the purposes of industry." Unfortunately Allen died in July after pouring out his fortune on improvements, most notably for a perfect arsenal of black powder, with which his men blasted away at the full crop of boulders that had been exposed by the erosion of the soil. Allen's son, also a sea captain, was as unstinting. "Great expences have been allowed to this ungrateful spot from regard to its favourite situation," Bentley noticed after six more years of flying rock, lengthening stone walls and expanding ornamental gardens, though he was as surprised as everyone else in 1810 when out of the blue the property was attached for debt — "the Mystery is yet unexplained as the reputation of Capt. Allen led him to no excesses & his wife could not be exceeded in prudence."

In 1816 the Allen Farm was bought by one Dustin, a butcher of Danvers, and remained in his family until Gardner acquired and carved it up in 1875. The evictees from Marblehead were joined by friends from Lowell and by others from Salem and Peabody. Roads were laid out and shade trees planted; Wenham Lake water was piped in, fountains were installed, a boating basin was seawalled up to Winter Island, and in the early 1880s the Neck was the base for the Salem Bay Yacht Club. By 1884 Captain Allen's "ungrateful spot" was a growing colony of a hundred summer cottages; the earthly remains of Fort Juniper had disappeared altogether, "and the yachtsmen and cottagers flirt and make merry," as one chronicler wrote, "where once the sad-faced patriot sentinel looked out over the bay in the moonlight and wondered at the inscrutable providence that kept him out there in the cold instead of suffering him to slumber in his comfortable bed in the town, but a mile away."

The exodus of the Lowell campers from Neck to Neck in the summer of 1873 coincided with the appearance at the Willows of the restaurant of François, a black chef who specialized in fish dinners, and an influx of outings and picnic parties. Under the prodding of the railroads and horsecar lines, city dwellers were just awakening to the excursionary possibilities of the North Shore "pic-nic." At Echo Grove in Lynn James Newhall counted thirty-seven of these ingestive communions with all outdoors and the insect life during the summer of 1871. That August the Eastern Railroad opened a branch from its Hamilton depot to the Methodist campground at Asbury Grove, founded in memory of Bishop Asbury, an early circuit rider, in 1859. The branch had been in operation only a few days when a breakdown on it contributed to the Revere Disaster, but the volume of traffic swelled unabated, and then in 1875 the Narrow Gauge launched its flood upon Revere Beach.

Consequently, when the Naumkeag Street Railway was incorporated in the summer of 1875 on the foundations of the Salem Street Railway, which had been running horsecars through town since 1862, the owners were quite aware of the nickel-and-dime potential of this novel traffic in picnickers and outdoor enthusiasts.

The Eastern Railroad's next move pointed the way for the Great Invasion of Salem Neck. After years of backing and filling, Eastern in 1872 had consented to run a branch line from Wenham to Essex, skirting the shore of Chebacco Lake, where the icehouses were expected to be a decisive source of freight. It occurred to an imaginative official of the railroad that the Neck, a stretch of lake shore of great beauty owned by the Low family, might make an ideal picnic spot for city people, and he set the wheels in motion. Eastern leased Essex's Neck from the Lows for ten years, named it Centennial Grove (this was 1876), built a dining room, dance hall and shooting gallery, laid in a fleet of boats for hire, let in one of the earliest of the "flying horses" (a couple of crosspieces with wooden horses at either end, pushed around by hand) and opened in the spring.

After its lease expired the railroad turned the park over to the owners to manage, having demonstrated brilliantly how a transportation company could quite artificially attract passengers by creating the attraction; one record summer two locomotives labored into Centennial Grove with a single picnic party that required forty-two coaches in two sections for the hauling.

If the railroads could do it, the horsecars should be able to at a fraction of the cost. Centennial Grove had hardly opened when the Naumkeag Street Railway sought and secured its franchise, laid tracks out to Salem Neck and dispatched the first bobtail, Car 33, off to the Willows on June 10, 1877. Patrick Kennealley followed with his peanut stand, yes, Pat Kennealley, inventor of the amazing, the famous, the one and only "double-jointed" peanut. And then the picnickers, happy droves of them. The Great Invasion was about to happen.

With the music from the fare boxes ringing in their ears, Naumkeag's owners within the next few months bought land at the end of the new line and built the Willow Park Pavilion, with dance hall on the ground floor, restaurant seating three hundred upstairs, decks of piazzas and an observation tower. For a theatre they reassembled the frame of one of the cavernous exposition buildings whose day had come and gone in Boston. They planted gardens and persuaded the city of Salem to spruce up its adjoining park. Finally, they stocked up on fireworks and opened to the public with a smashing debut on the tenth of June, 1880, three years to the day from Car 33's inaugural trip to the Willows.

By 1882 Willow Park had signed on the new Salem Cadet Band for Sunday concerts and the steamer *Three Brothers* for daily excursions. Horsecars ran from Salem every ten minutes. "There are none of the swindling prices so often charged at the sea-shore," advised a North Shore guidebook. Fifty cents covered a complete fish dinner with choice of chowder, "schrode," mackerel, cunner, flounder, baked bluefish Point Shirley style (hats off to the mighty Taft), salmon, codfish, haddock, lobster or red snapper. And a thin dime admitted the curious into the camera obscura, which "brings into striking prominence objects within a circuit of 20 miles." This popular adaptation of a centuries-old forerunner of photography may have made use of the pavilion's observation tower, from which a rotating lens would cast, by means of a mirror, an inverted panoramic image of the countryside and seascape down onto a white table placed in the middle of the darkened room below, to the delight of the customers. A more conventional camera was employed by Harry Esbach, who invited the sitter to enjoy the garden outside his studio while the tintype emerged.

From the very start the Willows was a smash hit on the North Shore. If you could get to Salem by train or horsecar connection, the trip out on the Naumkeag line was literally a breeze. The simple attractions (simple at first, but more sophisticated and exciting with each new season) drew great crowds, as many as eight thousand a day. The Shore's largest public resort outside of Revere Beach was cheap, wholesome and well run. It was also well regulated by the city, which took a proprietary attitude toward the exploitation of its traditional hanging and marching ground; the Neck was highly visible out there in the bay, and the amusement park was created by local interests primarily for the enjoyment of the citizens, of whom it could still be said, as Caroline King said of her childhood a generation earlier, that Salem summered as a rule in Salem "and the social life of the town was as full as in the winter."

Its bold stroke in devising an end for its own means contributed largely to the financial success of the Naumkeag Street Railway. Expanding east to Marblehead and north through Beverly, the line

*In the shade of the willows, derby hats and sweeping skirts are de rigueur at Salem Willows in 1891. Essex Institute*

*Hospital Beach, Salem Willows, 1891. Essex Institute*

*The end of Salem Neck at Juniper Point, with a steam launch all fired up to go, 1891. Essex Institute*

*Gazebo at Hospital Point, 1891. Essex Institute*

brought its bobtails to Asbury Grove via Wenham, causing one resident of that secluded nook of rural Essex County to complain that "with the first car which jangled down the quiet elm-shaded street, the peaceful calm of the town was ended, and in its place, the clang and hurry of modern life was to be for ever more." The effect on the campground of this so much more accommodating supplement to the steam railroad was a second boom. Crowds of "rounders" hustled aboard Naumkeag's ten-bench, fifty passenger cars at Salem for an afternoon at Asbury at thirty cents a head. The summer population of the Grove leaped to two thousand, and the count of rented cottages under the tall trees to nearly four hundred; camp meetings drew as many as fifteen thousand faithful, so that it became necessary for this unique summer community of seventy-five acres in the woods of West Hamilton to provide, besides the chapels and the tabernacle of the religious revival, a small hotel, stores, restaurants, an express office and its own post office.

The horse railroad reached the top of the hill in 1888, when more than six thousand nags clip-clopped through the streets of Boston. Then, suddenly, it plummeted down the other side into oblivion.

As early as 1885 Leo Daft had used electricity to run his queer little trams along Revere Beach, and late in 1887 the Lynn and Boston had tried an electric car on its Highlands circuit. But it was not until February of 1888 that Frank J. Sprague, an electrical genius whose name should be as much a household word as Edison's, succeeded in exterminating the bugs and got the world's first practical citywide electric streetcar system operating over the hills and around the curves of Richmond, Virginia. Horsecar executives (having their tracks already laid) grabbed the first train for Richmond to see for themselves. Boston's biggest horsecar line, the West End Railroad, made the decision to go electric, and the stampede was on.

That summer of 1888 scores of cities plotted to substitute an electric motor and an overhead wire for faithful Dobbin and his bag of oats. On the second of June the Revere Electric Street Railroad was organized. Six weeks later its two trolley cars, which looked to idle bystanders like ordinary bobtails, gave a satisfactory demonstration over the tracks above the beach, reaching the breakneck speed of thirty miles an hour and frightening several horses. On August second the Naumkeag Street Railway started regular electric car service to Salem Willows. On the twenty-fifth the Revere line was officially in business, carrying excited passengers the mile, almost, between Crescent Beach and the Great Ocean Pier in three thrilling minutes. The Revere *Journal* predicted flatly that the electric trolley car would prove to be very popular.

And that, to revert to waltz time, is how it came to pass that . . .

> *The place that I long for,*
> *The place that I'm strong for,*
> *Is sure to be in the race.*
> *The boys who will meet you,*
> *The girls who will greet you,*
> *Will all have a smile on their face.*
> *The dear ball-room floor is the place I adore,*
> *The waters with nice shady views.*
> *The music is grand, makes you dance, understand,*
> *It's the place where you'll never feel blue.*
> *It's not very far from old Salem,*
> *And from Lynn it's a half an hour's ride.*
> *You don't mind the trolley because you can jolly*
> *The nice little girls by your side. . . .*

#  What's Past . . .

BY 1890 BOSTON'S INSINUATION OF ITS NORTH SHORE WAS COMPLETE save for distant Ipswich, where the country miles of Argilla Road, skirting the drowsy drumlins above the salt marsh to the dunes and beach of Castle Neck, awaited an uncommonly compatible colony of Back Bay doctors and a few kindred professionals, presided but in no way lorded over by a Chicago plumbing multimillionaire who spent his money both wisely and well; and some islands — Baker's, Misery and Hog — that would be settled (and to a degree unsettled) in the unique style of islands.

The nineties rattled in on the electric cars and rattled on. In this third revolution of the wheels (the horsecars were merely the offspring of a marriage of convenience; the bicycle was the second), everybody wanted to go everywhere, and did. One frugal summer resident clattered and clanged the 285 miles from New York City, via Springfield, to Eastern Point for $2.85, and the open-air trolley parties rollicked along at the top of their lungs, before him and behind, on their way to the amusement parks held out, carrot-fashion, by the traction companies in the tradition of Salem Willows.

The phoniest Coney this side of the real one was four miles of crazy mirrors reflecting the strident, strutting, muscle-bound (it had its charmingly fresh and demure side) awkwardness of the nation in the glandular confusion of its adolescence. While the Willows waltzed divinely to the cadence of North Shore summer life, Revere

Beach stomped to the pounding pulse of the big city exploding to escape from its ever more unbearable self. Always obliging, the beach became a bedlam of the bizarre, a nightmare of the spectacular, and one of the great playgrounds of the world — a Jekyll-Hyde sort of beach, one face a mirror of distortion, the other a smiling fantasy of midsummer forever. Maurice Prendergast was there with his sketchbook — a slight man with a shy moustache, who parted his hair in the middle — and the ladies and gents with parasols and frothy hats and derbies, and the little girls in blue ribbons and pink petticoats, are alive today — more so, almost, than life itself.

Those beguilingly, deceptively halcyon years, bracketed by the closing decade of a British queen's long reign and the single Edwardian one of her heir, were the heydays of the big stealers and the big spenders, and there were those who looked about them darkly and supposed that America was being pocketed by the aristocracy of the dollar. Not quite. Legitimacy, not oligarchy, was at the top of the solid silver ladder, and from one coast to the other Boston's summer bastion was viewed as a social summit well worth the scaling.

And so the Henry Lee Higginsons and the Lorings found themselves shoving over for the Henry Clay Fricks and the Moores. Major Higginson counseled his friends that he who made his fortune before his prime should set an example of civic virtue by spending it before he died. Mr. Frick declared that he believed in high business conscience untrammeled by demagogic political agitation, by which he meant legislation of any sort, and he chartered a freight train to haul loam twice a day from Topsfield to his burgeoning Versailles at Pride's, and hired three hundred men to spread it around.

Everyone else who *was* anyone on *The* North Shore was spreading it around too, though no one could touch H. C. Frick, not even his wily crony down the road, "Judge" William H. Moore (never a judge), who had only two hundred men grading *his* estate but made up part of the deficit, anyway, by bringing his thirty-eight thoroughbreds, carriages and twenty-seven stablemen for the summer, every summer, on a five-car (sometimes seven) special, along with his own private family Pullmans.

The Lorings and friends in their silver-gray shingled cottages were quietly amused but scarcely impressed.

And then, the double blows — the descent of the income tax upon the land and the World War. So many foreign ambassadors were taking their ease on the North Shore when Germany declared war on the Allies in August of 1914 that no one else could get a cablegram out. French chauffeurs and Italian gardeners quit en masse to answer the call to arms, leaving whole households in an uproar. Patriotic yachtsmen got up an antisubmarine patrol out of Marblehead; the navy took over the Eastern Yacht Club; and the Myopia Hunt fielded a cavalry troop of polo players.

As the war ground on, matrons worried that the coal shortage would shut down their greenhouses. Norman Prince, the dashing scion of "Princemere" in Wenham, organized the Lafayette Escadrille and died in a French hospital from wounds after getting shot down in his hundred and twenty-second aerial engagement. And Miss Helen Clay Frick produced an amateur movie, *Home Fires,* for the boys on furlough from the trenches, showing a tennis match between Eleonora Sears and Alice Thorndike, hunting and golfing scenes at Myopia, polo at Princemere, whippet racing in Ipswich, and some shots of "Bunny" Wood's outing classes for little tots at Beverly Farms.

Then, the roar of the twenties, a mighty crash, and a chagrined and protracted silence. North Shore social note, 1933: "Real estate agents have become a positive menace to the prospective lessor. In fact this whole modern trend of having one's friends in business is simply harrowing to any one who contemplates buying anything whatsoever. Mention that you enjoy reading a particular magazine and you'll find a half dozen acquaintances selling it. Admit your gown is shabby and you'll learn your neighbor is running a 'shoppe.' Stores are employing post-debutante saleswomen in the expectation that their friends will purchase there. . . ."

But this is all for another book.

# Acknowledgments

MY PATIENT EDITOR, LLEWELLYN HOWLAND III, SUGGESTED THAT THERE are north shores and North Shores and proposed that I treat the subject along the lines I applied in a large book about the small place where I reside, Eastern Point. He understandably expected a smaller book about a larger place, as a practical matter, and was as much at a loss for words as I was at a surplus when, long past due course, he was presented with a manuscript that weighed in at five pounds and two ounces — about the heft of a small newborn — and yet failed to carry the proposition past 1890. "What! Two more?" Becky was wont to exclaim in mock amazement as one chapter after another underwent mitosis almost before her very eyes; but she knows about cell division, being a biochemist, and about the writer, being my wife.

As usual when exploring the uncharted history of the North Shore, I found the Essex Institute in Salem the most thoroughly provisioned of ships and its reference librarian, Mrs. Irene Norton, the most intuitive of pilots; I am also grateful for the help of Mrs. Marylou Birchmore of the staff and to Bryant F. Tolles, Jr., director and librarian, for his generous permission to make free use of the Institute's pictorial resources.

Others to which and to whom I am indebted include the Beverly Historical Society and Mrs. Nancy Coffey of the volunteer staff; Boston Athenaeum; Boston Public Library; Cape Ann Historical

Association and Mrs. Caroline Benham, curator; Eastern Yacht Club and Lawrence P. Pleasants, chairman of the house committee; Essex County Registry of Deeds; Lynn Historical Society and Harold S. Walker, archivist; Manchester Historical Society and Mrs. George Loring, curator; Nahant Historical Society and Mrs. Calantha Sears, president; Nahant Public Library and Mrs. Frank Samson, former librarian; Peabody Museum of Salem and Mrs. Barbara Edkins, librarian; Revere Public Library; Sawyer Free Library of Gloucester and Elizabeth Roland, reference librarian; Wenham Historical Association; Winthrop Improvement and Historical Association and Mrs. Christine Poor of the staff; and Winthrop Public Library and Mrs. Margaret Hinckley, reference librarian.

Frances L. Burnett of Manchester, Stephen B. Howard of Gloucester, William D. Hoyt of Rockport, Sandra Hubbard of Winthrop and Peter McCauley of Revere loaned me photographs from their collections or assisted me in gathering them around their communities, and to each I am especially appreciative of their time and expertise, as I am to Mrs. John Singleton Copley Morgan for an informative tour of Nahant.

Chief among written sources that have been recurrently consulted are the ponderous and truly invaluable town-by-town *History of Essex County* edited by Hurd; the rich *Essex Institute Historical Collections;* William Bentley's peripatetic *Diary* of his pastorate in Salem and his ceaseless travels on the North Shore from 1784 until his death in 1819; Samuel Eliot Morison's pathbreaking *Maritime History of Massachusetts;* and the *Dictionary of American Biography.* Town histories, odd volumes, newspapers, periodicals and numerous other sources have also been consulted; the more important are cited in the Notes.

# Notes

### CHAPTER 1: SO NEAR AND YET SO FAR

The history of the North Shore is a perfectly good example of the proposition that the history of America is the history of its transportation systems. And the canoe fell the first victim to progress.

### CHAPTER 2: SUMMER PIONEERS AT NAHANT AND DANVERS

A useful authority on the early days of Lynn and Nahant is Alonzo Lewis's *History*, first published in 1844. He was a surveyor and naturalist as well as poet and historian; after the author's death in 1861, James Newhall added his own comments to Lewis's unpublished notes and issued a revised edition in 1865.

Fred Wilson's *Annals* are keel and frames in the construction of the multi-chaptered Nahant. Wilson was a longtime leader in town and knew everybody; his father, Joseph T. Wilson, was a builder of North Shore summer cottages, town moderator and chairman of the selectmen, and local crony of Senator Lodge. Wilson is an abundantly necessary wellspring, but not fully sufficient without such humorous contemporary comments as those of the journalist James L. Homer.

Also called Lynn Beach and Nahant Beach, Long Beach is preferred here as the more descriptive.

### CHAPTER 3: COLD ROAST BOSTON

An enlightening recent source touching on Nahant's budding resort days is Seaburg's and Paterson's biography of Colonel Perkins, *Merchant Prince of Boston*.

### CHAPTER 4: TH' HAUNT IS NOT NEWPORT (THANK GOD)

Wilson and Lewis dominate the secondary sources on midcentury Nahant, while the literary company speaks for itself and would monopolize the chapter, if allowed, as Thomas Grattan almost did; his acidulous comments on Cold Roast are the most quotable ever penned.

## CHAPTER 5: ENTER THE IRON MONSTER

The strange story of once-fair Chelsea's settlement, annexation, disengagement, aborted promise as a resort, deflowering, dismemberment, and destruction and disbursement in the Great Fire of 1908 awaits a teller to do it justice.

That historian of steam, Francis B. C. Bradlee, has traced the ups and downs of the Eastern Railroad in considerable detail.

For readability, Thompson's *Sketches* is a cut above most town histories and is the principal source on Swampscott, with help from Alonzo Lewis.

## CHAPTER 6: BEVERLY AND MANCHESTER ARE ALL BUT SUBDUED

Warren Prince, the summer cottage builder, recorded the settlement of the Beverly shore in a newspaper series in 1884; it was further documented by Miss Loring's monograph of 1932, when she was president of the Beverly Historical Society. Mrs. Fraser surveyed Manchester in greater detail and over a longer span in her extremely valuable paper for the Manchester Historical Society in 1961, which was based on an account from the Salem *Register* of the summer colony of 1877.

## CHAPTER 7: GLOUCESTER KEEPS ON FISHING

Most of the Freshwater Cove account draws on reminiscent articles (unsigned but possibly by editor George H. Procter) in the Gloucester *Daily Times* of August 12 and 26, 1905. For the development of Eastern Point in this and Chapter 18, I have blandly plagiarized my *Eastern Point*, with some further information about John Perkins Cushing's tenure gleaned subsequent to that book's publication from Cushing's diary in the Boston Athenaeum.

## CHAPTER 8: THOSE FIRST YACHTS

Considering the importance of yachting on both shores of Massachusetts Bay to the advance of the sport in America, its history is a surprisingly neglected topic. William Bentley makes intriguing mention of activity catalyzed, perforce, by President Jefferson's Embargo. The *Personal Reminiscences* of the colorful Captain Forbes are as fruitful as they are entertaining, and his *Discursive Sketch of Yachting* (privately printed in a limited edition and hard to find today) is even more so. The best relatively recent source by far is William P. Stephens's rambling, happily written, encyclopedic *Traditions and Memories of American Yachting,* strung out through dozens of issues and then bound into a book in 1942 by *Motor Boating* — an important work which deserves reprinting and demands indexing.

### CHAPTER 9: WINTHROP AND THE LITTLE WIGGLER

William Clark's excellent *History* documents the high points of Winthrop's development as a summer resort. Chief conductors for the serpentine courses of the Little Wiggler and the Peanut Train in this and the next chapter are Bradlee, the *Trains* article and Clark. Winthrop is in great debt to her pictorial historian, Sidvin Frank Tucker. I should like to know more about Orray Augustus Taft, Alpheus P. Blake and Dr. Samuel Ingalls — enterprising entrepreneurs all — but they eluded me.

### CHAPTER 10: REVERE BEACH IS THE PLACE TO GO

Although doggedly compilatory and mysteriously organized, Shurtleff's *History* is the essential reference for Revere and its parent Chelsea. George Clarke's account of Revere Beach is a helpful overview, but the only way to catch the spirit of it is by thumbing the pages of the Revere *Journal*.

### CHAPTER 11: MARBLEHEADS SUCCUMBS AS SWAMPSCOTT HUMS

Robert Carter's account of his yachting cruise of the New England coast in 1858 is the first and freshest of all and should be in the book locker of every cruising boat. Its later counterpart on land — full of the contemporary viewpoint — is the series of guidebooks to the North Shore written by Hill and Nevins. Kimball's 1882 *Handbook* to Marblehead Neck, together with Searle's first-rate articles on the Neck and Cat Island and Peabody's on Peach's Point, and Roads's 1897 *History*, document Marblehead's late summer development, with a few nuggets from the long-needed updating by Lord and Gamage in 1972.

### CHAPTER 12: YACHTING GETS SERIOUS

Charles H. W. Foster's *Eastern Yacht Club Ditty Box* is a well-salted account of the growth of organized yachting at Marblehead and overflows with curious morsels of information, sailorman's anecdotes and splendid photographs of the club's pre-1900 fleet. Samuel Wakeman, via his Cohasset neighbor George G. Crocker, supplied me with unexpected information on the mysterious Nahasset Yacht Club.

### CHAPTER 13: MARBLEHEAD DEFENDS THE CUP

"Cutter Crank" Stephens, with his *Traditions and Memories* and *American Yachting,* is the mentor of us all for the trends leading to Marblehead's defense of the mug and the aftermath.

### CHAPTER 14: NAHANT OUT-BOSTONS BOSTON

With a little over three chapters, Nahant has more than its share of the North Shore; but it was, after all, the first and was loaded with luminaries during most of the nineteenth century until the money and show shifted to the Gold Coast.

### CHAPTER 15: OF AUTOCRATS AND ACTORS

Not until I chanced upon the 1908 *History of the Boston Theatre* did I discover that all the significant threads that connected the residents of Theatre Lane led back to that famous old playhouse and its owners. Eleanor Ruggles O'Leary's *Prince of Players* is a sensitive study of the unhappy Booths.

### CHAPTER 16: THE GOLD COAST

The outdated town histories of Beverly and Manchester throw little or no light on their resort phases. Stone's was published the year before Charles Cushing Paine bought into Beverly, and Lamson's is of interest largely on account of his jaundiced comments about the Manchester crowd. With the exception of Magnolia, Marblehead, Nahant and Winthrop, local chroniclers generally have neglected the rise of summer life along the North Shore.

Richard Harmond is the expert on the Beverly Farms separation attempt.

### CHAPTER 17: THE SHINGLED SHORE

I have relied principally on Professor Scully's revealing study of the Shingle Style, of which our "winterized" cottage on Gloucester Harbor is pleasant enough vintage 1889 — incomparable in June, perfectly wretched to heat in January.

### CHAPTER 18: FROM MAGNOLIA TO EASTERN POINT

Most of the Magnolia story arises from the short histories by Hartt and the Fosters, and a raking of *Magnolia Leaves*. My Cape Ann friend and neighbor, Professor O'Gorman, has quite thoroughly dealt with the Gloucester phases of Hunt and Homer during the course of his continuing study of the art colony of which they were the first settlers.

### CHAPTER 19: TWO GENERALS ON THE BEACH

Of the several biographies of Butler, *Lincoln's Scapegoat General* by West has the advantage of the longest perspective but leaves one with the feeling that the definitive picture of this puzzling personage has yet to be pieced together.

## CHAPTER 20: 'ROUND THE CAPE

No single source has the precedence in this ramble around the late-developing periphery of Cape Ann, though George Procter's memories of summer life on the Annisquam River — where I learned to sail in a Brutal Beast class we called *Pig's Knuckle* after we bought it from Jake Wirth, the Boston restaurateur — are especially evocative for me.

"When I was a lad," I wrote in my Gloucester *Daily Times* column of January 22, 1968, "we spent a few weeks each summer in my grandmother's cottage at Riverview, and every dawn I awoke (I can hear it now, just as clear) to the engines of the draggers laboring through Squam River for the Bay, and the lobster boats. Most of the vessels then had those slow-turning Wolverine and Atlas diesels. The still air before sunrise throbbed to the deep bass of their CHUG a da CHUG a da CHUG a da . . . receding as they passed by to round the bar below Thurston's Point, the swish of the wake slapping up along the flats. And then the next, growing louder as the first died out, coming up along by Rust Island, and the next . . . a meandering file of ponderous sea elephants, almost trunk to tail. Some days when it was thick I would leap from bed to the window, straining through the fog for a glimpse . . . but nothing to be seen beyond a shrouded maple, dripping wet. Only the sound from down below somewhere, muffled, dogged . . . CHUG a da CHUG a da CHUG a da. . . . Or a lobsterman going by, nursing along his old Lathrop . . . putt putt putt putt (silence while the flywheel spins) putt putt (silence) putt (silence) putt putt putt (silence) putt . . . and off down the river. . . ."

## CHAPTER 21: THE GREAT INVASION OF SALEM WILLOWS
## AND OTHER PICNIC PARTIES

Salem Neck, with hints of rattling good times at the end of the trolley tracks to come, seems a good spot to finish such a wandering tale as this. And who better to begin the ending than Dr. Bentley, who ended the beginning, in a manner of speaking, and enjoyed his summers on the North Shore as few have before or since?

# Bibliography

GENERAL AND REGIONAL

*The American Heritage History of Notable American Houses*. Ed. Marshall B. Davidson. New York, 1971.

Amory, Cleveland. *The Proper Bostonians*. New York, 1947.

Andrews, Wayne. *Architecture in New England*. Brattleboro, 1973.

Barrett, Richmond. *Good Old Summer Days*. Boston, 1941.

"Boston, Revere Beach & Lynn." *Trains,* January 1946.

Boswell, Charles. *The America: The Story of the World's Most Famous Yacht*. New York, 1967.

Bradlee, Francis B. C. "Boston, Revere Beach & Lynn Narrow Gauge Railroad." *Essex Institute Historical Collections,* October 1921.

—— *The Eastern Railroad: A Historical Account of Early Railroading in Eastern New England*. Salem, Mass., 1922.

—— "Some Account of Steam Navigation in New England." *Essex Institute Historical Collections,* January 1919.

Bunting, William H. *Steamers, Schooners, Cutters, and Sloops*. Boston, 1974.

Burgess, Edward. *American and English Yachts*. New York, 1887.

Coffin, R. F. "The History of American Yachting," in Fred S. Cozzens et al., *Yachts and Yachting*. New York, 1887.

Crowninshield, Bowdoin, B. *Fore-and-Afters*. Boston, 1940.

*Dictionary of American Biography*. New York, 1964.

Eastman, Ralph E. *Pilots and Pilot Boats of Boston Harbor*. Boston, 1956.

*Eighty Years' Progress of the United States*. Publ. L. Stebbins. Hartford, 1869.

Dwight, James. "Lawn Tennis in New England." *Outing,* May 1891.

*The Encyclopaedia Britannica*. 11th ed. New York, 1910.

Heuvelmans, Bernard. *In the Wake of the Sea-Serpents*. New York, 1968.

*History of Essex County, Massachusetts*. Ed. D. Hamilton Hurd. 2 vols. Philadelphia, 1888.

Kidney, Walter C. *The Architecture of Choice: Eclecticism in America, 1880–1930*. New York, 1974.

Long, H. Follansbee. "The Newburyport and Boston Turnpike." *Essex Institute Historical Collections,* April 1906.
*Massachusetts: A Guide to Its Places and People.* Works Progress Administration, Federal Writers Project. Boston, 1937.
Morison, Samuel Eliot. *The Maritime History of Massachusetts, 1783–1860.* Boston, 1921.
Mumford, Lewis. *Sticks and Stones.* Revised ed. New York, 1955.
Nason, Elias. *A Gazetteer of the State of Massachusetts.* Boston, 1874.
*Official Encyclopedia of Tennis.* United States Lawn Tennis Association. New York, 1971.
Rantoul, Robert S. "Some Notes on Old Modes of Travel." *Essex Institute Historical Collections,* April 1871.
Rowsome, Frank, Jr. *Trolley Car Treasury.* New York, 1956.
Scully, Vincent J., Jr. *The Shingle Style and the Stick Style.* New Haven, 1971.
*Standard History of Essex County, Massachusetts.* Publ. C. F. Jewett. Boston, 1878.
Stephens, William P. *American Yachting.* New York, 1904.
—— *Traditions and Memories of American Yachting.* New York, 1942.
*The Story of Essex County.* Ed. Claude M. Fuess. 4 vols. New York, 1935.
Sturges, Walter Knight. "Arthur Little and the Colonial Revival." *Journal of the Society of Architectural Historians,* May 1973.
Varrell, William M. *Summer by-the-Sea.* Portsmouth, N.H., 1972.

## LOCAL HISTORY

Babson, John J. *History of the Town of Gloucester, Cape Ann, including the Town of Rockport.* Gloucester, Mass., 1860. Reprinted, with introduction and historical review by Joseph E. Garland. Gloucester, Mass., 1972.
Babson, Thomas E. "Evolution of Cape Ann Roads and Transportation." *Essex Institute Historical Collections,* October 1955.
Benjamin, S. G. W. "Gloucester and Cape Ann." *Harper's New Monthly Magazine,* September 1875.
Brooks, Alfred Mansfield. *Gloucester Recollected: A Familiar History.* Ed. Joseph E. Garland. Gloucester, Mass., 1974.
Carroll, Thomas. "Bands and Band Music in Salem." *Essex Institute Historical Collections.* October 1900.
Chamberlain, Allen. *Pigeon Cove: Its Early Settlers and Their Farms, 1702–1840.* Pigeon Cove, Mass., 1940.
Channing, Walter. *A Topographical Sketch of Nahant.* Salem, 1821.
Clark, William H. *The History of Winthrop, Massachusetts, 1630–1952.* Winthrop, 1952.
Clarke, George C. "The Story of Revere Beach." Part I of *Kiwanis History of Revere.* Mimeographed. At Revere, Mass., Public Library, 1966.
Cobb, Albert W. "The Town of Winthrop." *New England Magazine,* July 1892.
Cole, Adeline P. *Notes on Wenham History, 1643–1943.* At Wenham, Mass., Historical Association, 1943.
Copeland, Melvin T., and Elliott C. Rogers. *The Saga of Cape Ann.* Freeport, Me., 1960.

Crawford, Mary Caroline. *Romantic Days in Old Boston*. Boston, 1910.

Dow, George F. *History of Topsfield*. Topsfield, 1940.

Dow, Mary Larcom. *Old Days at Beverly Farms*. Beverly, Mass., 1921.

Drake, Samuel Adams. *Old Landmarks and Historic Personages of Boston*. Boston, 1906.

Felt, Joseph B. *History of Ipswich, Essex and Hamilton*. Cambridge, Mass., 1834.

Foster, Charles H. W. *The Eastern Yacht Club Ditty Box*. Norwood, Mass., 1932.

Foster, Mrs. E. G., and Alice W. Foster. *The Story of Kettle Cove*. Magnolia, Mass., 1899.

Fraser, Mrs. William S. "Manchester Becomes a Resort." Manchester, Mass., *Cricket*, serialized 1961.

Gardner, William H. "The Town of Winthrop." *The Bostonian*, September 1895.

Garland, Joseph E. *Eastern Point: A Nautical, Rustical, and Social Chronicle of Gloucester's Outer Shield and Inner Sanctum, 1606–1950*. Peterborough, N.H., 1971.

—— *The Gloucester Guide: A Retrospective Ramble*. Gloucester, Mass., 1973.

*Glen Magna Farms: Gateway to Historic Essex County*. Danvers, Mass., Historical Society report, 1963–1964.

Gott, Lemuel, and Ebenezer Pool. *History of the Town of Rockport*. Rockport, Mass., 1888.

Gove, Charles E., Jr. *Queries of Old Nahant*. Manuscript at Nahant, Mass., Public Library.

Harmond, Richard. "The Time They Tried to Divide Beverly." *Essex Institute Historical Collections*, January 1968.

Harris, Leslie. *150 Years a Town*. Essex, Mass., 1969.

Hartt, Hildegarde T. *Magnolia Once Kettle Cove*. Magnolia, Mass., 1962.

Hawes, Charles Boardman. *Gloucester by Land and Sea*. Boston, 1923.

Homer, James L. *Nahant, and Other Places on the North Shore*. Boston, 1848.

—— *Notes on the Sea-shore; or Random Sketches by "Shade of Alden."* Boston, 1848.

Howard, Channing. *Stage Coach and Early Railroad Days in Winthrop*. Mimeographed. At Winthrop, Mass., Public Library, 1938.

Kenny, Herbert A. *Cape Ann: Cape America*. Philadelphia, 1971.

Kimball, F. R. *Handbook of Marblehead Neck*. Boston, 1882.

King, Caroline H. *When I Lived in Salem, 1822–1866*. Brattleboro, 1937.

Lamson, D. F. *History of the Town of Manchester, Essex County, Massachusetts, 1645–1895*. Boston, 1895.

Leonard, Henry C. *Pigeon Cove and Vicinity*. Boston, 1873.

Lewis, Alonzo. *The Picture of Nahant*. Lynn, Mass., 1855.

——, and James R. Newhall. *History of Lynn, Essex County, Massachusetts: Including Lynnfield, Saugus, Swampscott, and Nahant*. Revised ed. Boston, 1865.

Lodge, Henry Cabot. *An Historical Address Delivered at the Celebration of the Fiftieth Anniversary of the Incorporation of the Town of Nahant, July 14, 1903*. Nahant, Mass., 1904.

Lord, Priscilla Sawyer, and Virginia Clegg Gamage. *Marblehead: The Spirit of '76 Lives Here*. Philadelphia, 1972.

Loring, Katharine Peabody. "The Earliest Summer Residents of the North Shore and Their Houses." *Essex Institute Historical Collections*, July 1932.

*Manchester by-the-Sea, 1645–1970.* Town of Manchester, Mass., 1970.

Mansur, Frank L. "Swampscott Massachusetts: The Beginning of a Town." *Essex Institute Historical Collections,* January 1972.

*Nahant.* Nahant, Mass., Public Library. Lynn, Mass., 1899.

O'Gorman, James F. *This Other Gloucester.* Boston, 1976.

*Old Shipping Days in Boston.* State Street Trust Company. Boston, 1918.

Peabody, Robert E. "Peach's Point, Marblehead." *Essex Institute Historical Collections,* January 1966.

Pittee, Charles R. "The Gloucester Steamboats." *The American Neptune,* October 1952.

Pratt, Walter Merriam. *Seven Generations: A Story of Prattville and Chelsea.* Boston, 1930.

Prince, Warren. "The Pioneers of the Seashore." Beverly, Mass., *Citizen,* serialized 1884.

Pringle, James R. *History of the Town and City of Gloucester, Cape Ann, Massachusetts.* Gloucester, Mass., 1892.

Procter, George H. "How Bass Rocks Became a Summer Resort." Gloucester, Mass., *Daily Times,* August 23, 1911.

—— "Reminiscences of the Annisquam River." Gloucester, Mass., *Daily Times,* April 3, 5, 7, 13, 1909.

—— "The Summer Boarder Industry." Gloucester, Mass., *Daily Times,* August 9, 1911.

*Revere: 100 Years, 1871–1971.* City of Revere, Mass., 1971.

Roads, Samuel, Jr. *The History and Traditions of Marblehead.* Boston, 1880.

*Salem Willows Anniversary Booklet.* Salem, Mass., 1958.

Searle, Richard W. "History of Catta Island off Marblehead." *Essex Institute Historical Collections,* October 1947.

—— "Marblehead Great Neck." *Essex Institute Historical Collections,* July 1937.

Shurtleff, Benjamin. *The History of the Town of Revere.* Revere, Mass., 1937.

*Souvenir of Bass Rocks.* Bass Rocks Improvement Association. Boston, 1905.

Stetson, Helen L. "Sketch of Nahant." Lynn *Item,* March 22, 1902.

Stevens, W. Lester. "Cape Ann: An Artist's Paradise." *North Shore Breeze,* April 29, 1921.

Stone, Edwin M. *History of Beverly.* Boston, 1843.

Streeter, G. L. "The Story of Winter Island and Salem Neck." *Essex Institute Historical Collections,* January–June 1897.

Swan, William U. "A Century of Yachting at Marblehead," in Joseph S. Robinson, *The Story of Marblehead.* Salem, Mass., 1936.

Tapley, Charles S. *Country Estates of Old Danvers.* Danvers, Mass., 1961.

Tapley, Harriet S. *Chronicles of Danvers (Old Salem Village) Massachusetts, 1623–1923.* Danvers, Mass., 1923.

Thompson, Waldo. *Swampscott: Historical Sketches of the Town.* Lynn, Mass., 1885.

Webber, C. H., and W. S. Nevins. *Old Naumkeag: An Historical Sketch of the City of Salem, and the Towns of Marblehead, Peabody, Beverly, Danvers, Wenham, Manchester, Topsfield and Middleton.* Salem, Mass., 1877.

Welch, William L. *Walk around Salem Neck and Winter Island.* Salem, Mass., 1897.

—— *The Willows*. Boston, 1900.

Wilson, Fred A. *Some Annals of Nahant*. Boston, 1928. Reprinted by the Nahant, Mass., Historical Society, 1977.

Whitehill, Walter Muir. *Boston: A Topographical History*. Cambridge, Mass., 1968.

Winsor, Justin. *The Memorial History of Boston*. 4 vols. Boston, 1881.

Woodbury, C. J. H. "The Floating Bridge at Lynn on the Salem and Boston Turnpike." *Essex Institute Historical Collections*, January–June 1898.


## FIRSTHAND ACCOUNTS

*The Articulate Sisters* (letters and journals of the daughters of President Josiah Quincy of Harvard University). Ed. M. A. De Wolfe Howe. Cambridge, Mass., 1946.

Baedeker, Karl. *The United States*. New York, 1893.

"Belle-Life at Nahant." *Harper's Weekly*, August 28, 1858.

Bentley, William. *The Diary of William Bentley, D.D.* Salem, Mass., 1905. Reprinted Gloucester, Mass., 1962.

*Bowen's Picture Book of Boston*. Boston, 1838.

Butler, Benjamin F. *Butler's Book*. Boston, 1892.

Carter, Robert. *Carter's Coast of New England*. Boston, 1864. Reprinted Somersworth, N.H., 1969.

Champlain, Samuel de. *Voyages, II*. The Publications of the Prince Society, Boston, 1878.

"Coast Rambles in Essex." *Harper's New Monthly Magazine*, May 1878.

*The Conductor* (guidebook). Boston [ca. 1849].

Curtis, Caroline G. *Memories of Fifty Years in the Last Century*. Boston, 1947.

Curtis, George William. *Lotus-Eating: A Summer Book*. New York, 1852.

Cushing, John Perkins. "Diary." Manuscript at Boston Athenaeum, Boston.

*A Descriptive Guide to the Eastern Rail-Road, from Boston to Portland*. Boston, 1851.

*Eastern Ramblings*. Eastern Railroad. Boston, 1879.

Emerson, Ralph Waldo. *Journals*. Boston, 1909–1914.

Forbes, Robert Bennet. *A Discursive Sketch of Yachting; Forty and More Years Ago*. Boston, 1888.

—— *Personal Reminiscences*. Boston, 1882. Reprinted New York, 1970.

Grant, Robert. *Fourscore: An Autobiography*. Boston, 1934.

Grattan, Thomas C. *Civilized America*. 2 vols. London, 1859.

Higginson, Francis. *New-Englands Plantation, or, A Short and True Description of the Commodities and Discommodities of That Country*. [London, 1630.] In *Tracts of the Colonies in North America*, II. Collector, Peter Force. Reprinted Gloucester, Mass., 1963.

Hill, Benjamin D., and Winfield S. Nevins. *The North Shore of Massachusetts Bay* (guidebooks). Salem, Mass., 1879–1894.

Holmes, Oliver Wendell. *The Autocrat of the Breakfast-Table*. In *Works*. Boston, 1892.

—— *Our Hundred Days in Europe*. In *Works*. Boston, 1892.

—— *Pages from an Old Volume of Life*. In *Works*. Boston, 1892.

Homans, George C. "Sailing with Uncle Charlie." *The Atlantic Monthly*, July 1965.

*King's Handbook of Boston.* Ed. Moses King. Cambridge, Mass., 1878.

*King's Handbook of Boston Harbor.* Ed. Moses King. Cambridge, Mass., 1882.

Lawrence, William. *Memories of a Happy Life.* Boston, 1926.

Lodge, Henry Cabot. *Early Memories.* New York, 1913.

Lowell, James Russell. *Letters of James Russell Lowell.* Ed. Charles Eliot Norton. New York, 1894.

*Marblehead Neck Bulletin* (brochure). Marblehead, Mass., 1889.

"Nahant." *Boston Monthly Magazine,* July 1825.

*Nahant: And What Is to Be Seen There.* Boston, 1868.

*Nahant, or A Day in Summer.* N. p., May 1811. At the Essex Institute.

*Nahant, or "The Floure of Souvenance."* Philadelphia, 1827.

Phelps, Elizabeth Stuart. *Chapters from a Life.* Boston, 1896.

*Pigeon Cove House* (pamphlet). N. p., 1880.

Pulsifer, David. *Guide to Boston and Vicinity.* Boston, 1871.

Santayana, George. *Persons and Places.* New York, 1944.

Smith, John. *A Description of New England.* [London, 1616.] In *Tracts of the Colonies in North America,* II. Collector, Peter Force. Reprinted Gloucester, Mass., 1963.

Tucker-Macchetta, Blanche Roosevelt. *The Home Life of Henry W. Longfellow.* New York, 1882.

Webber, John S., Jr. *In and Around Cape Ann.* Gloucester, Mass., 1885.

Wheildon, W. W. *Letters from Nahant.* Charlestown, Mass., 1842.

*Willow Park Pavilion* (broadside). 1882. At the Essex Institute.

Wood, William. *New Englands Prospect.* [1634]. In Alonzo Lewis and James R. Newhall, *History of Lynn,* and Benjamin Shurtleff, *The History of the Town of Revere.*

## BIOGRAPHICAL

Ferguson, David L. *Cleopatra's Barge: The Crowninshield Story.* Boston, 1976.

Herreshoff, L. Francis, *Capt. Nat Herreshoff: The Wizard of Bristol.* New York, 1953.

Holzman, Robert S. *Stormy Ben Butler.* New York, 1954.

*Memoranda Relating to Nathaniel Souther.* Springfield, Ill., 1886.

Morse, John T., Jr. *Life and Letters of Oliver Wendell Holmes.* Boston, 1896.

Nevins, Allan. *Frémont: Pathmaker of the West.* New York, 1939.

*Other Merchants and Sea Captains of Old Boston.* State Street Trust Company. Boston, 1919.

Roscoe, Theodore. *The Web of Conspiracy* (the Booth family). Englewood Cliffs, N.J., 1959.

Ruggles, Eleanor. *Prince of Players* (the Booth family). New York, 1953.

Seaburg, Carl, and Stanley Paterson. *Merchant Prince of Boston: Colonel T. H. Perkins, 1764–1854.* Cambridge, Mass., 1971.

*Some Merchants and Sea Captains of Old Boston.* State Street Trust Company. Boston, 1918.

Ticknor, George. *Life of William Hickling Prescott.* Boston, 1864.

Truax, Rhoda. *The Doctors Warren.* Boston, 1968.

Tryon, W. S. *Parnassus Corner* (James T. Fields). Boston, 1963.
West, Richard S., Jr. *Lincoln's Scapegoat General* (Benjamin Butler). Boston, 1965.


## MISCELLANEOUS

Addison, Daniel D. *Lucy Larcom: Life, Letters and Diary*. Boston, 1895.
Andrews, William A. *A Daring Voyage Across the Atlantic Ocean*. New York, 1880.
Brainard, John G. C. *Occasional Pieces of Poetry*. New York, 1825.
Collins, Lou, and George Hardy. "Salem Willows for Mine Waltz." Salem, Mass., 1919.
Foote, Cameron S. "Who in Heaven's Name Invented the First Potato Chip?" *Yankee,* September 1975.
*Later Years of the Saturday Club.* Ed. M. A. De Wolfe Howe. Boston, 1927.
*Lynn and Boston Horse Railroad Company Annual Report, 1861.*
*Lynn Yacht Club 34th Annual Ball,* with history. Lynn, Mass., 1912.
Shaw, O. J. "The 'Sea Breeze': Polka Brillante." Boston, 1857.
*A Testimonial to Charles J. Paine and Edward Burgess from the City of Boston, for Their Successful Defense of the America's Cup.* Boston, 1887.
Thompson, Winfield M., William P. Stephens, and William U. Swan. *The Yacht "America."* Boston, 1925.
Tompkins, Eugene. *The History of the Boston Theatre, 1854–1901.* Boston, 1908.
Whitehill, Walter Muir. *Museum of Fine Arts Boston.* Cambridge, Mass., 1970.


## NEWSPAPERS AND PERIODICALS FREQUENTLY CONSULTED

*Cape Ann Weekly Advertiser*
*Essex Institute Historical Collections*
Gloucester *Daily Times*
Gloucester *Telegraph*
*Harper's Weekly*
Magnolia *Leaves*
*North Shore Breeze*
Revere *Journal*
Willows *Budget*

ndex

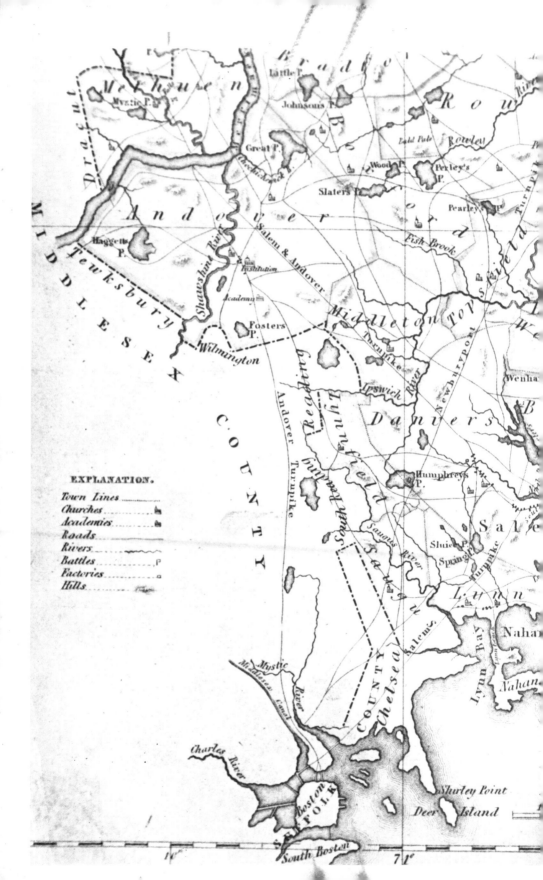